Project Rainbow

Having represented Great Britain from 1989 until his retirement in 2001, Rod Ellingworth founded and ran the GB Cycling Academy. Alongside Dave Brailsford, he was then instrumental creating Team Sky in November 2008.

William Fotheringham has been the *Guardian*'s cycling correspondent since 1994. He has covered twenty-two Tours de France and four Olympic Games and his published work includes the classic biographies *Put Me Back On My Bike: In Search of Tom Simpson* and *Merckx: Half-Man, Half-Bike*. He also co-wrote Bradley Wiggins's bestselling memoir *My Time*.

Project Rainbow

How British Cycling Reached the Top of the World

ROD ELLINGWORTH

with
William Fotheringham

ff

FABER & FABER

First published in 2013
by Faber & Faber Limited
Bloomsbury House
74–77 Great Russell Street, London WC1B 3DA

This paperback edition first published in 2014

Designed by Faber
Printed in England by CPI Group (UK) Ltd, Croydon, CR0 4YY

A CIP record for this book
is available from the British Library

ISBN 978-0-571-30351-9

FSC
www.fsc.org
MIX
Paper from
responsible sources
FSC® C101712

2 4 6 8 10 9 7 5 3 1

For Jane and Robyn,
for all the many days I have to
spend away from home.

For family and good friends
who have always supported me.

And finally for the bike riders
– without them we are nothing.

Contents

Foreword

Most coaches in cycling are either ex-professionals or scientists. That means their approach is either all about numbers, or they try to do it like they did in the good old days. They tend to go from one extreme to the other. Rod Ellingworth isn't like that. He has a unique ability to absorb you in what he is saying. He was a professional only at a domestic level in Britain, but he knows more about bike racing, its history, its tactics, than 90 per cent of the pros I've met. His love of cycling has always showed, throughout everything he's done.

The first time I met Rod was when I was a junior, and he invited me along to some training sessions he was putting on. It was wicked, so different from what I'd done before: no stop-watch, no numbers, just bike racing. He made it so much fun. It was Rod who made me want to be on the British Cycling academy programme. I turned up in Manchester on 12 January 2004. I hadn't been training all winter because I was working in a bank, and those early days were really hard. I was really unfit and was getting dropped all over the place. I didn't really know this guy who was in charge of us, but what I did notice was that he was putting as much time into me as he was into the guys who were looking better on their bikes.

That was something no one had done with me before. It had been the same story all my life – the coaches would put more time and energy into the guys with better numbers than the guys who were struggling. With Rod, it didn't matter where you were from, how bad you were going; he'd always wait and encourage you, full on. I've told the story before about how we were training up Gun Hill in the Peak District, and I got off my bike and cried. He could have told me to fuck off home, but instead he said I just had to keep trying. A few weeks later I won my first race with him.

At the academy he was firm; he would punish us whenever we got out of hand. They were long days, hard training, and there were guys who resented it – the ones who'd been mothered, the ones who'd always been given what they wanted. But I bought in, because he was working harder than we were. If we had to get up at six thirty to go to the track, he would have to get up earlier to drive in, leaving his girlfriend behind. He would spend time away with us in Belgium, which can't have been easy with a group of young guys, but it was all geared towards improving us as bike riders. Everything he did was aimed at that. That's why we progressed faster than any group of cyclists from any country, ever.

As we grew as a group, I kept working with Rod. Over the years, he has become more than a coach: he's a mentor and a friend. I improve most as a cyclist when he is working with me, hands-on. He'll turn up on his scooter in the pissing rain; at least I'm pedalling to keep warm, but he'll be just sitting there getting cold, for hour after hour. I complain about all the hours I have to spend in hotels because of my job, but I don't know anyone who spends more time on the road than Rod. He's a good man too; I like talking to him about normal things. He's cool, has good taste in music and knows about life outside cycling.

Rod was never a big-time professional cyclist, but he's never scared to tell me when I've fucked up, even though I've become one of the biggest riders on the planet. He's honest, straight talking, and doesn't believe he knows better than everyone else. He just knows what he thinks, and if you want to take it, you do. He has this way of getting everyone to buy in; if you make a mistake, he doesn't kick off and make you feel small. Instead, it's like the old cliché: he makes you feel disappointed in yourself. Rod has never been scared to learn from different areas – racing, science, psychology. He's not afraid that he might get it wrong, or that someone might know better, or of telling it like it is. No one else I know coaches in the way he does – by looking at every different quality in a person. A lot of coaches don't have social skills, but Rod knows how to read a person like no one else.

I always say that Rod is the most undervalued man in British Cycling. The current crop of riders who have come through the system he created and are doing big things – me, Ian Stannard, Alex Dowsett, Geraint Thomas, Peter Kennaugh – make up the biggest group of high-quality bike riders ever to come out of this country at the same time. No one else could or would have put the time and effort, the hours and hours of work, into building that system. No one else has done as much for cycling in Britain as Rod. All the other sides of the Olympic cycling programme use ideas taken from what he did with the academy.

It's still unbelievable how Rod managed to put that world championship team together. It took incredible vision to get the money to get that project up and running. It was a three-year plan, first aiming for Australia in 2010, then Copenhagen in 2011, and finally the Olympics in London in 2012. It's different building something with the national team: you're doing it for national pride, not for your professional sponsor. There are guys who have history with Great Britain. You need that buy-in, and Rod got it. At our first meeting he got all the riders together in a room, showed us something under a cover; it was Tom Simpson's rainbow jersey from the 1965 world championship. Everyone got goosebumps. You could see them getting behind the idea there and then.

When handing out any presents or accolades after that world title, I made damned sure Rod was on the list, because he was probably the most important part of the project. He was the ninth guy in the team and probably worked harder than anyone else. There is no way in hell that any other coach could have built a team to win the world road race championship for Great Britain. He doesn't do it for the accolades; he does it because he loves his country, he loves his sport and he wants the best for British cycling. He loves it and he wants it to succeed. If there is one person in British cycling who should have a knighthood, it's Rod.

Mark Cavendish
June 2013

Shouting at the Telly

Copenhagen, 25 September 2011

There were three of us in the Great Britain race car that day, for seven hours and seventeen laps of the circuit in Copenhagen. In the front with me was Brian Holm, Mark Cavendish's *directeur sportif* at the HTC team; Diego Costa, a mechanic with Team Sky, was sitting behind us. Normally a team car in a professional bike race has a television in the back for the mechanic, as well as one in the front for the DS, but we had only one, so the thing that sticks in my mind is Diego's hot breath down my neck as he looked over my shoulder at the screen, hour after hour, all the while clutching a pair of spare wheels in the back-seat space.

I'd thought long and hard about who to have with me in the car. Brian was there because being a *directeur sportif* isn't my forte and he's been full-time at it for over a decade in professional cycling. I had to drive the car because I was managing the team, but it made sense to have someone of his experience there. Brian is Danish but he does love Britain with a passion – that was why he had found common ground with Cav when he began working with him in his first full year as a pro. It made sense to have someone in the car in whom Cav had built so much trust over the years. Brian had won a lot more races sitting in a car directing Cav than I had, and there might be a moment when that made the difference. Plus we were in

Denmark, and Brian is a national hero in his native country. Cav was proud to have him in the car. There was a personal side to this for Brian as well: I knew Cav was going to be changing teams at the end of the season; for the first time in five years they would no longer be working together.

Brian hadn't been part of the build-up to the Worlds, but his years of experience mattered. That shone through when we were talking through the tactics for the day, about when the team would start to ride hard behind the day's main break, whenever that happened to form. They wouldn't start chasing from a set point whatever happened, say fifty or sixty kilometres out; they would get down to it when the break had formed and had got a certain number of minutes ahead. We discussed it with the riders: it was to be about four or five minutes, and we knew it was going to be a big group. I had been a bit uneasy with that – I didn't want to intervene as it was the riders' decision – so on the morning of the race, when Brian said he thought it was about right and there should be no panic, I thought, 'Perfect.' That kind of thing really bolsters your confidence.

And then there was Diego, an Italian, from Piacenza. I'd chosen him because although we've got plenty of British mechanics, he's the best I know in the race car. You have to think about it – what's the mechanic's job in the car? He's got to study the race and help the two guys sitting in the front work out which riders are in which group. That's down to listening to the short-wave race radio. Diego speaks perfect French, Italian and Spanish, and he'd learnt English in two years. He's very particular about his work; not a great person in a team, but good on his own. And I've never seen anyone as fast at getting out of the car and fixing a puncture; just being very confident about it – no panic, just gets it done. That alone could be the difference between winning and losing.

Diego was going through a rather particular time in his life. He had just got a new girlfriend and was constantly on the phone to her. So when we got in the car at the start of the race and I said, 'OK, guys, unless there's a major crisis, no phones now,' he was pissed off and wouldn't talk to me for the first two or three hours. I didn't give a shit; he still did his job. That's something I always do – I wouldn't answer the phone to my wife when I'm in a race car unless it was an emergency. It's our job to make that clear to our other halves. I remember years back I was in a race, on the radio to one of the riders, and he couldn't hear me because someone in the car was on the phone. It makes a difference.

We'd thought about the telly as well. Chris White, the performance analyst who had been working with us since the start of the road Worlds project, had hired it and had made sure it was going to work. He'd done a load of checks around the course to see where the signal dipped in and out. So you would go under some trees and you'd know you were going to lose it. That in turn meant you didn't start fiddling with the dials, because there was no panicking that you were going to lose the channel and how would you get it back? You're ready for the picture to come back at a certain point, and then you're straight back on it again. It all helps you keep calm.

We had good reason to be nervous. We'd been working towards this one day for the last three years, since I'd gone public with the idea that Great Britain could build a team with the aim of winning the elite world road race championship, the biggest one-day race in the sport, the one that rewards its winner with the right to wear the rainbow-striped jersey for the next twelve months. Britain had only won it once, with Tom Simpson back in 1965, and had never looked like winning it since. This could be our once-in-a-lifetime chance: this might be the only time in Cav's career that he would get the flat course that suited him. The build-up hadn't been straightforward, but we knew he was ready, and that might not happen next time. We also knew the team had bought into the idea, in a way that no British team had done since the day that Simpson won it nearly half a century ago.

The project had got under way in 2008, but it had been seven years since Mark Cavendish had first told me that he wanted to win the Worlds, back in 2004, when we started working together. It sounded unlikely then, but a few years later it had begun to look like it might be possible one day, as he'd landed his first big win – the Scheldeprijs – started his first Tour de France and won some smaller races. He'd ridden the 2007 Worlds just to get in amongst it, to feel it, to experience how the Italian and Spanish teams worked, how teams come together from their day jobs working for other outfits and have to race as a unit from scratch on that one day. That was the key to the whole project. Assembling a team for the Worlds is like English footballers playing together for their country in the World Cup after kicking the stuffing out of each other in the Premiership all season – you have to work hard to get it right.

It might not have crossed many other people's minds, but it was clear to us back then that no one in cycling was faster than Mark Cavendish – and that made life a lot easier when it came to winning a one-day race like the Worlds – plus we knew the riders had the engines to ride as a unit and keep the race together for him on a flat course. I felt we had the talent, so the question was: how do we do it? It helped that the bulk of those cyclists in the team that day had come up through the Great Britain academy which I had founded – riders like Ian Stannard, Geraint Thomas, Cav himself, of course – so they all understood how I worked and how Cav operated. And the older guys like Steve Cummings, Bradley Wiggins, Jeremy Hunt and David Millar were all smart and had always got the picture too.

Before the start of a one-day race there is a lottery for the car's position in the convoy; we had been given a really bad draw – nineteenth – and were supposed to be sharing the car with the Irish, although Great Britain were in the top ten in the world rankings. I said there was no way we were going to share with Ireland if we were out to win the Worlds; I've got nothing against the Irish – I am half Irish myself – it was the pure principle of it. So Dave Brailsford, the GB Performance Director, protested against it, and did a bloody good job. He managed to get us moved up the order, but we were still well outside the first ten, which meant that if anyone needed a wheel change or a fresh bike, it would take us that little bit longer to get to them. For most of the race that wouldn't matter, but at the end it could cost us everything.

We knew that even if Cav had a problem right up to the last five or six kilometres, he would still be on for the win; he could crash or puncture, and we could still bring him back, but if he did have a problem after that, there would be no use being car eleven or twelve. We'd have to be right there behind the bunch if something happened. It had taken a bit of planning to get round that one, but we had worked out that with a bit of front we would be able to do at least half a lap as car number one in the convoy. This was where Brian had come into his own. Just before the end of the lap there was a right-hand corner, then the finish straight, and after that the road narrowed to go past the feed zone; no cars would be doing any overtaking there, and then there was a fast section where the peloton was flat out and the cars would all be split up.

Brian said to me, 'Right, when I say "Go", you go with all guns blazing, horn blaring, making a big noise – and time it so that the second you hit that right-hand corner before the finish straight, you're car number one in the convoy.' So we were flat out, screaming past the other team cars. I was hanging onto the wheel, Diego breathing down my neck all the time as he kept his eyes on the telly. And as we flew past the other team cars, everyone was looking at us, thinking, 'What do they know that we don't? Why are they moving up now?'

So we got to the front and stayed there through the narrow section, right up to the foot of the next climb. At that point there was a chance the other cars might try to push past us and put us back in our place right down the pecking order. But then Brian came into his own again: 'Right, let's go and talk to my mate in the doctor's car.' Being a legend of Danish bike racing, Brian knew the guy who was driving that car, which spent the race sitting right behind the peloton, ahead of car number one in the convoy – Italy or Spain. So we went and talked to him for ages, looking quite worried, as if we might actually have a reason for talking to the race doctor. I remember the Italian team manager Paolo Bettini coming past in his car at one point, and he was clearly thinking, 'Oh yes, I know what you're up to.'

We got to a certain point in the race – I think it would be with a good hour to go – and I said, 'Right, guys, no stopping for a piss from now on.' It's hard to stop anyway at the Worlds: you're on a circuit, it's all barriers, and there are people everywhere. I was clenching and twisting my hands on the wheel all day. I was literally just watching that telly for seven hours. You're not meant to watch it as you drive, but it's hard not to. There's nothing else you can do; you're just sitting there, hoping.

I don't think I've ever felt so nervous. I'd gone through the full gamut of emotions since I started working with Great Britain. You start out with the riders, you go to your first race with them, they're starting to win . . . There had been nervous times – the Commonwealth Games in 2006, when Cav won the scratch race, and the world track championships in 2005, when he won the Madison, and in 2008 in Manchester, when he and Bradley Wiggins were taking a lap on the field in the same event and the whole stadium was on its feet cheering them on. This was way bigger than any of them, but there we were in Copenhagen in this little car, all on our own, not a sound apart from the race radio and the three of us yelling at that little screen.

1 : All I Ever Wanted

I first went to the road Worlds when I was nine. I'm right there in the video footage of the 1982 pro championship in Goodwood, Sussex, but I'm not riding my bike. I'm standing in the middle of the road along with my brother Richard and my best mate Simon at the very moment when Bernard Hinault retires from the race. How the hell I got there I still do not know, but what I do know is that on my head is a Sem-France-Loire racing cap, as worn by Sean Kelly, who was my hero when I was a kid, partly because my mother is Irish.

Cycling has always been my life. All I can remember is wanting to be a cyclist or a fireman. My dad was a cyclist, one of the founder members of the Clayton Velo Cycling Club in Burnley, where I was born. All our holidays were centred around our bikes: the Cyclists' Touring Club's New Forest cycling week, the Harrogate cycling festival. We never went abroad; if we had a break, it was always in the UK so we could ride our bikes. Goodwood, the second and up to now last time the world road championships came to the UK, was another one of those trips: we camped out the whole weekend, watched Mandy Jones win the women's race for Great Britain and watched the amateur race on the Saturday. Shortly before Giuseppe Saronni flew up the rise to the finish to win the pro race on the Sunday, we swarmed into the grandstand. We didn't have tickets or anything, so everyone just stormed in.

I grew up with cycling. After we moved from Burnley to Grantham in Lincolnshire in 1976 or 1977, Dad would take us to watch the city-centre criteriums in Nottingham and other places. He was the organiser of the town-centre races in Grantham, and my granddad was the one who did the time-keeping at the local ten-mile time trials for our club, the Witham Wheelers. They still run an annual road race named after my great-granddad, the GT Ellingworth, in late May. We were constantly at bike races.

After my parents split up in 1979, I stayed with Dad. It was a cycling house; life there revolved around it. It was where the lads would come and meet before going training or riding the evening chain gang. We had a VW camper van, and that was the centre point at races – all the guys would come over, sit around and have a cup of tea while they were putting their numbers on. Richard, who's older than me, began racing before I did – my dad made me wait until he thought I was old enough – so every weekend we were off supporting him in whatever schoolboy circuit race he was riding. I rode my first race in one of those circuit events, run by the English Schools Cycling Association. I was mad about road racing and the Tour de France. We used to get *Cycling Weekly* magazine every week – it was at the time when they had really good front and back covers, so my whole room was covered with them, and they were all over my school books as well. There was no 'Do I like it or not?' It was everything to me.

I was lucky that my granddad was really good at getting us to go out and do things, to ask for stuff. There were two moments when this made a real difference to me as a young bike rider. The first was in 1988, when he persuaded me to ask the headmaster at my school to fund me for a youth-training week run by the ESCA during the holidays. It was a week when you would learn the kind of stuff that British Cycling's Talent Team do now – skills, race tactics, and so on – but it cost about £150 and it wasn't something we could afford. I remember my granddad saying, 'Why not ask at school?'

At that point cycling was nothing as a sport. I was doing a sport which wasn't really recognised, which had no presence in schools, and no one there knew anything about it. When you do that kind of sport, you're always seen as a bit different. You're the one who bangs up and down the A1 in those stupid time trials. But I wanted to go on that youth weekend, so I went into school, aged fourteen or fifteen, sat down with the headmaster to show him all the information and asked if they could put up the money. And they did. They even bought me a cycling jersey, got the school name printed on it and presented it to me in front of the whole school at assembly. I was super-embarrassed. But getting that jersey was massive for me. I went to the races and pushed a bit more, so that I could go back to my headmaster and tell him how I'd done.

The other thing my granddad got me to do was write to the local council, because they had started doing a grant scheme called 'Gifted Young People', under which they would give funding for people to do arts, sport, whatever. So I went for that and got £50 for 1987, and the grant ended up going all the way to 1996, when I was getting £5,000 and a car. One way or another, that relationship lasted all the way through until I finished cycling in 2001. I was lucky the school and the council took an interest in me, but it only happened because my granddad asked me to approach them. There are times when if someone doesn't point you in the right direction, you don't know what to do.

So cycling was my life. As soon as I started riding in the local club runs, I was one of the ones who would finish with the fast group, and they'd all be asking, 'Who's this kid?' I always remember I did twenty-nine minutes five seconds for my first club ten-mile time trial, because my dad had said he wondered if I would get inside thirty minutes, which is the big barrier for anyone riding their first 'ten'. I was thinking, 'Too right I can get inside thirty minutes.' And I started riding track leagues on Tuesday and Wednesday at Nottingham and Leicester, alternating with the club tens and schoolboy criteriums on Saturday and Sunday. At that time there were loads of city-centre races, which always had kids' events; if you look at the calendar now, there are about a third the number of races there were then.

I enjoyed going to school because I loved the social side of it. At that time I was flicking back and forth between my parents. One minute I was living in one place, then in another, and that's a crucial time in your school life when you begin secondary school. I couldn't really be bothered with the studying. I just wanted to go cycling. There were three things I wanted to do at school: study French, because I wanted to go to France and be a cyclist; technical drawing; and PE. I was in the first year that took GCSEs, and at that point PE wasn't one of the options. There was no exam.

If there had been, my life might have been different, because although I wasn't smart at school, doing that might have pushed me to do other doings, such as sports science. I loved PE. Every subject we did they would give us monthly marks out of four, pushy, we think big, we believe that everyone has two arms and legs just like the rest of us. But that's something we have grown into; back then the attitude was, 'You'll never make it into that kind of racing. No one from Britain is ever that good.'

I think that things must have been tough for my dad. He was made redundant one year and he was living on his own with me. We certainly didn't go on family holidays abroad, although I did go to Malta once with my mum. Perhaps Dad wasn't overambitious, and as a result of that I wasn't that sure about going off and racing abroad and making it as a European pro like Kelly or Yates. And at that time there was a good little professional racing scene in Britain. In a way, it held a lot of people back – riders like Chris Lillywhite, Chris Walker, Rob Holden – because they could earn a bit of money without going abroad, and I got drawn into the tail end of that.

I was never among the very best. I would win races, get a decent result here and there. I could always handle my bike and get in the right place. But I never looked at how to train properly, how to eat the right things, how to race to your full potential. When I think now of what I did, perhaps I wasn't smart enough to look at everything and break it down. But I was in there, racing was my life, and I just enjoyed it. I went with it.

There was one evening in October 1988, when I was sixteen and had left school. The phone rang; Dad answered it, and I remember him speaking a little bit posh, a bit proper. 'Who the hell is that?' I thought. Dad came in and said, 'It's Doug Dailey on the phone.' You think of people with radio voices, and Doug is one of those. He has a very distinct, powerful voice; he just bellows it out. Doug was involved with British Cycling from the mid-1980s to 2012, and at that time he was national coach. He never changed; he remained a key part of the national team for all those years, fully committed, and was just the same then as when I worked with him later.

'Doug Dailey here, Rod,' he said. 'I'm very happy to tell you you've made the national junior team.' And what got me was that he added, 'You've not just made it onto one – you're on both the road and track teams.' It was brilliant. I got a letter telling me to go for a medical in Edgbaston, and I'll never forget the journey there, clutching the letter all the way. So I rode in the junior world championships in Moscow in 1989, and then in Middlesbrough in 1990. It was all a bit of an experience. At Middlesbrough we were going OK in the team pursuit, heading for about fourth, when Matthew Charity crashed, and that split us up.

After that I started racing in Europe a little. There's a guy called John Barclay who took groups of riders to race in Belgium. He's a bit of an institution in British racing – he's been doing it for years and is still taking guys out there. He had a bloody great Peugeot estate which could hold six or eight of us, bikes on the roof, bags in the boot. You'd be asked to go through word of mouth. You'd meet at a service station on the M25 on a Friday afternoon, get the ferry, stay in a youth hostel or a barracks or something, pay him a bit of petrol money, race your race and then be dropped back on the Sunday evening.

There were trips with the local Centre of Excellence – regional set-ups which received small grants to help their riders progress, with racing abroad and training camps at home – with riders like Mark Dawes, Mark Armstrong, David Standard, Paul Spencer, Lee Burns and Andrew Roche. When I think of what I've seen since, some of them were definitely world class

– Mark Armstrong won the junior Liège–Bastogne–Liège in 1990, for example.

On one of the trips I realised how the Great Britain team worked back then. The guy who managed us there told me that at the end of each season there was a meeting where they went through the invitations for the next year's international races. They would ask, for example, 'Who wants to do the Tour de l'Avenir?' and whoever wanted to be team manager would just say, 'I'll do it.' There was no experience in the management, no coaching structure, no pathway for the riders to follow. As far as full-time employees went, there was only Doug. There was help for those at the top leading up to the Olympic Games, but nothing for the people below that. I did quite well when Alan Sturgess was the junior coach, but there was no long-term development pathway. You couldn't see where it might take you if you weren't part of that elite group.

British Cycling had no real base – it was run out of Jim Hendry's place in Kettering. There was no money. They were doing all the races off the back of nothing. There was no question of 'Ride these four races to get ready for this next one.' You would do one race at random, then another, then the world championships. I remember watching the Worlds one year and seeing a rider I knew called Steve Farrell always sitting last wheel in that massive peloton because he didn't have the skills. They wouldn't bring in riders who could help the team, put other guys into the right position; it was all about who was best at smashing each other over the Yorkshire Dales in the Premier Calendar races – riders like Farrell or Mark Lovatt, who were as strong as an ox. And the guys who did have the skills, the strength and the knowledge – Chris Lillywhite, Chris Walker

– never rode for the biggest pro teams, so they never got to use their ability at the highest level.

By 1993 I was riding for Dynatech, which was an amateur version of the Raleigh professional team. I was pushing for a place in the Olympic and Commonwealth Games but never quite made it. There weren't that many options. There were plenty of lads from the UK trying to make it abroad – in Belgium, France or Holland, even Italy – but you never heard of them. There might be a little write-up in *Cycling Weekly* now and then, but otherwise they would just be lost. There was no level you could aim for in between racing in the UK and racing abroad, which was a long way above British racing. You couldn't just race to improve, and there was no advice to be had. So I decided to be a professional. I wasn't in the Olympic clique for the road or the track, so it seemed that I might as well.

The key influence for me in the mid-1990s was Shane Sutton, an Aussie who was still racing as a professional with Keith Lambert's teams, which had been sponsored by Banana Group and Falcon. Shane went on to coach Wales and played a big role with Great Britain from about 2003 onwards. I was about twenty-one or twenty-two when I got to know him well. He was a huge influence on me in terms of how a team works, how to respect your teammates. He was a very good racer, a very good tactician, and I learnt more from him than from most of the people I ran into. He was always very, very disciplined, unbelievably strict. We would go on trips to Australia, and if you were late for a training ride or late leaving for a race, you'd go home.

By 1995 I was racing for a team sponsored by Ambrosia Desserts and run by an ex-pro called Mick Morrison, who'd been part of the pro scene back in the 1980s. The team had a proper professional licence – which ruled me out of selection for Great Britain – and sometimes we would go racing in Belgium when there was a gap in the UK calendar. There was one particular spell when we went and stayed in Mechelen in a house owned by Tim Harris, a pro from Norfolk who lived out there – and still does – and who was giving a bunch of guys a bit of an opportunity. The guys living in that house were trying to get noticed by the Belgian teams, and they were living pretty rough. They were doing it the hard way, living off what they could earn in the bike races, and I had total respect for them. I was sharing a room with a thin, blond guy from Yorkshire called Rob Reynolds-Jones, who was nicknamed Log, and Ben Luckwell, an older lad from Bristol.

It was a three-storey house above Tim's furniture place. It was freezing, with about eight or nine of them living in there, but they had a whale of a time. The toilet was in a big bathroom with a curtain across it. I was sleeping on a mattress – Rob had the bed – and next to it was a mineral-water bottle with the top cut off. I was lying there looking at it; it had marker-pen lines on it, with one about five millimetres from the top. I said, 'What the hell is that?' And Rob said, 'You don't want to be going down the steps to the toilet in the night. If you tried going down there in the dark, you'd break your neck.' So the bottle was what they would piss into. I said, 'OK, so what are the lines?' 'That's the world record.' That's what they'd got to one night – I don't know how on earth they'd have got it down the stairs in the morning without spilling a load of it.

Then there was one night when I woke up going, 'What the heck is that?' Something had run over me, just below my neck, something a bit furry. And Rob just said, cool as mustard, 'That's Ratty.' 'Oh my God, are you joking?' But he wasn't.

This was in 1995, about a month before the world championships, which were in late August. They were in Colombia that year, and most of the better pros in Europe weren't going because the course was too hard, so they were all riding the *kermis* races – the little events they have in conjunction with village fairs over there – that we were riding to prepare for the Commonwealth Bank Classic in Australia. One of the guys in the team was Glenn Holmes, who I knew well from back in England, and we would both get completely and utterly smashed to pieces in the races. Basically, we couldn't keep up. Sometimes I would make it into the front group. You'd be in there with riders who had won the Tour of Flanders, riders like Steven Rooks, Johan Museeuw and Jelle Nijdam; I'd get in because I could ride my bike well in the crosswinds, but I'd then get dropped because they were going so fast. I was thinking, 'Oh my God, what is going on?'

Glenn and I got back to Tim's house one night, just shattered. He looked at us and said, 'Not as glossy as it looks in the mags, is it, lads?' We were getting our heads kicked in week in, week out. I rode the Tour de l'Avenir that year, and there were riders there who'd ridden the Tour de France a few weeks earlier. I was going in with Boots multivitamins and couldn't work out what the hell was going on. I remember Glenn saying to me on that trip, 'I thought the goalposts were here, and now I can't even see them.' He was a good bike racer back in the UK, and it was a massive blow to him. I don't put it down to him not being good enough; it was a matter of not having the right structure going into the racing. And there was the doping culture out there: we had no idea what the hell we were up against. Back then, you were in the UK, on your island, and you had no clue what the rest of the world was doing. You could earn a reasonable wage in the UK without going through the hard times that Tim and his lads went through. People would knock them, but I'd tell those people they should be out there.

So I thought, 'Sod it, I'll go and race in France.' There was a guy from Newark called David Miller, who'd been national criterium champion in the 1980s; I knew him well, and knew he raced for a team called UV Aube in the town of Troyes, in eastern France. I got in touch and said I'd had enough and needed to go out there. I had a routine to my year: race the Australian season over the winter; then work at a training camp in Spain with Graham Baxter, who ran holidays for club cyclists and liked to have pros along to lead the rides and give advice; and finally the British season. I felt I needed to go and race in France just for the experience. Perhaps I had realised that I was never going to make it at the highest level.

France was fantastic. I loved every minute of it, even though it was hard: there was no phone to call home, I didn't speak the language to start with, and there was no coaching. It was simply a matter of 'Just be there at this time. We'll pick you up and go to the race, then we'll drop you off.' But my attitude was that I was going there and I wanted to live the life. I couldn't afford to go home anyway. I was working in the winter doing little bits here and there, but I wasn't getting paid to race in France. After three months I was doing OK: I wanted to learn the language and I managed that, and I started making some prize money. Then the club started to pay me £20 a week, which meant I could afford some food. In 1998 I met Jacques André, who was the real force behind cycling in Troyes and ran the rival club to UV Aube, UVC Aube. He'd run UVCA since the 1960s, and had had some very good British riders who had gone on and done well as pros: Vin Denson, Alan Ramsbottom, Derek Harrison.

Jacques was a barber who had his own shop in a suburb of Troyes. He loved the Brits. He told me one day that he thought we were fighters, that we never gave in, but on the other hand, when it came to cycling, we had no idea how to train and race. He was a strong character. He would send me home in the winter with a handwritten training plan of what to do every day until I came back to Troyes. We had a fair few arguments because we're both very opinionated people – for example, he didn't approve of me going to Australia in the winter – but it always felt as if we respected each other. He'd drop in most days to the flat above a newsagent's where I lived – he'd come to buy his paper, pop in and open the fridge to see what I was eating. In that part of France the roads are made for motor pacing – rolling roads, very straight, lots of steady climbs – so he'd take me out for hours and hours and hours behind the car.

The club had a minibus, and we'd all cram in to go to the races. I had my own seat, right behind Jacques in the second row. Over the years Jacques had learnt a few words of English, and he thought he was really good at it – but he talked too fast, so it was hard to understand. The way it worked was that each generation of foreign riders at the club would introduce the next, so after me came Dan Lloyd, who went on to ride the Tour with Cervélo, Yanto Barker, who is still racing, and Jon Tiernan-Locke, who is now at Sky.

I was winning ten or twelve races a year, always getting in

the group who made the money in the criteriums. But it wasn't about the money; it was about going and doing it, about the whole experience. So from 1997 to 1999 I was lost to the GB system. I'd missed the boat earlier because of the pro thing with Ambrosia, and I knew I wouldn't be a pro with a career like Paul Sherwen or Robert Millar, both of whom had gone abroad as young amateurs and ended up with long, successful spells riding the Tour de France.

I came home in the winter of 1999 because I had heard they were taking on firemen in Grantham. I had thought I would go on cycling until I was about thirty, and then think what to do with the rest of my life. I didn't have a clue what to do, but I had always wanted to be a fireman, so I won my last race in France and came home. I went into the fire station, with no interview set up, and spoke to the station officer. He turned me down there and then. He said they weren't going to train up someone who had been swanning around the world for the last ten years. He said, 'We'll commit to you, and then you'll go off again.' I just thought, 'This is great.' I hadn't been successful and I hadn't made any money, but that hadn't meant I wasn't committed to what I was doing. And it didn't mean that I wouldn't be committed to the fire service if they let me join.

I sat down on the wall outside the fire station in Grantham and wondered what on earth I was going to do.

2 : First Blood

It was deadly quiet that morning in January 2003. I was sitting in an apartment in Bendigo, about thirty kilometres north of Melbourne. The Great Britain team had gone out early doors for an easy ride on yet another day of blinding heat, and I was sat in my room at my laptop. I'd been appointed as a GB coach a few months earlier and there was plenty to catch up on. We had a group of about ten riders at a two-month warm-weather training camp, among them the under-23 group that I was looking after.

Then I heard the clip clop of cleated cycling shoes in the courtyard. One of the riders had come back early – too early, half an hour into what was supposed to be a three-hour ride. I jumped up, a bit concerned, and looked out of the window: Russell Anderson, one of my lads was out there. I couldn't make out what was wrong; perhaps he would come and knock on the door. I sat back and waited. The knock came soon enough. Standing in the doorway, he was a bit white in the face as he held up his arm to show me his elbow. The cut was a deep one; the blood had dried where it had run down his arm, and I could see the thick red mark on the skin around the gash. He'd taken a nice chunk out of the joint.

Straight away, the coaching instincts kicked in: 'Let's get you cleaned up, into the shower and then off to hospital to be stitched up.' Russell was quite a tough lad and wasn't particularly disturbed by the cut. He wasn't the type who talked much anyway; quite reserved, he tended to grunt in that Scottish way. It wasn't easy to have a conversation with him at the best of times, let alone talk about any deep stuff.

'Bloody hell, what happened?'

'Tom White and me were messing about, locked our bars, and we both went down. Tom's OK, but I thought I'd better get this sorted.'

He was all apologetic, but I said, 'It's not a problem, you've not broken anything.' I always say that if you fall off while racing and break something, that's part of the game; if you fall off in training and it's a silly accident and you break something, you're cursed; but if you fall off and don't break anything, there's no harm done. And then, while I was cleaning up the wound, he said it: 'It didn't hurt as much as I thought it would do.'

'What do you mean?'

'It's the first time I've ever fallen off on the road.'

He had had a crash on the track, but I remember thinking, 'How can you not have fallen off on the road?' I asked him, 'Have you never flown into a corner, busting a gut to get into it first, so that your wheels go from under you?' It's all about learning your limits, all about finding things out – 'God these are crap tyres, but those work fine,' that kind of thing.

The thought passed quickly. He got cleaned up, they put some stitches in, and that was the day over. The lads were taking the piss out of him, as riders always do. But this was a moment when it suddenly came home to me that something wasn't right. How can you get to nineteen, be wearing the Great Britain cycling jersey, getting paid full-time to ride your bike, when you've never experienced crashing onto tarmac?

It made me think, 'We've got to toughen these guys up.' Cycling is a hard world, a sport where you get hurt regularly. It wasn't that you had to make the young riders crash, but you needed to put them into situations in training which would challenge them. I cast my mind back to club runs in the winter in the old days, when you're going round a corner and the first few riders hit a patch of ice. Boom! Down they go, the guys behind hit their brakes, and in a second everyone is in a pile on the deck. Someone bends their bike (you hope there's a bike shop in the nearest town where you can straighten it out with a hammer), and you hobble home and get in the bath to clean the raw burgers on your elbows and knees. These are all things you go through as a young lad. You're constantly pushing yourself. Or you should be. But I didn't see that in the lads I was looking after. They were so into their training efforts, so into doing things in such a structured way. Russell was symptomatic of the problem: he had a lot of talent, but wasn't being taught right.

There was another constant moan I had: the lack of discipline among the young guys. There was an incident that summed it up for me with Paul Manning. He is now a successful coach at British Cycling, but even then, as a medallist in the Sydney Olympic Games in the team pursuit, he was a leader, an elder statesman. He didn't earn that status by shouting at the top of his voice but because he was well organised, always clean and tidy, and rode his bike so well. And critically, he was always on time. The riders would go out training early in the morning because of the heat, and Paul would be there at ten to six if they were going out at six. I'd be there early too, and there was one morning – it would be at one or two minutes past six – when

Paul said to me in that dry Black Country drawl of his, 'Rod, I don't think it's fair that I have to wait for these young lads.'

'Paul, you're right. What's going on?'

That was another moment that took me to the core of the problem. These lads were swanning around on ten grand a year, couldn't even ride their bikes, couldn't position themselves correctly in a race, and they couldn't even come down on time for training. What the hell was going on?

I thought, 'Something has to change here.' But ironically, Paul was the opposite of what I was aiming for. He was a fantastic athlete, but he was an athlete rather than an all-round bike rider. In a team pursuit – and this was the key discipline as far as we were concerned – he was always sitting a wheel's length off the back of the other riders and looking round the rider in front. His success came out of a structured approach and from his physical qualities as an athlete. I always wondered how much better he might be if he could sit closer to a wheel, if he was a more complete bike racer.

I believed you had to have a passion for cycling above all else. The young lads I had to coach didn't really seem to enjoy it, but I'd loved cycling as a teenager, really loved it. You had to know about the sport, and you had to have a thirst for every bit of information you could get. To take another example, none of the young lads we had knew how to stick on a tubular tyre. I said, 'How can you not know that? Did no one ever teach you?' I knew that John Herety, the former top professional who was the road team manager, was just as frustrated, but he had to spend so much time with the older riders that he never really had the chance to think about how to turn the younger ones into better cyclists. Not that anyone had said I had to do it.

My brief was to coach them and to learn from our head coach, Simon Jones. The objective was to turn the riders into Olympic medallists. My idea was to go back to basics: develop the lads into good bike riders first and then turn them into athletes. And there was something else you could do: develop them as young people at the same time.

A couple of years had passed since the afternoon when I had walked out of the fire station in Grantham, sat down on the wall and wondered what I was going to do with my life. I was with my best mate Simon – 'Bear', as I called him. He asked me what the next step was, and I remember saying to him, 'I don't know. I'll just keep riding my bike, I guess.' I was fortunate that Richard, my brother, had his own businesses: a recruitment agency and a track-day company, where you go around racing circuits in fancy cars – a Ferrari and so on. He's ambitious enough, and he said to me, 'Why don't you form a little company, base it around your cycling and set yourself up as a bike rider?' I thought that was a good idea, so I moved into his house in Harlaxton, just outside Grantham. Richard put in a bit of money, so did I, and we called the company RJ Management, after him – Richard Jeffrey – as I didn't want it to be named after me. We printed up some brochures, and I went down to the dole office. Again I got lucky. I'd never signed on; I hated it but I knew I was doing it for a reason. I sat down opposite the dole officer, and he said, 'Are you Rod Ellingworth the cyclist?' He knew of me because of the involvement I'd had with the council since way back when. So I explained what I was doing, that I didn't want to go for a job, and he said I could just come in, collect the dole money and get on with what I was doing.

Richard and I had a whole list of companies to approach – food, health, travel – that I thought might like to be involved in cycling. Unlike today, nobody knew much about the sport. We sent out the brochures, did follow-up calls. What I'd done with the council in the past began to kick in, and so did the work – school visits and so on – that I'd done with Ambrosia when they'd sponsored me. The council were really getting behind pushing cycling; they had a meeting every few weeks about developing it – bike paths and so on. I came up with a plan for school visits, I organised National Bike to Work Day and National Bike Week with them, kids' routes, stuff like that, and they would get me in and use me to see if this or that would work.

I wasn't making a lot of money. I think in a year I'd bring in about eight to ten grand – nothing really, but enough just to get by. I had a car from the council and I used my contacts to get everything I could for free: I was still involved with Raleigh, and they got my bikes and so on; and Impsport – a local company from Lincoln – sponsored me with clothing. And I was still racing at the time, so I'd pick up a few hundred quid in the criteriums. I picked up some work on a couple of television programmes on the Disney Channel and the BBC – there was one BBC kids' programme about aerodynamics with me talking to a puppet which still gets shown – and I did cycling-proficiency and road-safety videos, that kind of stuff, little bits here and there. I was just getting by, with no idea where it would take me.

It was about then that Simon Jones, who was the Great Britain head coach, approached me about riding for the national team. It was just before the Sydney Olympics in summer 2000, and they were looking ahead to the next Olympic cycle, trying to bring in all the riders who in the past had ridden in the team pursuit at either senior or junior level, to assess their potential for Athens. That opened the doors again. Jenny Gretton, who was the East Midlands coach for the Talent Team – the Great Britain under-16 cycling programme that aimed to 'uncover' the next generation of Olympians – knew I was doing all these little things and was looking for what they called 'an expert rider' to come along to team camps at weekends, so I started doing that as well. That was the first time I experienced coaching from the other side – as a coach, not a rider – and I thought, 'Bloody hell, I actually quite like this.' I did a few weekends and days with them over that period and really got into it. What appealed was the fact that the kids actually listened and would then go and do something, such as a turbo-trainer session. You'd be explaining to them how to get the best out of themselves, and I enjoyed that.

I applied for a job as British Cycling's Talent Team coach for the north-east later on in 2000. I was training on the track under Simon Jones, staying in the top end of the Peak District with Tim Buckle, who was a couple of years younger than me and ended up going to the Commonwealth Games two years later. I didn't hear a word back about the job and I was pretty pissed off when I learnt who they were taking on. I had nothing against the woman who did land the job, but I didn't understand why they didn't call me in to talk to them. Ian Drake was the Talent Team coordinator; he's the chief executive now, but he was the guy who set it all up at the time. I didn't know him from Adam, so I called his secretary and asked her to explain why I hadn't got the interview. I was really pushy – 'Listen, all

I want to know is why I didn't get it. I'm pretty up for this, so I want to have some idea.'

Next thing, Ian Drake actually rang me himself. Although I didn't know him, he clearly knew me. It turned out he was from round Nottingham way, so there was an East Midlands connection there. He explained that I had no qualifications, no experience in coaching, while the other people had been to university or had been coaching in part-time jobs. I asked him what I had to do. He said I needed a coaching certificate and some experience. He also told me there was a pot of money available for coaching within the East Midlands region, so I went to them and they paid me to do a course. Funnily enough, Simon Jones was doing the course with me – he was the head coach but he had to do his level-two coaching as well, for insurance reasons.

I'd done nothing like this since I left school twelve years earlier and I felt the course was too scientific, but one of the last sessions was a practical day, when you had to run a session of your own. My subject was mounting and dismounting the bike. When you look at it, there all sorts of different ways you do that, depending on the discipline: cyclo-cross, track, road. (In cyclo-cross you are constantly getting on and off the bike; in a criterium you need to get away from a standing start at high speed; while on the track you have to be able to come down on your fixed-wheel bike, slow down and stop without falling off.) You had to go away for the evening, think about it and put your session together. 'Brilliant,' I thought, and I went into all the different ways of doing it. Ian Drake was one of the supervisors, and he said it was one of the best sessions he'd ever seen and I'd gone into areas he had never even thought about.

I didn't pass all my theory, but because I'd done so well on the practical side I got the coaching badge no problem.

With that behind me, I started practical sessions to build up experience. Just then, after the Sydney Games, British Cycling was starting to bring in a series of tests aimed at filtering talented kids into the system. To give just one example, the coaches would spend a whole day at a school in Nottingham, a kind of open day for cycling in which different groups of kids could come in and do the tests. So I started helping them out, and a couple of other regions as well when they needed people. I threw myself at everything and anything the Talent Team could give me.

Something else which bridged the gap from being a rider to being a coach was that from the mid-1990s I had been involved over the winters with a cycling-holiday company run from Yorkshire, Graham Baxter Sporting Tours. Graham would always bring out a pro or two to work on his training camps for amateur cyclists, to lead the rides and give advice and lend the whole thing a bit of glamour. The pros at the camps used to do talks in the evening as well, which was all good experience for coaching, but there was more. Over the years I realised there were things that didn't work. For example, you would take the rides out and there would be riders spread all over the countryside. I said to Graham we could make it much more structured. Most people were coming out for a week at a time, so why not have seven set routes, seven main climbs for them to go over during the seven days? You could have all the groups setting off at once, splitting them up by ability when it got hard, and have them all followed by cars, so that if people had a problem they would know there was someone behind them. You could have a big map on the wall with the route for each day. I got totally into it and felt I really took responsibility. I didn't realise it at the time, but all this was helping me learn to manage people out on the road.

Gradually I was being drawn into the Great Britain set-up. Leading into 2001, Simon Jones asked if I would be interested in riding some stage races with the younger lads, guiding them a bit in the role of road captain, which meant giving orders to the team from inside the peloton as they raced. It's a role often given to an older rider, as there are many times when a team can't be in touch with the manager in the following car. Jonesy was looking ahead to the Commonwealth Games in 2002; he had a big group which he'd widened out after Sydney, and he was trying to whittle them down a bit. There were riders like me, Tim Buckle, who is now a coach at British Cycling himself, Phil West, who is still working in the sport on the promotion side, and Steve Cummings, who went on to ride for Team Sky and BMC.

I was very much one of the guys on the periphery, but already I was beginning to ask questions about how they did certain things. For example, to qualify for Great Britain in those days you had to do a standing-start three-kilometre time trial and a flying kilometre on the track, and be within a certain time. That's all it was, that was the standard – and that was all we would do at a track session, those bastard tests. It was horrible. It was demoralising, and limiting. If you had the talent, you could do it, but I never made it. I never really had the heart for it – it would just crack me – while others would waltz through it because they were so talented. The coaches would relate your time to your age, and also to the temperature at the track – the warmer the air is, the faster you go – and would deduct a certain amount. The development riders – an eighteen-year-old lad, for example – could go a few seconds slower and still get funding, whereas my attitude was that even at eighteen or nineteen you should be trying to be the best in the world. They should be trying to win world championships, because this was track racing, not road racing, where endurance matters so much. All you need on the track is sheer guts and speed.

In 2001 I started doing the training camps in Majorca with Great Britain, then the stage races which were used to build up the track riders' foundation of fitness for their specific speed training: the Flèche du Sud in Luxembourg, the Cinturón in Majorca, the Route du Sud in France and the Tour of Rhodes. I roomed with Bradley Wiggins sometimes; out of the four stage races I did with GB that year, he won three of them, and was second in Rhodes to Fabian Cancellara, who was a prospect then but has now turned into the best Classics rider in the world. For a young lad Brad was already quite striking: he would be first up the hills, and first in the bunch sprints as well. He was just so talented, and he led off the bike too: he'd come round the team's rooms in the evening and he'd be really behind us all, always saying, 'Thanks for all the work you did today,' and so on. Road captain was a role I really enjoyed, seeing all the young lads race and watching them progress. On one race, along with me, Tim and Brad, we had the mountain-bike team for company: they knew nothing about racing on the road, didn't know about the tactics, so showing them the ropes was really good fun.

As 2001 progressed I realised I was getting closer to Simon Jones in terms of how it was all running. I was constantly challenging him, continually saying, 'You're too training focused; these lads don't race very well.' I could understand lads like Brian Steel and the other top team pursuiters riding the road races, because it was preparation for the track – but why not just try to win rather than merely getting in the miles? Surely they would prepare better if they raced? It did my head in. I remember going to Jonesy and pointing out that it was pretty limiting for the lads who did the team pursuit because there weren't many racing opportunities. Why didn't I get a few lads in a team with me? I would help them out and we would ride the team-pursuit national championship together. I knew I wasn't going to go anywhere, but for my teammates, Tim Buckle, Steve Cummings and Phil West, it was worth a go, and it was another opportunity for the lads to get on the start line, which didn't happen very often. I called the four of us Team McEll. They weren't a sponsor as such but my brother's company. I was trying to sell every bit of the jersey to various companies, but I couldn't sell the main part, so that was the name on the front, and the name of the team.

I think of one week in August 2001 as *the* week, because so many significant things happened. The four of us won the team pursuit national championship; it was quite a big thing because we'd been through a long period of time together and we'd had good fun. It was also the first time I took Jane out – we've been together ever since – and I applied for a job as the north-east Talent Team coach. I handwrote the entire application because I had no computer. It was massive: I put down everything I'd done, every little bit, and went on and on and on. As well as the interview, I had to do a fifteen-minute presentation on how

British Cycling should develop youngsters in the sport – and that made me as nervous as anything. With my brother's help, it took a week to get the presentation ready. I'd never done anything of the kind before, so I dropped everything, even riding my bike. I literally stopped cycling there and then.

Ian Drake and Dave Brailsford were on the interview panel, along with the head of HR at British Cycling. Dave had been part of the Olympic set-up from almost the very start in 1997, and had known me through those years of being on the team. There was one key question he asked me: 'Are you prepared to put your all into this job?' I think he was a bit concerned about how some former bike riders simply can't leave the sport behind and end up compromising by keeping on riding just enough for it to be a distraction. I remember that I told him I would do it 100 per cent, and I've always stuck to that; that's why I haven't raced my bike since. I got the call from British Cycling a week later. I was as nervous as anything leaving Jane's house in the morning on my way to see them. Dave said, 'We want to offer you a job' – at which I thought, 'Oh my God, you're joking' – and then added, 'But the problem is . . . you have to choose between three jobs.' They needed Talent Team coaches in the north-east or East Midlands, or a Talent Team manager in the south-east, where the whole set-up would have to be built from scratch.

Dave gave me the bit of paper: the Talent Team coach's salary was £15–22,000 and the manager's was £23–30,000. I was twenty-nine and I thought, 'Fucking hell, I've never had this much money in my life.' I said I would come back to them in the next hour, sat in the car park, rang my brother and thought it through. If I took the coach's job, I could stay in the East

Midlands or go and work in the north-east with Jonny Clay – another former bike rider who I knew really well – but then I thought, 'Let's say the British Cycling thing folds. If you've been a coach in cycling, that's one thing, but if you've been a manager, that's more recognisable, and you're more likely to get a job somewhere else.' I didn't have a clue what I was meant to be doing because I had to start the entire set-up from scratch, but I said I would do it. I rang Jane and told her to meet me in a restaurant in Manchester to celebrate.

So my career as a coach with the Great Britain Olympic team began in March 2002. I spent the first part of the year living in Vicky Pendleton's father's house in Stotfold, up on the Hertfordshire–Bedfordshire border. During the week I was getting up at 5 a.m., driving down to the lock-up at Welwyn Garden City, getting all the kit together and driving on to one school or other in central London, where I would run filtering sessions from nine in the morning to three in the afternoon. These sessions were the core of the Talent Team programme. You had an endurance track marked out around the outside of the playing field and a sprint track marked across it; you had to put so many youngsters through. They were all timed and they would all compare their times online, so there was a national table. It was a system that Ian Drake had come up with, when Peter Keen, who had founded the Olympic team, began to get concerned about where the next generation of Olympic cyclists would be found. Pete was aware that they wouldn't just come out of the British club system, and the idea was that the times would enable regional coaches to figure out who were the best, and they could then get them into the system and work with them.

You tested the riders out on the playing field and then invited the better ones in for a day of testing on the rigs. There you did more quality testing and interviewed them so you could get to know them. The next stage was a training camp, when you got to know their characters a little bit better, and then you selected them onto the Talent Team, so many riders per year from each region. As a talent-identification system, it worked: Lizzie Armitstead, who won the silver medal in the road race at the Olympics in London, was one who was spotted through that filtering process; Ed Clancy and Jason Kenny, both gold medallists in London and Beijing, were others who began there. Ian Stannard was one from back then – and I'm still coaching him now – Alex Dowsett, who is currently riding for Movistar, was another, and so was Russell Hampton, who went on to be part of the academy.

I got into the job. I really enjoyed it, even though for the first few weeks I was sitting in an office in the Gosling Sports Park next to the outdoor velodrome at Welwyn Garden City trying to figure it out. I'd never done anything with budgets or finance – I'm still not the best at that side of it – and I didn't have a clue. I was told, 'Get a desk, get computers, get everything you need,' but I'd never done anything like that before and I was on my own. Then we employed Helen Mortimer, who'd been a mountain-bike racer, as a coach, and that helped. I was really excited about the idea of talent ID – I thought, 'Bloody hell, it really works' – but what I hated about the system was that it was very rigid.

The programme Ian Drake had come up with was a fantastic concept, but I remember thinking there was more we could do with rider development. So what particularly appealed to me were the training camps we ran in the school holidays; that was where I had a bit of freedom. We did four or five days down at Calshot in Hampshire, where they have an old indoor track from the six-days, and one day I did track, the next day grass track or road or cyclo-cross or mountain biking. So over two or three days the kids had a morning of each discipline. I was running the grass-track sessions, and I had the kids on the grass doing Madisons – a relay event for teams of two, who change over when one rider 'throws' the other into the action. It was an Olympic discipline, but we taught it to improve the riders' skills, teaching them the basics of how to come in for the change, how to avoid overlapping the wheels, how to get into position for the sprint. It wasn't actually my job to coach, but I was getting into the idea of it all.

I never lost contact with Simon Jones, and when the assistant national coach moved on late in 2002, Jonesy said something to me about doing the job. At first I thought, 'Bloody hell, I've only just got into this role here at Welwyn,' but I did feel that what I was doing could be directed at older riders, not just the kids, and Helen Mortimer was doing really well. She understood what I wanted to do and was ready to step up; I was thinking she could do the job, and I could go and work for Simon. Then one day I was walking through the track centre in Manchester when I met one of the *soigneurs*, and she said, 'Congratulations on your new job.' I didn't even know I had got it.

Simon and I had been in contact a lot, and I think he enjoyed the conversations we used to have – he was after a little bit of cycling knowledge, more of the bunch-racing skills that the Great Britain team lacked. Simon was a special character; there are stories of him wrestling Chris Hoy when he'd had a drink or two. I liked his drive, the fact that he knew his own mind. He didn't care if people didn't like his decisions; he would just say, 'This is what we are doing,' and on they would go. He was the one who changed the team-pursuit squad – their way of training, the structure of it. The trouble was that he couldn't see beyond the team pursuit. There were other Olympic events on the track – the points race, the Madison – but they were outside his orbit and it used to frustrate me. The lads who rode the team pursuit would be going to road races to build their strength for that four-minute effort and they'd be finishing at the back in bunch sprints – but there was some fantastic talent and finishing speed among them. And I'd be thinking, 'Why don't you make them race?' That was what I had been trying to do when I was road captain at those stage races in 2001: we competed, we took it on, and Brad got his first professional contract with La Française des Jeux because he won those races.

I hadn't really known it was coming my way, but I took the job of assistant national endurance coach. In those days Peter Keen was heading the whole Great Britain set-up, and I wouldn't imagine he was a supporter of me coming on board. I always had that feeling because he was so into the sports-science side. Simon was the coach, John Herety – a former professional from the 1980s who still runs the Rapha-Condor-JLT team – was the road manager, and they were both my bosses, although it never felt like that. Simon and John never got on, but I didn't give a monkey's about that – it was their problem and the one thing we had in common was that we wanted to be successful. That's a key thing about British Cycling: the BC way isn't my way, the Simon Jones way, the Dave Brailsford way or anyone's way of doing things – it's just how everything has developed. At the centre of it is one thing: we put the riders first. As for me, I was already thinking, 'God, we could do so much better at road racing and at bunch racing on the track.'

The training camp in Australia at the start of 2003 was my first trip away with the lads. I was keen to see them race because I didn't know them that well. There were a lot of races on the programme, although they weren't at the highest level. The lads were riding the track leagues at Bendigo and Castlemaine; they went down to the Vodafone stadium in Melbourne for a couple of races; there were handicap races on the road run by the Bendigo club on Sundays; and the Victoria Carnival races over Christmas and New Year. Those races would help me understand the level they were at, and even before Russell Anderson had his crash I didn't like what I was seeing.

One evening, Russell was racing in the Bendigo track league. I was filming it – I was recording every race so that we could do feedback sessions with the riders afterwards. It was a beautiful warm evening, with a gorgeous sunset because there had been fires up in Canberra. It was about forty-five degrees. Russell got in the break, went to the front and did his turn; as he swung up the track to let the next rider in line through, this guy was overlapping his back wheel and he fell off. Bendigo is a big track, 500 metres round, so it was about thirty seconds until the next time Russell came round. When he got to the other rider lying on the deck, he back-pedalled, slowed right down and came to a stop to see if he was all right. You can hear me on the video camera shouting, 'What the fuck are you doing? Don't you dare stop.' I was quite short with him. 'What were you doing?' He said, 'It's only track league. I wanted to see if he was all right.' He didn't know if it was his fault or not – and it was another of those things that made me wonder, 'How much does this guy know about cycling?' In a race, you don't worry about what happens behind you – if someone hits you from behind, as long as you weren't doing something stupid, that's their problem. You've got to get stuck in.

It wasn't just Russell, it was the whole group I was working with in 2003: Owen Wallace, Russell Anderson, Kieran Page, Steve Cummings, Ben Hallam, Tom White and Kristian House. I was continually thinking, 'Something isn't right here.' I don't know if that came from my background, the ten years I'd spent before that not earning anything and scraping by, but it seemed to me that these riders had a GB jersey on and it was far too easy for them. They didn't lack for anything. I couldn't see any sign that they were hungry – that's what it was.

Throughout that year I'd watch them training on the track. They were never pushed. These young lads would come into the track centre and their bikes would all be there for them, the right gears on, tyres pumped up, ready to go. They'd have exactly the same kit as the Olympic team, but the only thing they had to achieve to qualify for the Olympic development squad was to hit those age-related times. It wasn't as if to get on the national team they were having to win five races, win one of the biggest one-day races in Britain – the Premier Calendars – or an international race, or show their ability to handle their bikes in the bunch. The philosophy was, 'Can you do this time and within an hour back it up with another?'

I remember one day we were going off to a race; I think it was the Girvan Three-Day in south-west Scotland. I had

Russell Anderson and Kieran Page in the car with me. They both had their headphones on and wouldn't talk. I was thinking, 'For the next few hours they've got a chance to get a whole load of information about bike racing out of me . . .', but they weren't interested. Kieran was reading the newspaper and talking to me about some general news in there, and I was thinking, 'Mate, you're nineteen or twenty, you're in the GB national team, you're sitting next to the coach – why aren't you talking about cycling? You're in the wrong game, pal.'

I remember asking them, 'What have you got planned for next week?'

They said, 'Nothing.'

'How do you mean "nothing"? What races are you doing?'

'We're not racing.'

'When are you racing next?'

'The so-and-so stage race' – in a month's time.

'What are you doing in between?'

'Nothing, you guys haven't entered us for anything.'

'But don't you want to race?'

'We don't want to race unless you make us race.'

That was something I simply couldn't get my head around: how could you not want to race if you were a bike racer?

They were doing only twenty or twenty-five days of racing a year, but they didn't have to win those races as long as they could keep doing their qualification times, and I was thinking, 'So what? What does that get you?' They had the same kit and clothing as someone who was a professional bike rider or an Olympic medallist. None of it added up for me. They didn't have to work hard enough for it. They didn't have to prove anything. They'd made it. And everybody was wrapping them up in cotton wool. They were scared to push these guys.

People had got comfortable. The words 'minimum standard' make you think. To get in the team you had to hit a minimum time standard. It wasn't a question of 'Here's the fastest time in the world. Let's pick the riders who get closest to that.' It was: 'Here is a minimum standard to get you on the national programme.' There's an important difference. That way of doing things doesn't create winners. It creates people who say, 'Right, as long as I can do four minutes twenty-four seconds for 4,000 metres, or whatever, that's great; I've got my money and I can live a nice comfy life.' I didn't even feel that our senior squad were what they should have been. When you looked at the Aussies, the team we were trying to beat, they were staying in Italy together, living the life of bike racers, and that meant they knew each other inside out. Our guys would go home, come together for a few races, get looked after like pros and go home again. It looked as if there was no real bite to them, no major commitment. Their basic understanding of cycling was poor. They were nice kids, but they didn't have a clue. They weren't really into it. They had no passion for cycling. We were a million miles away from where I wanted to be.

3 : Man with a Plan

I seemed to spend most of 2003 writing. I've always been into writing my ideas down. I constantly give myself lists of things to do; I don't care how the end product looks on paper, I get it all down so I can understand it. From the moment I came back from the hospital with Russell I started putting my ideas down. I could see a massive window of opportunity. I could change it all so easily, and I could make it bloody good fun for the lads. I would get so absorbed by the process that John Herety, who was rooming with me in Bendigo, would ask, 'Could you not stop working and just calm down?' But I had to do something. I'd just got the job and was so enthusiastic; it felt as if I was jotting down ideas around the clock. I'd learnt a lot from Simon Jones, and now I was ready to put the programme together. I really enjoyed that time. I was so immensely into it, looking at everything and believing I could make it all better.

I wanted to make sure I was going to do a good job; if I didn't make a success of working for Great Britain, there was nothing else for me to do. I remember saying to Jane that this was the only option I had: 'I've got to be ready for this, I've got to put everything into it.' This was either going to work or else I was going to have to get a normal job that I didn't want to do. I was bloody well ready for it. I'd always committed to my bike riding; I'd always known, for example, that if I wanted to go out on the Nottingham club run, I had to be out of the house at eight in the morning and no later. If you didn't put that commitment in, you wouldn't get anywhere, and if I made the same kind of effort now, I'd be OK.

I believed that there was a bottleneck in the British senior men's endurance team. Riders like Bryan Steel and Chris Newton had been around for a long time, and in my mind they were blocking the system; how could the young lads beat them if getting into the squad was just about going fastest in a straight line? If you're trying to get to Olympic-medal standard in the team pursuit, how do you show whether you're good enough when there are only a couple of races in the year? I wanted to take these young riders away from the senior squad and make the European under-23 track championships their main goal, with the under-23 world road title their other focus. Those were age-related goals, so they would be competing against their peers. I wanted to get the young riders away from the older ones, away from that senior bubble. They had to have their own programme with its own coach, completely separate from the senior team.

The stepping stones were there. The best example was Bradley Wiggins, who had won the junior world pursuit title in 1998 and broken through to the senior squad for the Sydney Games; two years later he had gone on to a successful career on the road and a place in a professional road team. If the two ends of the spectrum are the athlete and the pure bike racer, Paul Manning would be your athlete through and through, while Phil West was a good example of a bike racer who really loved his cycling. The best ones – Brad, Rob Hayles, Chris Hoy – combine being a great athlete with massive racing ability and a passion for cycling. That's because to be good on a bike at any level you have to be able to hurt yourself. If you are really fit, you still hurt, but you just sprint faster or go across the gap to a break more quickly. The pain is the same. The best cyclists find it easy to hurt themselves because they have that passion. In the case of Brad, cycling had always been his life: he'd read all the magazines, had the posters on his wall. You can imagine him riding around Herne Hill pretending to be in a six-day or riding through the lanes pretending to be in the Tour de France. And he's a great athlete on top of that. He's the complete package. That was the kind of cyclist I wanted to produce.

To get some ideas from outside, I had a look at other sports – athletics, netball. I visited the Winter Olympics performance director and went to the English Institute of Sport in Bath. I wanted to speak to people who worked with similar age groups, developing athletes. The Winter Olympics was a new development programme; netball the same. Athletics was interesting: there were around nineteen national coaches, so how did they work together? I left the majority of them thinking they were not as structured or as disciplined as I was intending to be. They also had lots of issues with external coaches, which was something that wouldn't be a problem for us.

British Cycling's development manager at the time was Simon Lillistone, who would go on to head up the whole cycling programme at the London Olympic Games in 2012; back then he managed all the junior programmes. So through 2003 I stayed in the office with Simon late into the evenings working through the whole concept of an under-23 academy – what it would look like, how it would work, what discipline level we would start at. The idea was that I would coach it, and he would have an overview and manage things like logistics.

Discipline was a big part of it. I knew what I wanted: a crack squad of lads who behaved themselves, knew where the line was, had a good time and loved their sport but respected the people around them. If you don't have a basic regard for the people in your orbit, you're not going to get anywhere in any field. It would be simple and strict. I wanted them to look at it like this: you clock in in the morning, you clock out at night; this is full-time; this is a job; you're responsible and accountable for your actions. I wasn't interested in whether these guys were tired and couldn't perform on the bike. I was interested in a system, a regime, in getting these guys feeling like they were part of such a strong unit that one day that bond would bring them so close together that they would perform as a team.

It had to feel like they had gone through a journey, a massive experience in their lives. Everyone who's gone and lived abroad and experienced that loneliness has that in common, even complete strangers. It was the same concept. The Aussies were coming all the way to stay in Europe, living in each other's pockets. They would have a bond. They would live and die for each other. When it comes down to a key moment in a bike race – for example, when someone is doing a big lead-out for you – you want to know what that guy is thinking. You've got to trust him. That was what I wanted. The question was how to create that within a team.

From the British Lions – and from the time the school gave me that cycling jersey at assembly – I got the idea of having a welcome ceremony for the riders. When a player joins the Lions, he is awarded his Lions cap in front of his teammates. Everybody is there and they all applaud and so on. So at the start of every year I would do a presentation for the academy riders and all their families. I would tell them what we were expecting, set the targets, lay out the plans for the season, and so on. I wanted them to feel that they were joining a family. We took them on a tour of the velodrome; it was a way of saying 'Welcome' and getting the riders' families to buy in. I wanted them and the riders to have the background on how we worked, and the parents could take the information pack away and refer back to it. And the new riders would be awarded their jersey there. I knew the importance of that first jersey because I had kept mine, one of the classic GB ones in blue with red sleeves, which I may have been supposed to return!

The long-term goal was that the academy would produce at least two riders who would progress to the 2008 Olympic Games in Beijing. In the short term, however, the whole set-up was to be based around preparing riders to be professionals with European teams. The two objectives were completely compatible. I've always felt that the track is a young man's game: it's fast, it's about enthusiasm, it's punchy, intense. An athlete can't do that for ever. I see track racing as a stepping stone to being a pro on the road. The track is a good way in for a young rider, because you learn all your skills and you can become an Olympic champion; throughout that time you can learn, which is fantastic, and then you can go on and earn your money by becoming a pro. At that time there weren't too many pure team-pursuit specialists like Ed Clancy and Steven Burke. Nowadays, the discipline has moved on in terms of sheer speed, but back then the team pursuit was for riders like Rob Hayles, Chris Newton, Paul Manning, Jonny Clay – we all know they could have been fantastic pros on the road in the Bradley Wiggins mould.

At the time, Simon Jones was very much in favour of putting

the team pursuiters in top-level road races, because Brad had gone on to be a pro and so had Rob, and you could see the benefits in other areas of track endurance as well. So the idea with the academy was to start the riders on the track, then move them onto the road. Getting them to progress to being pros was in the plan. It was overt. Peter Keen had said before he founded the World Class Performance Plan in 1997 that it was about 'building a team that was ultimately a prelude to a full professional team . . . preparing people for life in teams where they will earn a lot of money'. Even then Dave Brailsford had the idea of running a pro team off the back of the track squad.

So there were many different things that went into the British Cycling academy plan. In drawing it up, what I concentrated on was this: you've got twenty building blocks to be a road professional or a world champion on track or road, so how do you tick them off? By riding at under-16 level you get the first couple of blocks, in the juniors you do the next two or three – but what do the blocks look like, what do they consist of? They include things like personal organisation, bike mechanics, being able to handle a Madison session, do a standing start . . . You could make a list of everything it takes. I was thinking that you've got to get these lads ready to compete. They need to be track competent – they know how to do every event on the track, but to get that good they may well need to do stage races, and in order to get the most out of that, they need to be able to look after themselves on the road.

One big change would be that when it came to track training sessions, these lads needed to have their own designated times and not just piggyback on the seniors. We had to get back to absolute basics. I'd seen sessions where a coach would be on the motorbike with the young riders in a line behind him, and he'd be indicating when he wanted to come off the blue line, in the middle of the track, down to the black, at the bottom. It would be: 'Moving down . . .' My attitude was the opposite: 'Put them on the fucking block, get them going flat out, get them hurting themselves.' There was all this talk of progression, to get them up to a certain level. I just thought, 'If they aren't fit enough, hard luck. Let them get stuck in.'

I began thinking about the education side. Around this time, the GB sprinters Vicky Pendleton and Ross Edgar had been to the college run by the Union Cycliste Internationale in Aigle, Switzerland. I got some ideas from Vicky, mainly about how the day was divided up between cycling and education. In terms of the latter, I wasn't interested in someone going off and being at university, learning history or whatever. This was about cycling – their education in the sport. Learning foreign languages, particularly French, was an obvious one. We would also go into how to look after yourself: stretching, injury prevention, what you do when you have an injury, the medical side in terms of saddle sores, road rash. I got in touch with Jo Harrison from the English Institute of Sport – I was the first one of us to make proper contact with them – and got her involved. She'd been doing little bits sporadically, but this was the first time we evolved a real system. She ran the education side, and we used all the EIS facilities – they organised the language courses, for example, and a food-hygiene course at a college in Stockport.

The racing side would be based in the UK to start off with. We had the idea of maybe going abroad one day, although we didn't quite know how it was going to happen or where it would be. The idea was to give the riders quite big goals: the European under-23 track championships and the under-23 world road championships. We were a million miles off winning those in 2003, but these were targets that were age-related, so there was no reason why we couldn't aim to perform there. So initially it was a domestic programme – Premier Calendars, the national championships, and so on. But what I tried to do was to have at least one European trip every month.

The rest of it was based around the European under-23 track championships and the under-23 world road race championships, and as many days racing as possible. I had a bit of an eye-opening moment in Moscow in 2003, when I took a team to the Europeans. We went with only six or seven junior and under-23 riders, which wasn't very many considering that by 2003 we had become one of the leading nations on the track. There weren't many nations as good as us at the elite level. I counted the riders from other countries, and the Germans or the Spanish had twenty or twenty-five across all the disciplines. We didn't field riders for all the races, only certain ones, and I remember coming back and saying, 'I don't understand this – where were our juniors? Where were our points-race riders, our Madison riders?' We had a budget; I took that and pushed massively for a change, to take big numbers, and from 2005 we started performing in the Europeans. We were one of the best nations at senior level, so there was no reason why we couldn't be good enough at under-23.

Right from the outset I wanted to set the bar high. I believed they should be competitive at their age. That was why I was so set on making it an exclusively under-23 programme and why the road Worlds and the European track championships were always two of our big hits: they are age related, so a rider couldn't say, 'Oh yeah, that rider who beat me is older and has got more experience.' We still weren't competing that well on the road, but I thought to myself, 'There's no reason why we can't make these guys good enough on the track.' We'd never done anything in the under-23 road Worlds – Yanto Barker was fifteenth in 1998, and that was as good as it got – and so we didn't set our targets massively high on that side. I certainly did on the track, though, because ultimately our aim was to win Olympic and world championship gold medals. That's our business. About that time, the track calendar, and the track Worlds, moved to the winter, but the Olympic Games was still a summer event, so the riders would have to get used to coming off the back of stage races to prepare for the Games; that meant that the Europeans, which were also in summer, were really good for their development.

For the first year we started in January, and the programme was a mix of road and track, all thrown in together. It didn't work in terms of the riders producing great performances, because they were doing too much of everything. We were doing two or three track sessions every week, even if they'd got a big road-race objective a week or two later; I just wanted to throw them into anything and everything. These guys had to put as many numbers on their backs as they possibly could in a year, so there were seventy-five to eighty-odd days of racing: track, time trials, Premier Calendars, internationals, World Cup stage races.

In the second year we changed it to a template that we pretty much stuck to from then on. It was in two halves: from October to June it was mainly about the track; between October and February it was totally track, and we always had a track World Cup as an objective – conveniently, at the time the Manchester

World Cup was often in February. Then we'd go on the road and prepare as if it was an Olympic year, aiming for the under-23 European track championships, which were in June. After that they'd have a holiday, a week at home – I didn't want to give them too much – and then it was all about the under-23 road Worlds at the end of September, after which they'd go away again for a couple of weeks. The next year's academy would then start in late October or early November.

The racing side had to be about competing as many times as we could, and getting the riders to experience all that comes with racing. In the plan I even explained that you don't just do sixty days of racing; you've got sixty days plus the travel back home talking about the race, buzzing with this and that – 'I nearly crashed there', 'Did you see so-and-so do this or that?' – so if you only do twenty days, you only get a third of that. That discussion is when the rider naturally reviews their race – talking to their dad, talking to their mate who's taken them there, talking to the coach who's driving them rather than sitting with their headphones on. That became a massive thing in the academy – we always talked about the racing afterwards. It was bike race, bike race, bike race, next bike race, next bike race, next bike race. It wasn't about who was going to be prime minister.

Simon Lillistone put together the budget – about £110–120,000 to run it for the entire year. Equipment was something I looked at in a different way: I didn't want them on the top-of-the-range Shimano Dura-Ace bikes used by the seniors, so they started on Ultegra kit, which is one step down in the hierarchy. I wanted the riders to feel the academy was a stepping stone. I even wanted them in different clothing, but we couldn't do it because when they raced, it had to be in GB kit. I wanted them to have only one road bike; that would mean they would have to learn to look after it and not take it for granted. If they had specific race bikes and a training bike, their training bikes would be treated like shit, left in a right state, whereas if they had only one, they would have to look after it because it might let them down in a race if it wasn't well maintained. The idea was to make them feel, 'I'm here, but I've got to go up to there. I've got to get somewhere, earn my right to be in that top group.'

Money was an issue. I felt they got too much, and they weren't having to pay their way. I wanted them to come and live in Manchester instead of living at home, which was a massive shift. That came from watching riders at coach-led racing weekends and the Talent Team weeks. At those training camps a coach could be a massive influence on the group. To get them working in our way, we needed them there all the time. We could have made it happen without using the riders' money, but I wanted them to feel that they were investing in their future. So I took half their funding off them. They were getting £6,000 a year; I took £3,000 off them towards their accommodation. UK Sport may have had their doubts at first, but once we explained how it worked and what the money went towards, it was fine.

That left the riders with £58 a week to live on, which I thought was just enough; from that, all they had to do was buy food. Everything else was provided. Taking them away from home was in turn going to create the whole question of how you learn to live as a bike racer: how do you look after yourself? How do you feed yourself? How do you stay healthy? If they wanted to be top professional cyclists, they might well have to live abroad – in that event, what do you cook? How does it fit in with the nutrition side of things? How do you look after your clothes and your cycling equipment?

To be a pro, you have to learn how to look after yourself and how to be around other people. In a pro team on the road you have to share a room with someone, maybe for three weeks on a Grand Tour. So how do you live in close quarters with people you don't know? To take three of the riders who shared a house in the first year of the academy, Bruce Edgar, Cav and Ed Clancy, there was plenty of discord between them: Cav was so particular about things, Ed wasn't so fussy, and Bruce would leave stuff everywhere. They were such different characters, and you had to manage that – the different ways they had been brought up, the different things they thought were acceptable. It was a big life experience for them as well.

The academy weeded out people who weren't going to fit in with the group. The riders only had four to six weeks away from each other in the whole year. It was intense. That was where it was slightly flawed. I think Ed Clancy suffered early on; Alex Dowsett suffered later. Ed did get through OK, though, and went on to win gold medals at the Beijing and London Olympic Games. I'm confident it made him into a better bike rider. He wasn't massively sociable at the beginning, but he learnt to be because he is such a good guy. I think it helped him develop and taught him how to work within a team, how to accept people. But it wasn't perfect, because you might have a talented individual who struggles in that team environment twenty-four hours a day, seven days a week.

The whole thing was about setting the riders up to fend for themselves. Take race entries. I had had that initial exchange with Kieran Page, when he said, 'If you don't enter me for a race, I don't do it.' I had asked what he meant: 'Who does enter you guys for races?' It was somebody in the office at British Cycling, but we changed that. We used to do it on a monthly rota: one of the riders would have the responsibility of entering the entire team into all the races for the next month; they would have to come into the velodrome, get the cheque from the administrator in the office, print off the entry forms, write all the forms out for the month and send them off.

I wanted them to be able to organise themselves. If we were going off somewhere on a Sunday morning, I'd say to one of them on the Friday night, 'Right, it's your turn to organise the race. Ring me on Saturday. I want to know what time I am coming to pick you up, and I want to know how long it's going to take us to get to the start. You need to have all the start sheets and the maps to get there.' Some of them couldn't read a map at first. I used to make them sit next to me in the front of the car, and they'd run the day – tell me where we were going, left here or right here, here's the HQ. All I did was drive. They would clean the bikes at some stage races, particularly the British ones. We wouldn't take a *soigneur*, so they'd have to make their own drinks, get their own food, and if stuff didn't get put in the car, I didn't put it in. I had to keep an eye on the staff to make sure they kept their hands off; instead, they would work with the riders, teach these kids how to make their race food. The idea was partly to make them self-reliant, but also to ensure they would appreciate the work the staff did.

I also wanted to join up the development programmes – Talent Team, juniors, under-23s. I started thinking about the junior programme, the classroom stuff we had had to do for the under-16 Talent Team, which I had just come from working on.

The Talent Team was pretty structured; you couldn't put much of an individual touch on it. I had nothing against Marshall Thomas, the junior coach at the time, or Simon Jones, but their way of coaching was all training programmes: Marshall would have the juniors on the track, but there was no oomph, no discipline, no hard work; it was all disc wheels and fancy stuff, no spokes, just go as fast as you can.

That was when I came up with the concept of coach-led racing. That started from the question of how do you teach riders about bunch racing? You either do it through training sessions or you just race and give feedback afterwards. I was massively into the latter. But there wasn't enough racing on the calendar, so we had to produce our own races. Having worked for the Talent Team, I knew it would link in well with that, because the riders need to see a pathway ahead of them. I knew that the regional Talent Teams could feed into a national structure, taking the two best riders from each area. We had a small budget with which to house twenty-five riders on a Saturday night in Manchester, bring them in early on Saturday, send them home late on Sunday. We needed someone to film every race, someone to drive the motorbike, someone to do the lap board – and there the idea was to use the national junior and Talent Team coaches so that they would learn from the weekend as well. I even put together a plan where you could have local coaches sitting up in the stands watching, then do questions and answers with them at the end. That's the great coaching question: how do you put on a session for twenty-five kids? The point is, you need lots of coaches to cover the bottom level, and if you can educate them while running the sessions, you kill two birds with one stone. I did these about once a month, and kept them going when the academy started.

At the same time there was some discussion about the Revolutions – Saturday-evening track meets, very glitzy, at the Manchester velodrome through the winter. These were just getting going, and Face Partnership, the organisers, wanted to include youth racing, so we met them and said that what we wanted from the Revolutions was just kids' racing. My idea was that they could ride a Revolution every month, then two weeks later they would be back on the track doing coach-led racing at the weekend. That in turn meant that through the winter they weren't going ages without racing. Every month there would be kids doing track league on a Tuesday, riding a Revolution, track league again, then coach-led racing.

I pulled together the under-23 squad, the national junior squad and two from each of the regions around the UK – about twenty-five riders – and put together a basic timetable: points race, scratch, team pursuit, Madison. Nothing else. Short sharp races over the two days. To make it a proper camp I got lots of different jerseys and split the riders into four- or five-man teams. The idea was that you would give them a little job to do: here's a task, how do they deliver that as a team? Because what you are looking for in a team is people who will follow instructions rather than go off and follow their own agenda. If you're riding the Tour de France, it's stage fifteen and you've got to do a job for the team, that's what you have to do.

You want people sticking to the plan, not thinking they can just drift off and do something else. For every single race I had a slip of paper for each team: 'You nominate one leader, you keep the race together and lead it out'; 'It doesn't matter how, but you have to split this field up, so keep attacking'; another team would be told, 'You have to counter-attack when the bunch comes up to any breaks.' These kids were all guns blazing. I'd film everything, and we'd sit down after every race – it was all timetabled – and do feedback. I'd pick each team and we'd rewind it – 'Tell me, Joe, what were you thinking here?' – and go over little technical parts – a Madison change, an attack. So I got the kids talking, saying what they were thinking, and so on.

It was at one of these sessions that I first became aware of Mark Cavendish. He was invited with the junior team at the back end of 2003; what I remember is that he had a sprinter's bike – steep angles, round steel handlebars – and it was hard to figure out whether he was a sprinter or an endurance rider. He didn't stand out particularly from a physical point of view. He wasn't chopsy; I didn't have to tell him to quieten down. What I do remember was that I was packing up afterwards in the car park, and he came out and said, 'Please can you invite me to the next one? That's the best thing I've ever done. Thank you very much.' I thought that was pretty interesting, for someone that age to appreciate what was going on around him.

I had been constantly running ideas past fellow coaches like John Herety, Simon Jones, Dave Brailsford and Peter Keen, as well as Simon Lillistone. David Millar also played a part. Throughout 2003 he was around Manchester, and in and out of the velodrome. Millar is pretty much the last of the old-school British pros in Europe, the ones who'd gone out there and done it on their own. He was part of the decision to put the academy riders in two houses in Fallowfield, right in the middle of Manchester's university district. The area was full of young girls floating around, and heaved with students out on the piss, down the nightclubs, with everything open all hours. It's all going on; it's exciting for a young kid, and these lads were moving out of home for the first time. They were like any other student. Dave said, 'Bloody hell, the worst thing you can do is stop these kids from going out. When it's really time to press on the pedals later in their careers, they need to have worked through all that young-lad stuff.' We took that on board and thought we would bung them in there, then if they wanted to go out, they could. If people are good enough, they'll go training because they love cycling more than going out. And if they've trained hard enough, they'll be too knackered to go out anyway. We weren't scared, but it was quite a brave move.

I always had four British professional bike riders in the back of my mind: Roger Hammond, Dave Millar, Jeremy Hunt and Charly Wegelius. Those guys had done it the old-school way, going out to race in Europe and earning their pro contracts without much help. That's how I had tried to do it. So I spoke to all of them at some stage. I was quite good friends with Charly, who had been our best under-23 in the late 1990s before going on to a long pro career. I talked to him about the system at Mapei, where he started his pro career, and I took some ideas from that. Even Chris Boardman had a look at the academy plan, as he was quite involved with British Cycling at the time. His view was that he didn't know whether this would work for him; he didn't think he could have handled it but he liked the idea. Then there was the Australian Institute of Sport: I had spent a load of winters out there and looked at how they had done it with Charlie Walsh. Shane Sutton had shown me the discipline side when I was racing with him for GB, while

John Herety was a guy who had been through it all and had never forgotten about the dream of being a road pro and what that can offer riders. While I can take responsibility for driving the programme, the academy and the wider junior programme was a mixture of everybody's input. That was the heart of it all.

In August or September 2003 I presented the academy idea formally to Doug Dailey, John Herety, Dave Brailsford and Peter Keen. Simon Lillistone helped me with the presentation, putting it together and making some of the ideas more clear. John was totally behind it from the start. He'd already added to it: for example, he'd shown me which were the good under-23 stage races so that we could give them more days of racing. Doug thought it was a fantastic idea. I talked Pete through the feel of it, the technical side, and he was quite amazed at how it was all put together. But he said, 'You can't start this in 2004 because it's Olympic year. It would take too much time. Great idea, but the timing isn't good.' He wasn't against it, but he was worried about the timing. Dave said we should definitely do it. If it hadn't been for him, it wouldn't have got off the ground.

Pete and Dave were very different in their approaches, although they were working together. Pete wanted to do everything by the book, so if the funding was there, it was there; if it wasn't, it wasn't. Dave was more of a risk-taker – and he was taking a risk with this, because what experience did I have? He was acting on a hunch, thinking perhaps I was the right person to do this. The classic Dave way is not to go, 'Here's a programme, go and do it'; you go to Dave with an idea, and he will look at it, get involved, and then say, 'Right, let's go and make this happen.' He likes people coming to him with ideas.

He really gets behind you and supports you. So Dave said, 'Go and put this together, let's see what it looks like.'

For the very first academy intake we advertised the places, and we selected a group of people for a full day of interviewing. I wanted it to feel as if they were coming in for a job interview, so on their applications they had to say why they were doing everything. We ranked them according to where they were and invited the top ones in. I did a presentation for them and their parents so they knew what we were trying to do. The interview panel consisted of me, John Herety and Simon Lillistone. The questions were all about the riders' goals, why they thought they could make it, what their current situation was. One of the questions I asked was, 'How did you get here?' Questions like that give you a general awareness of how the riders are – are they on the ball? Can they get their bikes ready for a race? In the years after that we didn't bother with the interviewing process; we didn't need to. I became a lot closer to the junior programme, which meant that we could pre-select the riders beforehand – we would advertise, they would apply, and we could select them from the information we already had. But that first year we didn't know anyone.

There were six who made it through: Cav, Christian Varley, Bruce Edgar, Tom White, Ed Clancy and Matt Brammeier. Of the six, Cav was quite bolshie about what he thought he could do. He said, 'I want to be a pro.' He was quite clear about what he wanted – if it wasn't the academy, he was going to Belgium. He didn't behave as if our way was the only way, which impressed me. He seemed very streetwise. He knew exactly how he'd got over from the Isle of Man to the interview; he'd been doing that journey since he was a kid. He seemed sure of himself but wasn't particularly cocky. At this point, he was working full-time in a bank; he'd just had his tonsils out and was quite sick and wasn't riding his bike. I remember him calling me and saying, 'I'm not going to let you down. I'm really looking forward to this opportunity. If it wasn't this, I was saving up to go to Belgium.'

If you talked to Marshall Thomas, the national junior coach, it was as if Cav was the devil. Marshall didn't like Mark, and Mark was very resentful because he didn't get selected for the Worlds. It's well known that Cav wasn't a lover of sports scientists; he didn't like their methods and he didn't want to do times on the track. His view was that he had won national championships across the board, on road and track, sprint and endurance, so why wasn't he being taken to the Worlds? He was right. One of the reasons we did choose Mark was that this guy could win bike races, the same as Ben Swift a couple of years later: you put them against the clock and they weren't that good, but they knew how to win races.

Ed Clancy was the other way round: perhaps he couldn't win races all the time, but his physical qualities were something quite special. He wasn't particularly open and aware in the interview – he was very much on his own, very quiet, a tough one to crack. But get him on the bike and he really, really wanted it. He is an athlete who is built more like a track sprinter than a road racer, which is why he has been so special at the team pursuit. The academy really challenged him; racing on the road cracked him at times, but on the track you could see he was good. He was very quiet – the lads would be walking down the street, and he'd be walking ten lengths behind them on his own. He always wore the same Ferrari T-shirt because he was dead into his Formula One. I think he only had the one and he never washed it. As much as Cav and Ed are good friends now, they went through quite a hard time together. But Cav could see that Ed had something special about him, and Ed could see that about Cav. I don't think the academy was perfect for Ed, but he learnt a hell of a lot there.

Ed could have gone to university, but my view was that the riders could go and do a degree in something or other, but it wasn't going to help them with cycling. I always believed these guys could earn from cycling, and now they are doing that. They may never have to have a normal job; a lot of them will finish their careers and remain in cycling because it's been their lives.

The hardest year at the academy was the first year after I put the plan together. The discipline level and the commitment to the work for ten months a year was at boot-camp level, whereas later on it was cut down to a three-month period. It was just a bit too intense. The boot camp wasn't called that until the end of 2004, but basically that's what Cav and all the others went through the entire year. Their daily routine changed a lot from the first year to the second. In the first they were like guinea pigs, and it was as much about me learning as them taking things on. The objective during the winter – one of the key things – was that these lads would do more track riding and skills-based work than any other under-23 in the world.

The challenge I set for the riders was this: could these guys get their track skills to a level where they would be like ducks in water? When they were moving back from being road pros to racing on the track at the Olympics or the Worlds, they would be out of the water for a couple of years, then they would land on the water and have to swim immediately. It was a challenge for them. Riders like Peter Kennaugh and Geraint Thomas were all part of that. I think it helped them; think of the success in London, where they were both part of that GB team that won the team-pursuit gold: they knew going into the Olympics that they could go and do lots of stage racing, then drop back in and with one or two sessions look pretty good on the track. I'm sure that's because of all the work they'd done in their early days at the academy.

So for me it was important that they got into it. It was a full-time job, eight till five. I wanted them clocking in and clocking out. What I'd experienced myself, and what I'd seen in my early days of coaching, was young lads thinking that they'd made it just because they'd got on some kind of a full-time team. They'd be training but in the afternoon they'd spend half the time in a cafe or shopping, spending all their money. My attitude was that I was going to keep these lads so flipping busy they weren't going to want to go out. Some days they would have to leave their house at about ten to seven in the morning. Even though some of them had cars, they weren't allowed to drive to the track; it was a rule that they had to ride in, because to me this was all about riding their bikes, and that half-an-hour ride meant an extra hour on the bike every day. The track would open at seven thirty, they'd ride on their rollers in the gym for twenty minutes and then we'd be on the track from just after eight until ten o'clock. After that they'd have a lesson over at the English Institute of Sport for two hours, then they'd come back and do two till five on the track, and after that they'd ride home. So they were getting home at quarter to six or six o'clock, and then they would have to do their washing, sort out the food, and so on.

One item on the education list was anti-doping, which we ran through Brian Barton at British Cycling. There were quite a few workshops for the young lads, as the feeling was that this was a new generation of bike riders and we had to teach them to race in the correct way, to do the correct things and to understand what they could do within the rules. Could they take a cold supplement, for example, or did it need to be declared? It was a matter of teaching them the basics, such as 'whereabouts' – the system of declaring where they were at given times for random testing, which had just come on stream. There were older riders even within the British scene who kicked up a massive fuss about having to do that, because it was a bit of a pain. But the young lads never knew any different – it's what they've had to do their whole careers, so they don't make it an issue.

What we were looking at was: if someone offers you a supplement or you want to take one, how do you find out if it's acceptable or not? You go to the doctor and you're not sure about a medicine, then what do you do? It wasn't, 'This is what the pros are doing, this is what you may come across.' Because we didn't know, and I'd have just been talking rubbish. A lot of the anti-doping groups – like 100% Me, one of the schemes run by UK Sport, which was one of the backers for the academy – would get people who had done the dirty to speak on film saying how much they regretted it, how they felt they'd let their parents down, their wives and husbands, the damage it had done to their health. It was quite impactful stuff. You would be thinking, 'Phew, you don't want to be doing that.' We would constantly get people in doing presentations and so on; some of the lads thought it was a bit of a pain, but it was critical for them at that stage.

I wanted the academy to be structured like a university, so it was all timetabled: what time they were leaving for the track, what time the first session was, when and where the education lessons were, what track sessions there would be, what time they would be leaving for a race. It would all be there so there was no doubt about it.

The biggest, hardest days for them consisted of a track session from eight o'clock in the morning till ten, then education, two till five on the track, stay for track league and then ride home. They would get home at eleven o'clock at night. Or it would be three hours in the morning on the road, then ride to the track, a two until five track session, then ride home. That made for five or six hours of actual riding in a day, but they didn't realise it because it was split up into different disciplines. But when you think about what Mark Cavendish, Ed Clancy, Geraint Thomas and all these lads did as young guys, they put a fair few kilometres in their legs.

I knew the academy would get bigger, but I only wanted six riders at first. My whole idea was that I wanted to develop a programme that would enable them to move forward. I remember saying to Marshall Thomas that if none of the group actually made it, it wouldn't be an issue. I didn't really care. What we had to do was look at the system after a year and ask, 'Is this going in the right direction or not?' The lads all knew it – in the presentation we made it clear that we hadn't done this before, that we were trying something different and they were there to try the system out. They were very much the guinea pigs.

4 : Keeping Tabs on the Guinea Pigs

As I drew up the academy plan, I began talking to a new arrival at British Cycling. Steve Peters was a forensic psychiatrist who had worked at Rampton and who had been brought in by Dave Brailsford to help the team out. He was to become extremely influential. I hadn't had anything to do with guys on the mental side of sport since I was a junior, when the national squad had worked a little with John Syer, who was Chris Boardman's sports psychologist. I'd enjoyed working with John – he was the guy who had got me on to writing things down, making lists – so I was looking forward to working with Steve. Plus it was another chance to ask someone outside cycling how I could make the academy function.

Steve has a distinctive way of working. He looks you straight in the eye, and he's very quick when it comes to asking or answering questions. He talks fast. Sometimes you wonder whether he's trying to catch you out. It's as if he knows he can read what you're thinking, but is steering away from it to concentrate on the job in hand. And he has this way of turning questions back at you: what would *you* do? What do *you* think? That means the conclusions you come to are yours, not his. What I wanted to know from Steve was how much work I could give the young guys who would be coming into the academy.

One day late in 2003 we were sitting up in one of the

hospitality boxes in the Manchester velodrome, having one of our very first discussions, when he looked at me in that intense way of his.

'Rod, in this position you're the coach, but you could be their mentor, their father figure. You may have to act like a friend, you may have to be the person who's going to punish them, the person who's going to put an arm around them when they need it. Are you ready for this?'

He paused and let the question hang in the air, which is typical Steve, and I sat there in the silence, thinking, 'Shit, is he really asking me this? I'm barely thirty-one years old; am I actually ready to be father figure, brother, friend, coach – all these things that he talked about?'

I looked at him and said, 'Yes, I am.'

'OK, now we can carry on . . .'

The most important principle that Steve and I established was this: rules and consequences. We felt you've got to make your standards clear with young people: these are the rules, and if you break them, there are consequences. It wasn't just about the riders. We talked a lot about what I had to do. I would need to be consistent. Steve taught me to start by getting everybody into a room, and I would say, 'Right, guys, what are the rules that we have to have?' I knew what I wanted, but what Steve had taught me was that you've got to have open-ended questions, so that the lads would be the ones who arrived at the answers. Each year you would say, 'OK, these are the rules from 2006. Are there any new ones?' We had house rules, on-race rules, rules about how we would operate, how I would behave as a coach towards them, how they would behave as athletes towards me. What it amounted to was that the riders wrote their own rules, with my guidance, and agreed on the consequences of failing to follow them.

A classic example was that they had to be on time for every session. I told them to imagine that they were riding in the Olympic Games. You've trained for four or eight years, the bus leaves at nine o'clock in the morning, and you miss the bloody thing. There was one occasion when Ben Swift, at a track World Cup in Moscow – on his eighteenth birthday of all days – missed the bus, and I left without him. That was my point to Ben: 'You've learnt your lesson here. You've trained for this all year and then you miss the bus. You don't miss the race because there may be another bus in half an hour, but you get to the race more stressed than you need to be.' It's all about being prepared for the race: we turn up perhaps an hour or an hour and a half before the start, and there is a difference if you turn up just half an hour before you start warming up. More importantly, if a rider is part of a four-man team and isn't on that bus, then the other three are going to be affected. They will be wondering, 'What's happening? Is he sick? Has he overslept?' So we would say, 'OK, guys, what's the punishment for poor timekeeping?' It was all written down – there's one notebook I've found where I've scribbled: 'Consequence not bad enough, need something that will hit them hard.'

There were rules for me too: for example, I could never come into their bedrooms unless they said I could, or unless I knocked on the door and asked to be let in. They knew that, and I stuck to my word. I think some of it sprang from me saying how I wanted to work. I didn't model it on anything, but I wouldn't want any Tom, Dick or Harry just waltzing into my room. A rule we did have was that the living areas in the houses and the kitchens had to be spotless. You leave your cup out and someone else has a moan about it, I'm going to tell you, because that other guy has every right to moan about you leaving your rubbish everywhere. You've got to keep a happy ship.

When it came to discipline, I wanted to go straight in – 'whack' – and make bloody sure they knew where the line was. We were not going to mess about. I wanted to come in hard at the beginning, then back off a little bit; not let the standards go, but back off in the sense that I wouldn't need to be all over them. I remembered that the best teachers at school were the ones who would discipline you from the word go and then relax several months later. So at the beginning I was going to be all over the lads 24/7. I wanted a good, shipshape group. I like the ethos of the Russian system or the army – that hardness, being a unit. When you think about it, when you go to a bike race it's similar to going to war. You've got to do as you're told. There are workers and there are winners, and they all have to do their job. If one person doesn't, that can mean the whole thing fails. If you want to be good, you have to be on the ball.

For most of the academy programme, 2004 was about seeing what worked and adjusting things that needed to be changed. There were plenty of times when the riders broke the rules; there were various consequences, and a lot of those involved making the riders do a heap of work on the bike. I was criticised a little bit for that; people would say it was a bit over the top. For example, there was the time we went down to Cornwall for a round of the national under-23 series; as always when it was an under-23 race, I put the pressure on because they were riding against their own age group. You ask them, 'You've put all that special kit on, you've got all this backing, now I want you to perform – are you up for it?'

The first break went away after two or three kilometres, and we never saw it again. At the finish line Matt Brammeier was about five seconds behind Evan Oliphant, so we were close to winning it. My whole point was not about their work ethic from kilometre eight up to the finish – it was the first eight kilometres. Not going with a breakaway at eight kilometres had nothing to do with physical or tactical ability; it was just because the riders were lazy. What I'd noticed was that the lads had gone off the start line at the back of the bunch, as if they thought they were the big hitters. They came into the car park afterwards, and I was steaming – 'Pack the car,' quite stern – and they all knew something was up.

As they were putting the bikes in the car, I said, 'Line up,' so they did, with the other riders and parents all around, packing their kit away and so on. I went up to each and every one of them, looked into their faces and said, 'Right, did you see the break going?' They said, 'Yes.' So I asked, 'Were you tired at that moment?' Every single one of them said, yes, they saw it, and no, they weren't tired. I've always said if a rider physically can't do it and has tried his best, you've got to look at the coaching or other things that weren't good enough. But if you're just lazy or not taking it seriously, then you've got a problem. So I said to them, 'Right, guys, I am not happy you messed up. Basically, you've shown yourselves up. You're the Great Britain bike team and you've shown yourselves up. Get in the car, I don't want to hear another bloody word from you.' We drove from Cornwall all the way up to Manchester with hardly a word said. I told them, 'I'm not stopping other than for fuel,' so if any of them wanted a piss they had to piss in a bottle and empty it out of the window.

We got to Manchester late at night. Normally Monday would be an easy day – ten o'clock start or something, rather than nine o'clock as it would be on a training day. This time I said, 'Right, be ready to ride your bikes at eight o'clock – it's going to be a long one.' Even though I'd spent my weekend driving the little bleeders down to Cornwall, the next morning I got up early – I lived forty-five minutes away at the time, so I had to guarantee I was there waiting. They rode for five hours around the circuit we used regularly, which was out in Cheshire, near Jodrell Bank. It was a bit rainy, a drizzly sort of day but not belting it down, and one of the lanes we were going down was really muddy, a farm track which wasn't easy to ride on. Once we got onto the little circuit, they did about three hours of through and off, each one taking a turn at the front so they were sharing the pace as if they were in a breakaway or chasing the break from the bunch. I wasn't bothered how fast they were going; they just had to do the work. I drove behind them, and every now and then I would cut across the circuit and hide behind a bush or something to make sure they were doing it. Then they rode home. The point was simply this: 'If you miss a break, I will make you do something you don't like doing.'

Another example was in the Girvan Three-Day in south-west Scotland, one of the first stage races they did with me. Cav won the first stage, and he won it really well. He was at the back of the lead group going up the last climb and he didn't get any help to come back up because we'd got some riders in the break who didn't wait for him; he came back through the cars and absolutely blasted it in the sprint. We had a GB senior team and a Persil team – they were the under-23s' sponsor – in the race, and I was looking after both. On the radio, Tony Gibb, a GB rider who had a good sprint on him, was saying, 'I want the lads to lead me out,' but Cav was saying he was going to sprint for himself, so I left them to it. Cav absolutely floored all of them by lengths. The plan was that we were working for Gibby, but Mark said, 'I want to win this race' – and he knew he could, so fair play to him. If we hadn't won, I'd have gone mental with him, but he pulled it off and it was one of his first big wins. At that stage, we didn't know what the lads were capable of, so that was one of the first big moments.

The next day Mark was in the yellow jersey, and the question then was: what are we trying to work on? I wasn't expecting these young lads to win the race overall, but I was expecting them to work on their race tactics. So one of the plans for the next day was that we couldn't afford to let a big break go – if there were any more than six or seven riders off the front of the bunch, we would have to close it down straight away. Well, flipping heck, twenty-five or so kilometres into the race there were twenty riders up the road and they'd gone. All the academy lads were sat there, and I was thinking, 'What on earth are you doing?' I said, 'Right, guys, get on the front and ride' – and that was including Mark, who was the race leader. They rode at the front of the bunch for the whole stage, until Cav went out the back and they all got dropped. Afterwards I made the point: 'Guys, I don't really care about the result at this stage. What I do care about is that you didn't stick to the plan.' They knew what happened if they didn't close down a race at once:

they were going to have to work a little bit harder, and a little bit longer.

There was another moment like this on a trip to Belgium, when Simon Jones was with us. We did two or three trips to Belgium for the *kermis* racing, blocks of about ten days at a time, racing every other day. We used to stay at Tim Harris's house – the same Tim Harris I'd stayed with during the 'Ratty' episode in my racing days. Tim loved the idea of what we were doing, and his partner Joscelyn would look after all the lads. Tim and Jos's house was in Tielt-Winge, not far from where Eddy Merckx was born, which was a good story to tell the lads. It was an early stage of getting the lads to spend time abroad, and the Merckx connection was part of getting them into the culture of the sport.

The riders had a recovery day, during which they rode for three hours. It was all about them getting as many kilometres in the bank as they could. They asked if they could have a cafe stop. I used to put in the programme whether they could have one or not, and if I heard about them having one when they weren't supposed to, there'd be trouble. There were at least two hours of riding before the stop. In the great scheme of things it doesn't make a big difference, but for me it was about listening to what was set out, obeying what you were meant to do. I didn't give a monkey's about anything else: if someone says, 'Do this,' you do it rather than whatever you want to do. A lot of people get it wrong: it's not dictatorial, there's a reason for it. If you stick to one thing you have agreed on, and you all believe in it, you will achieve more. If you're thinking, 'Oh, I'll have a cafe stop after one hour, not two,' and someone else thinks differently, your group is split.

It was a rest day, so I hadn't gone out with them, and what happened was that there were these other British lads who lived locally – three or four of the guys who were racing full-time in Belgium. They all met at Tim's house and went out together. I thought it was good for the lads to be mixing with them, because I remember what it was like being out there on your own. Off they went, and when they came back, they were having dinner, and I came in and they were showing Joscelyn photographs of their cafe stop. I think it was on Cav's camera. I walked behind them and saw the screen and said, 'Hey, give us that camera.' Cav looked at me, and I just saw on his face that something was not right. I asked them, 'How was the ride, lads?'

'Oh yeah, good.'

'Where did you stop?'

'Oh, we stopped after about two and a half hours.'

I looked at the phone and I looked at them and said, 'Right, guys, where within half an hour of Tielt-Winge is a fucking nice big square like that?' And they all just looked at me. 'You lying bastards. Right, in one hour I want you with your kit on. Meet me out the front.'

I just did it off the top of my head. I didn't know what I was going to do as it was about two o'clock. I was cursing. I couldn't believe they had lied to me. All the effort and time you put into them, and they can't tell you the truth. Jonesy was saying, 'You can't get them to go out,' and I said, 'You flipping well watch me.' So we went out, and they did another three hours, and as I did after the race in Cornwall I made them do blocks of through and off. The next day, however, Cav won an under-23 *kermis* in absolutely fantastic style – he got across to a break and took the sprint. Jonesy, who was the head coach, of course, was saying, 'Really, I'm not sure you should be doing this; this is too much work.' My answer was: 'They had so much time sat on their backsides in that cafe, I think they've got plenty of energy.' The point wasn't that they hadn't done the ride; it was the fact that they'd lied to me. If they had said, 'Rod, we stopped after an hour and a half because the other British lads wanted to,' I would have been annoyed, but I wouldn't have made them ride again.

Another classic one came as we were driving home from a Premier Calendar: the Peter Longbottom memorial in late spring of 2004. The lads had done quite well – they didn't get a result, but I thought they rode well together – and we were talking about the race when I took a phone call from Simon Lillistone: 'We've got a problem. The owner of the house has had a complaint from the church opposite that there's some kind of obscene drawing in the window.' It was in the house where Matt Brammeier lived. With the lads listening in the back, I said, 'You're joking, Simon, you're having a laugh,' and I saw the lads going a bit quiet. I said, 'What, a drawing?' and all of a sudden I saw them snigger. I thought, 'You little bastards.' We pulled up outside the house, and they were all laughing.

My first reaction was, 'Whoever's done this, bloody hell, you've got a talent for drawing.' There were two pictures: one was of a donkey with a great big knob, but the other one was horrendous – a big fat woman with her legs wide open and everything showing. I stopped myself from laughing and told them: 'That's horrendous. A house in a residential street, and you draw that. Who the hell did it, and why? You've got too much time on your hands.' There was a disciplinary hearing with Simon and Dave Brailsford, because we'd also had a complaint from the guy who owns the house. Dave gave them an earful. What I did was make them ride for a whole session – a full three hours – round the top of the velodrome.

That might not sound so bad, but riding round the top of the track rather than on the black line at the bottom means you've really got to concentrate. On a really good track like Beijing you don't have abrupt transitions between the straights and the bankings, but in Manchester it's not quite as seamless, so you go a little higher in the straight and lower in the bankings to keep a nice even pace. The higher up you get, obviously you can't do that transition because you're stuck against the barrier; you can't even it out. Physically, it's much harder than riding lower down the track, and if the guy at the front doesn't ride nice and fluidly in and out of the turns, the guy at the back will constantly run up on the wheel ahead; he'll always be back-pedalling to slow down, then accelerating again.

At first I had them riding with a bottle in their back pockets, but the track manager came over and said, 'You can't have them drinking on the track.' So I made them drop down and put their bottle on top of the drinks fridge. I wouldn't let them stop, so every fifteen or twenty minutes I'd shout, 'Drink,' and they'd come down off the track, grab the bottles as they were going around, then put them back and go back up to the top. I stood there for three hours on the side of the track, shouting, 'Closer, closer, get closer . . .' They were in pieces by the time they finished. Cav got off and said, 'I'm sorry, Rod, I'm never, never going to do this again. My balls are killing me.'

In year one a lot of my consequences were physical things, which over the years I learnt I had to be a bit careful with. Steve

Peters provided a few guidelines, but my idea was to punish the riders when they broke the rules, but also to make it hard work. I needed to build the programme's reputation. I wanted them to feel, 'Oh my God, this is so hard,' because I wanted those lads to tell all the young kids below them that this was really difficult. My bottom line was always that if they were not prepared to work this hard, they were not going to make it. I wanted this principle to flow year after year, and the only way of doing it was through hard work.

I'm sure the lads tried to wind me up. And I don't think they liked me. I really don't think they liked me but I didn't care. I was just doing what I knew I wanted and I was going to get what I wanted with this programme. My goal was to produce a crack squadron of bike riders, mentally drilled, trained like the SAS. In cycling terms, they could go in and kill anybody at any moment. I wanted a driven team. But over the year what also happened was that I developed into someone who was better able to lead them.

I was working out a lot of this stuff for myself, but crucially I never felt isolated. Dave Brailsford was always behind me, and Steve Peters was continually supportive. I would take problems to Steve on a regular basis. For example, I would get quite wound up sometimes when we were in a restaurant, sitting around the dinner table; on occasion they would behave in a way that I didn't think was acceptable – just being lads. I'd have a go at them, and they'd make a bit of a snide remark at me: 'Bloody hell, who are you?' – that kind of attitude. I brought this to Steve one day, and he said to me, 'Rod, you aren't their father. This is parenting. Actually, if they are like that now at eighteen, you will never change them. Don't try and change what you can't change. You've got to recognise what is changeable and what isn't, where you can be an influence and where you can't.' He said I was at fault there – I was trying to make a point but I was over the top. I had to recognise that not everybody could be like I wanted them to be and that sometimes I would be wrong.

The most striking example of the timekeeping rule and the cleaning-the-bikes consequence came when we did the Triptyque des Monts et Châteaux, an under-23 race in Belgium. It was our first proper international stage race as a team – I went as manager, because John Herety fell ill – and we got our heads totally kicked in. Thomas Dekker of Holland, who would go on to be a pro with Rabobank and Garmin, won the race. He absolutely floored us. We had a seven-man team, and six out of the seven had crashed by the end of the second day. Bruce Edgar had completely torn himself up; he went down a barbed-wire fence, and it was as if someone had slashed a razor blade over his arms and legs, like when Johnny Hoogerland hit a fence during the 2011 Tour de France. I'd had a busy time with running riders to the hospital and so on, but again it was one of those occasions when I said, 'Right, guys, we are leaving at nine o'clock in the morning.' It was a miserable, miserable day, and Mark Cavendish and Christian Varley rolled up at five minutes past nine. Everybody else was sat in the vehicles ready to go, and they just came into the car, saying, 'Sorry we're late.' I said, 'No worries,' but I was seething.

We went off and did the race, got back in the cars and pulled up at the hotel; there had been crashes and they were all nearly in tears because they had been raced so hard. I said, 'Right, before you get out of the car, Mark, Christian, go get your tracksuits on, you're washing the bikes.'

'Hey?'

'Go and get your tracksuits on, be down in ten or fifteen minutes. You're washing the bikes.' They got up and went chuntering off. I told the mechanic, Mark Ingham, 'Get everything out, your hosepipes, buckets, everything, but don't touch the bikes.'

'Yeah but . . .'

'Mark, don't touch the bikes.'

I stood there, arms crossed, while they washed every single bike, including all the spare ones. There were people coming over saying, 'Bloody hell, what are you doing?' I remember the American team in particular kept coming over and asking what I was up to making the lads wash the bikes. I said, 'Well, they were late.' The whole point was: show up on time. The same thing happened at the Tour de Lorraine with Ian Stannard and Daniel Martin, which was a junior race where I was covering for their usual coach, Darren Tudor. They were late down for the start, so I made them clean all the bikes. Dan wasn't particularly happy, but I didn't give a monkey's what people thought. It was all about the riders sticking to the rules we had drawn up.

Dan* is one rider from Britain who has gone on to a very successful professional career without going down the academy route, but there is a good reason for that. We were very track focused at the time he came to us, and we didn't have a completely road-orientated programme at the time; there were really no long-term objectives on the road because the programme

* Daniel Martin has a British father and Irish mother, and currently races under an Irish licence.

was still very young. In 2004, when Dan was a junior and won the national road race championships, he was already a massive talent, but he wanted to specialise in that area without doing the track, which was fair enough. For 2005 we didn't have a full-time road programme, which led to the question of what he was going to do for the two months in the summer when we were away doing track racing. My position was that if he didn't want to do the track, he couldn't join the programme. I think Dan and his dad, who is a former top international himself, were both pretty pissed off, and I agree with them that it must have felt like they weren't getting the support. The problem was that we couldn't cater for a sixty-kilogram road rider at the time. A year later, when we went to Italy, it might have been different; that year, 2006, we brought in Ben Greenwood, so Dan would have fitted in. If we had been a year more advanced, it might have worked for him. Unfortunately, we just weren't ready to cater for a young climber.

There was one thing that I never slipped up on, right from the beginning. Every week, with every rider, I did a formal one-on-one session. It was thirty minutes in a room with the door shut, just me with the cyclist. It was a set format: ten minutes on what training or racing we'd just done, ten minutes on what we were about to do and then ten minutes on anything else they wanted to talk about. It doesn't sound a long time to talk about the training and so on, but I was spending so long with them that we'd be constantly reviewing what we did as we went along. Mainly it was a confirmation of what we'd already talked about: 'Have you had any other thoughts about what we've said on this race?' 'Actually I think I slipped up there.' 'You struggled in that session. Do you have any idea why?' It was a time when they could go, 'Listen, this is just too hard, I can't do this' – or whatever the problem might be.

It gave them a chance to raise the kind of thing that they might not be up for discussing in front of other people. This had come from Steve. The ten minutes at the end would be, 'Have you got any other business?' I always tried to give them the confidence to tell me what was annoying them. The classic one was when Ian Stannard came to me and said, 'Rod, I know this is small, but Steven Burke is pissing me off. Every morning, every day, he has an egg, and he always leaves the fucking shell on the side in the kitchen. He never cleans it up, or if he does he takes the eggshell but leaves a bit of egg behind. And I always have to clean it up.'

Rather than me having a go at Burkey, saying, 'Hey, Ian's told me this . . .', what I would do is ask Ian when Steven had eggs. 'Well, he has eggs every morning, or twice a week for his lunch, always on a Tuesday.' I'd then make sure to go into the house at two o'clock on a Tuesday. I used to do house visits all the time. I'd make excuses to go round and chat to them, but actually I was checking out the house. So if I was in there, I'd be able to say, 'Burkey, come here. What's this rubbish down here? Is this you?'

'Oh yeah.'

'Come on, mate, tidy up after yourself.'

So I would invariably go round after them, rather than getting in whichever of the lads it might be and saying, 'So-and-so said this or that.' I would make sure I caught them out. So if someone said to me, 'This guy is out on the piss every single night and he's keeping me from getting my sleep,' what I would do is keep going past the house until I caught them. The idea was to make out that I caught them by chance rather than have them think someone had let me know.

I wanted them to be truthful and upfront with me. I would tell them, 'I'm going to push you guys to the ceiling now. If you crack, there's no problem; you're all going to crack at some stage. But the biggest key to it is to tell me when you are cracking, tell me when it's getting too much. I'm not just going to keep throwing this at you. Our job is to keep making you better, so we'll perhaps back off, but part of the process is learning about why you have cracked. Did you go to bed early last night? Are you eating OK? Are you sleeping OK?' You had to teach them how to plan, how to organise themselves for a big performance. It would come down to basic coaching questions, such as: 'How come you were on your feet all that day when you were meant to be resting?'

'Oh, I had to go out shopping.'

'Why didn't you do that the other day?'

To take one example with Cav, one day we were down at the track in Newcastle-under-Lyme, in Staffordshire, doing our European track championships preparation. Cav was absolutely useless. He couldn't even keep up with the other riders in a team pursuit. From the start, the riders had to keep a diary with a simple scoring system. On the timetable, the date would be at the top, but I'd also have 'hard day', 'moderate day' or 'easy day'. They would mark themselves against that day out of five: if I put a hard day and then it was exactly what they expected, it would be a three; if it was easier than they expected, they'd write a two, or very easy they would write a one; if it was harder than they expected they would write a four, and if it was super-hard they would write a five. If I'd put 'easy day' because it was a two-hour recovery ride, you'd expect them all to put three, but some days some of them would say it was a one because they could have done a bit more. A surprising pattern started: they'd constantly put fours and fives because their days were harder than they expected.

I think a lot of people believed I just leathered them, like the Australian system – the stronger ones rise to the top. It wasn't like that at all. If someone said to me, 'I'm tired, I can't do this session,' I never raised my voice. I never made it an issue. I always went back to the drawing board and asked why. It was a matter of working out with them how they could get better. I was super-hard on them, super-strict on them, disciplined them, but I think I also put my arm around them at the right times. This time, we couldn't find out why Cav was tired, why he wasn't performing, so I sat down with him and said, 'Right, Cav, what we're going to do is go through every single day for the last month. We'll look at what you did, and we're going to talk about how hard that day was.'

It turned out that out of thirty days he'd done twenty-one days of recovery. He had been sick at the beginning of the period and had hit the training too hard for a while. You could see that his marks were too high for the type of effort he was doing. As a result, he had ended up taking a load of recovery days. He'd made loads of excuses up: 'I'm tired', 'My girlfriend had been over that day, so I didn't go out properly the next day' – excuse after excuse. He was completely different once he saw how many days of training he had done simply by going through his diary. So there was no point in me thumping away at him.

The training diary was key to a problem we had with Ed Clancy: he had been ill, and he looked anaemic. Fortunately, the riders had to write down what they ate every day. Ed had it all on paper, so I went back for a month and we had a good look. I wrote out across the top of a piece of paper all the food I thought he should be eating: milk, cereal, potatoes, carrots, and so on. I put those big bits of paper on the floor and went, 'Right, cereal,' and put a mark where he'd eaten cereal; milk, tick, potato, tick, pasta, tick, pasta sauce, tick, beans, tick . . . I kept a tally.

It was dead simple: there were no vegetables, no salad, no tomatoes, no tuna, no fish, a little bit of chicken. It was all cereal, milk, pasta with pesto sauce, beans and bread. Ed didn't know how to eat properly. It was no wonder this guy was sick. Your first thought is, 'Bloody hell,' but it's only like young people going to university. The solution we came up with was to get Nigel Mitchell, the nutritionist at the English Institute of Sport, involved in what they were doing. Nigel would go shopping with them, teach them what to buy, explain why you needed it and how you cooked it, and we developed menus; they would be on the wall in the kitchen. Then we looked at cleaning – different-coloured cloths for this, that and the other – and that also went up on the wall. It was quite well structured in that sense, but it's only natural that young lads want to take short cuts.

Later, we moved to a roster which the lads worked out for themselves. You had one cook and one helper, and the next day the helper would be the cook and he'd have a helper. That helped a lot because what they did was have two or three things that they would cook, which Nigel would do with them. He would make sure that these meals included a nice variety of ingredients. They got really good at cooking those particular things, so it made their shopping easy.

They knew it would take them exactly an hour to prepare, and a lot of times I'd pop around and the atmosphere around the dinner table was bloody good. The lads would be starving after training all day; they'd be hanging around the house, while the two guys were in the kitchen working flat out at getting the food ready. So the other lads would be walking past the kitchen, someone else would be watching a film and looking over his shoulder, and the atmosphere was always bloody good. When they were away on a stage race, I always encouraged that. To me that was a part of the day when you learnt about the history of the sport. They would want to talk about how it was back in those days – 'What about Bernard Hinault?' 'Well, he did so-and-so . . .' I used to make a big effort never to be too busy to come down to dinner and make sure I spent that time with them.

I had all sorts of rules and regulations but my principle was this: 'Once you clock out of here at night, you go and do whatever you want, but I'll expect you here at seven thirty in the morning. If you're pissed or simply can't do the training session, you'll go home. If you carry on in that way, you'll be kicked off the programme.' It simply boiled down to this: 'What do you want?'

'I want to be a professional bike rider. I want to win the Olympic Games.'

'Right, let's get you back down the track.'

I never, ever got heavy with them over going out; I just used to make it quite clear what was at stake. There was an example once when Geraint Thomas and some others went out for his birthday. The next day I took a call from Mark Cavendish, saying, 'Rod, I couldn't sleep last night. They all went out on the piss and came in and woke me up. I don't mind them coming in late, but I mind them waking me up.'

'Cav, I agree with you 100 per cent. We'll do something about it.'

Gee was supposed to be riding the Five Valleys road race, but I pulled them all out of it. It was a bit extreme, but I thought I'd have to make the consequence a hard one. It hit Gee because he was responsible, and it was the biggest race in his home area, South Wales.

They were all young lads wanting to get out and about. There were plenty of issues, and I'm pretty sure there were a lot more than I knew about. We had all sorts. There were times when I walked into the houses by the front door, and girls would go out by the back one. We used to have a rule about this, because both Cav and Matt Brammeier had girlfriends, quite long-standing ones; the rule was they weren't allowed to stay in the house – at the end of the day the place was paid for with our money, and it wasn't fair on the other lads. If they wanted to go and spend the night in a hotel, but still be at the track to train the next morning, that was fine. That eventually got quite difficult for them, so we ended up having a rule that they could stay two nights a month or something.

Policing that wasn't simple, but I used to go round to the houses all the time. Jane and I would go for an evening out in Manchester, and she would curse at me. It would be midnight or thereabouts, and we'd drive past the houses to have a look. I'd sit outside, get out of the car and listen to see if I could hear any music. If I did, I wouldn't say anything there and then. I'd just go to work in the morning, see who was there, and in the course of the conversation say, 'Did you have a good sleep last night?'

'Yeah, yeah, Rod, really good.'

'Oh, what time did you go to bed?'

'Ten o'clock.'

'Lying bastard – no, you didn't.'

And they would be saying, 'How do you know?' And I'd never tell them.

Or I'd see some of them walking down the street late at night, and I'd just keep driving. 'Did you have a good night last night?'

'Yeah.'

'What did you do?'

'Watched a film.'

'What time did you go to bed?'

'Ten o'clock.'

'No, you didn't, you lying bastard.'

I think it helped that early on they could feel themselves progressing as bike riders, even if they weren't doing it on the big stage yet. They were loving it. But I didn't care whether or not they were OK with it. These were the rules; this was what we were doing.

About six or seven years after the event, I learnt that Cav's girlfriend at the time, Melissa, had come over from the Isle of Man once, and I had had absolutely no idea. I came into the house he, Ed and Bruce shared one Sunday.

'Hey, guys, how are you doing?'

Ed was watching Formula One, and there were about twenty laps to go.

'Brilliant, can I have a look?'

So I sat down watching the Formula One with the lads, talking to Ed about it. Afterwards it was, 'All right, lads, see you tomorrow at training. Bye.' And unknown to me, Melissa had been in the cupboard all that time. I had knocked on the door, and they had gone, 'Shit, get in the cupboard.' She was there for maybe an hour, and they didn't say a thing.

I'm sure there was plenty else that went on that I still don't know about.

5 : The Guinea Pigs Come of Age

I always say that when Cav joined the academy he had his track-suit tucked into his socks. I can't remember whether or not that was actually the case, but that was the kind of character he was back then. He turned up at the Manchester velodrome in his scally car at the start of January 2004, and drove round the car park at high speed. I was thinking, 'Who the hell is that? What sort of car is that?' He gets quite embarrassed by it now because I think he really thought it was cool at the time, but it was dropping to pieces: the tyres were bald and it had a sticker saying '007 Goldfinger' across the top of the windscreen. It was fantastic – 'Cav-tastic', we called it. I was thinking, 'Oh my God, who is this?' and he got out in his tracksuit. You couldn't make it up.

I'd seen Mark race at the national track championships in 2003, when he was still a junior but racing with the seniors. Chris Newton knocked James Taylor off in the points race, James went up the track and Cav went down under him and hit him coming out of turn two; he went straight over the handlebars. I thought, 'He's going to be in trouble,' but he got up and tried to carry on racing. My next thought was, 'Good on him – he could have stopped there.' He was this fat little barrel on a yellow Dolan bike with sprinter bars. I remember wondering, 'What is he trying to be – a sprinter or an endurance rider?' I asked Marshall Thomas, who was the national junior coach at the time, about him; Marshall felt he didn't have the numbers; in other words, he didn't show the power readings they liked to see when he did tests on the rig. 'Yeah, he wins some races at home but he'll get to international level and it won't be enough.'

To select the riders for the academy in the first year we did a matrix: we listed the riders' qualities, such as their ability to listen, ability to win races, were they fast, were they technically good or not, were they practically good enough, were they organised. Obviously, a lot of it was quite subjective; I did it together with John Herety and Simon Lillistone, and we weighted the scores to reflect the fact that I thought winning bike races was the most important quality. If they can't win races at the level they can race at, you can't expect them to win anything else, so that ability should be weighted fairly high. Ed Clancy came out on top, but Cav was only a point or so behind him – the total added up to something like forty points – and their achievements since then would indicate that we got it pretty much right.

At the time I never thought, 'Oh yeah, Mark Cavendish has got speed like I've never seen before,' but what caught my attention was what he said. One of the first things he told me was, 'I never got selected for the world junior championship and I would have pissed it.' You look back now and you think, 'God, yes, he probably would have done.' He wanted to win races, but the main thing he kept saying was, 'I am not going to let you down. I really want to do this, but if I don't get selected I'm going to Belgium anyway.' It wasn't said arrogantly and it was one of the things that made me think it was worth having this lad on the programme. His enthusiasm has never dropped in all the time I've known him. I don't think I've ever seen him lacking in desire. He's always pretty enthusiastic about his bike racing, and he was as opinionated in 2003 as he is now. He holds himself quite highly in his opinions. He's not always right, but my feeling was, 'Bloody hell, this guy is really, really streetwise.'

I started working with the riders and advising them in November–December 2003, and Cav wasn't doing anything on his bike at that stage. He'd had his tonsils out and he was in terrible shape. He was still working at the bank on the Isle of Man; that was one thing that made him stand out from the others – you could tell he'd actually had to go to work. It just made him a little bit different, more grown-up perhaps. He knew his way around, knew how to work people, how to keep people on side, but he was constantly fannying around, particularly with Matt Brammeier. I don't think either of them had as bad an upbringing as they both like to make out. Mark was a pretty bright guy at school. He's not stupid, and that was quite evident early on. I deliberately split them up when we allocated the houses because there was no way we could have those two living together. I constantly had to keep my eye on them.

Cav's parents were divorced. I think that there had been issues with his dad, and perhaps Cav was ready to look for a father figure, someone to lead him quite strongly. Geraint Thomas was completely different – he just wanted a coach, somebody to advise him. Ed Clancy was different in another way: he fought against the discipline. You could see in his face that he didn't like it. I don't think Ed enjoyed the academy to start with because socially he wasn't really in with the group. Matt Brammeier and Cav had such strong personalities that they led everything, and the way they did that was to take the piss out of everybody. Ed was quite a target at first, but fair play to him, over time he let his legs do the talking.

Early on in the academy timetable I was testing the guys. We would do a regular session out on the road – four or five hours during the week around Manchester. We'd head out southwards towards the Peak District, towards Whaley Bridge, over the climbs round that way and then over to the Leek area. In every hour's riding, we'd do fifteen to twenty minutes of through and off, when the riders would be constantly rotating in a line, each doing a few seconds at the front before letting the next one past. It wouldn't matter where they were when they had to start their fifteen minutes of through and off – in the middle of a town, starting a 20 per cent descent or 20 per cent climb. They would start anyway.

The point was that this wasn't a physical training day; we were working on skills. One day they might end up in a team which had the yellow jersey in a stage race and they would have to be riding at the front to defend it. That would mean riding through and off going through a town, shouting out when you're at the front to indicate the dangers – 'Watch the lights', 'Car on the left'. If you're riding hard on a descent, you've got to look after your teammates, and it's the same if you're on a climb – in that case the question is how fast do you go to avoid putting them into the red. I used to explore all the muddiest lanes for them because they would need technical riding. I used to find as many little lanes and shitty little roads as I could. During that year Paul Manning came out with the lads. Simon Jones was in the car with me, and we were going down these lanes, with the riders going through and off. Paul came back to the car and said, 'Rod, we just can't do it along here.' I said, 'No, Paul, you've missed the point. This is just about them: if they are slip-sliding round little corners with gravel in the middle that's fine, because they've got to shout those dangers back down the line.' There is no better way of doing it than learning like that.

One day we'd come out to the south of Manchester. We'd done a loop, then went up Long Hill towards Buxton and turned right down into Goyt Valley. Mark went out of the back of the group on Goyt Valley, which is about a five-and-a-half-kilometre climb. He was in pieces; he hit a stone and both hands came off his handlebars, but he just managed to grab hold before he went down, while the other lads just tootled over the top. This was happening an hour and a half into five hours' riding, and he was already shot – snot all over his face, cheeks all big and red. I thought, 'My God, this guy is really going to struggle.'

So we were near Leek, the roads going constantly up and down, and then we hit Gun Hill, and straight away he was off the back of the group. I drove around him and watched the others, who all split up because the climb is quite steep. They popped over, and I pulled up to wait just over the crest of the hill. I was there for what seemed like ages, and all of a sudden I saw him zigzagging up the hill. When Cav is suffering, he climbs with his head over the front of the bike; he was really labouring. He got to the back of the car, and I thought, 'What is he doing? He needs to come around the car,' and the next thing he had disappeared. There he was, his bike on the floor, his head in his hands – he was crying, properly crying.

'Bloody hell, Mark, are you OK?'

'I know I'm letting you down, and please don't not believe in me. I'm so much better than this.'

Those are the moments when you could be a bit sharp: 'Fucking hell, what is wrong with you? Get on with it.' But you could sense there was something more going on in there, so I went through it with him. I didn't care that the other riders had gone off; I just took him through it: 'That's fine. What's going to make you a better bike rider? What do you have to do?'

He sat there looking at me. 'Well, I've got to get fitter.'

'Yeah, you have. How do you get fitter?'

'Well, I've got to ride my bike more.'

'Exactly. What are we doing now?'

'I'm riding my bike.'

'Perfect. What's expected of you today is for you to do this five-hour ride. Was there a set speed? Did we ever say you've got to do that distance in a certain time? No. Come on, we'll just get on with it. You'll get there.'

He just went, 'Oh my God,' and I said, 'Come on, get back on the bike. I'll get you behind the car, and from there it's a lot easier to get home.' He was absolutely fine, but I would think that in the past at times like that he must have always had people shout at him.

There were times when I did raise my voice, though. I used to do a track session called 'Go Till You Blow'. They were all on the same gear – eighty-eight inches – which is quite a low gear for the track, and I would be on the motorbike. I would tell them, 'This motorbike is going to go anywhere on the track, and the pace is going to build.' I'd start at forty kilometres an hour, with the riders in a line behind the bike, and gradually go faster and faster until they were absolutely flat out; at the end it was just a matter of who survived. Every single track session I did would end – in theory – with half an hour of that. Ed Clancy survived every single session and would always be on his own at the end. I don't think I ever got to half an hour; I'd always hit twenty or twenty-three minutes and stop, by which time the only one left behind the motorbike would be Ed, because he had the pure leg speed needed for it.

The problem with riding behind the motorbike is what we call 'the damage'. That's when a rider swings out of the line because he has cracked, and the rider behind him has got to close the gap. It may be only a bike length and a half or two perhaps, but to close even two lengths you've got to go several kilometres per hour faster, which isn't easy if you're going at sixty or sixty-two kilometres an hour and are close to your physical limit. Everyone thought it was fun. Some of the lads would be on their knees, but they needed to be on the edge. When they were racing – the final kilometres of the world Madison championship, for example – they would have to be in control and know what they were doing, even when they were at their physical limit. So on the motorbike I would try to mimic the moves that happen unexpectedly in the peloton on the track. Sometimes as you're coming around the banking the back of the string of riders just flicks up, so I used to take them all over the track: up and down, straight up to the top of the banking, ride up there for a couple of laps, then belt down as if it was a points race or a Madison. We ended up with loads of people coming and watching the session – they would all want to know who was going to last the longest.

In the first weeks Cav couldn't even last ten minutes. The riders always crack when they swing up from behind the bike and try to get on the back of the string; you see them sprinting flat out and all of a sudden they're gone. The first time Cav got dropped, he ended up sat there in the middle of the track. It was one of the few times I've shouted at him, and it was because I was on the motorbike and couldn't be heard otherwise. I yelled, 'Get back on your bike, get back on your bike!' And back on he got. We got the riders off the track, and I spoke to him on his own: 'Mark, what's wrong with you? Why couldn't you hang on?'

'I'm tired. The others are better than me. They're fitter than me.'

'Exactly. Well, how are you going to get better?'

'I've got to keep riding my bike.'

'Right. Are you going to get better sat on your fat arse down there?'

'No.'

'Right. What I want to see, even if you never manage it, whenever that motorbike comes past you try and make it onto the back of the line every single time, because that's pedalling your bike.'

I told them all that, and I'd try to help them when we did 'Go Till You Blow'. If there was someone who got dropped quite early, I'd see them half a lap ahead and I'd drop right down onto the black line at the bottom of the track and hold my speed, and at least give them every opportunity to get on the back of the string. If they could get another two laps out of it, that was better than nothing. If a rider was going round the top of the track and was absolutely knackered and needed to take five or six laps out, that was fine, but I wanted to see the effort every time. So if Mark was trying to get to the front each time the motorbike came past, I would give him a good pat on the back afterwards: 'Well done, you bloody trained, you nearly made it that time, nearly got on the back. You stayed in two minutes longer. Well done, brilliant.' It was something that Simon Jones taught me, something I totally believe in and still preach to this day: never praise the result; praise the effort.

There were little episodes like this early on with Mark, but all of a sudden he started winning bike races in spite of his lack of fitness. When he won that stage in the Girvan Three-Day that was an eye-opener, and the way he won it made it a big moment for the academy: our first win on the road. It's one of the ways in which he is special: he is a race winner, a rider who can be unfit but still win. When some riders are knackered, they can't even get out of the saddle. Mark is one of the few who are just naturally fast at the end of races, so even if he is absolutely on his knees, he can bring it home. Some people think that natu-ral-born sprinters don't have to try too hard and that explains why they've got all that speed left at the end of the race, but it's not that. If you put Mark in a race, it's a different kettle of fish from training; he'll always get more out of himself racing. He's always been like that – maybe 15 per cent better when he com-petes. It's partly that he simply enjoys racing. He loves the envi-ronment, and if you're happy doing something, you get more out of yourself. I don't think he particularly liked training early on, but he doesn't mind it now, as long as it's well structured.

Mark is the best athlete I've ever seen when it comes to turning things around, when you compare how he trains to how he races. Geraint Thomas is just very consistent – good at training, good at racing. Ed Clancy is pretty similar but he would struggle with a lot of the training we did at the academy.

That wasn't down to him: it could have been because I didn't have a full understanding of what a sprint athlete was going through. Steven Burke would much rather train than race, and he'd be much better at training than at racing. But one thing that's common to all of the riders who have gone through the academy and actually made something of their cycling – not just Cav and Ed, but Andy Tennant, Burkie, other guys – is that I've never had to push them forward. I've only ever had to hold them back to stop them doing too much. If you say, 'Do four hours,' they'll go and do five; if you say, 'Do three efforts,' they'll do four. You never ask them to do five efforts and find they've only done two, unless there is something wrong with them. You never have to get them out of bed – they're all pretty good at getting themselves going.

Things really started to move forward for us in late 2004, when Geraint Thomas joined the academy. The first time I'd seen him was at the youth national track championships in Manchester in 2002 or 2003. I was with my old teammate Tim Buckle, who was working as a Talent Team coach at the time. He said to me, 'Look at this kid, look how aerodynamic he is, look how small he makes himself across the front.' I remember looking at him and thinking, 'Bloody hell, he looks good as a pursuiter.' Through 2004 Geraint began getting involved quite a lot, even though he was still a junior; he was good enough already to race with us at the European championships, he'd won the scratch race at the world junior championships and he was riding above his category in the under-23 races in the UK. We all knew this guy was a real talent. He was the first British rider to win the junior Paris–Roubaix, although Ian Stannard still thinks he could have beaten him. They were together at the end of the race, but Ian went straight on at the point where they had to turn right into the velodrome, where the race finishes; Gee went right and won. They still argue about it to this day. Everyone winds Ian up, saying, 'Oh, you went the wrong way'; and everyone winds Gee up, saying, 'You wouldn't have won if Ian hadn't taken the wrong turning . . .'

Gee joined in October 2004 as a junior, the first one of the 2005 intake, and that took the academy up another level because all of a sudden we had added another very high-quality bike rider. Everything seemed to flow better, and that winter it all progressed. We committed to riding a lot of the amateur six-day races in Europe, and the lads learnt so much there. I used to go on my own with Cav and Gee and stand in the centre of the track with a spanner, a pair of wheels and a set of Allen keys. Most of the amateur lads would do their race, which would be before the pro six, stay up and watch the pros, then get up at eleven or twelve in the morning and race again. There was one day in Bremen when it was raining. Geraint and Cav had ridden three hours in the morning, and when they got in they met a couple of Belgian guys who had just got up. The Belgians asked why our lads were out on their bikes. I just said, 'They can't bloody lie in bed all day.' We had a good routine: ride in the morning, lunch, talk about the racing, race in the afternoon, dinner. After that they'd ride to the race from where we were staying with their lights on. They used spoked wheels because it was about them putting in the hard graft and learning how to race, not just winning. We'd watch an hour of the pro racing, then go home. That week Cav and Geraint won every single night, in spite of two massive falls.

A turning point for the academy came that winter, when we invested in going to Australia for two months ahead of the 2005 world track championships in Los Angeles. We went down to Cronulla, south of Sydney, and this is where the lads put in a lot of work. They really grafted. There were five of them: Ed Clancy, Matt Brammeier, Tom White, Geraint Thomas and Mark Cavendish, and we also had Matt Crampton, the sprinter, with us. This was where the academy really took on a life of its own. I didn't have to discipline these lads any more; they were in the rhythm, they could see that it was working. When we were doing all the six-days, they had started to feel good about it, and at the track World Cup in Sydney they were getting medals. They could see they were starting to get results.

On some days in Australia they were doing 260 kilometres: for example, they might do three or four hours in the morning, ride to the track, which took an hour or so, do a track session and then ride home; on other days they would do a little spin going to the track, train there, ride home, then ride a criterium in the evening, riding to and from the race, which might be half an hour or forty minutes. They were on their bikes all the time. It was decent weather, and they were out on their bikes at six o'clock in the morning. There was healthy food and plenty of climbs. We had days out as well, because they were there a long time. They were young lads and they needed to get more out of it than just the racing, so we went round Sydney harbour and over to Bondi beach.

It wasn't all good times. We were transferring from Cronulla to the hotel for the World Cup in Sydney, and the lads were going to ride down – it might have been thirty-five or forty kilometres. I'd been pretty specific about not leaving anything behind, because I didn't want to have to come back to the hotel in Cronulla. I left twenty minutes or so after them, stopped at a petrol station and was just getting in the car when Matt Brammeier called: 'Rod, ever so sorry, I've left my racing licence in the drawer of my hotel room.' 'You're bloody joking, Matt.' I spun the car round, went back and got his licence. I was ten minutes into the journey back when Matt rang again. I nearly didn't answer it – my first thought was, 'Sod them, they'll just have to do without whatever else they've left.' I picked up the phone and said, 'What the bloody hell have you forgotten now?' He was in a total panic: 'Rod, Geraint's on the floor.'

I hadn't known Geraint that long, but what I did know about him was that he didn't stay on the floor just because he had a big crash. He had crashed in every single six-day he had ridden with me; there was a massive one in Ghent when he was getting back onto the string of riders after lapping the field, and at the top of the track someone flipped up and shoved him into the barrier. He fell right at my feet – didn't even hit the banking, just straight onto the concrete, head first. I stood looking at him fiddling with his bike, and he was on the floor wheezing because he'd winded himself so badly. But he got back up, carried on and rode the race. So with Geraint I knew that something must be really wrong if he was still lying on the floor. I asked Matt: 'Have you called the ambulance? Calm the lads down, stay where you are, make sure the road is safe.' And as I turned up they were just putting Geraint in the back of the ambulance.

They had been riding two by two. Gee was in the third couple, with Matt Crampton and Ed at the front. Ed felt really bad about what happened, but it was just a bit of bad luck: there was a massive steel spring lying on the hard shoulder of the dual carriageway where they were riding. It stood half a metre high but it was wound up – and they hadn't seen it. At the last minute Ed had shouted, 'On your left.' Tom White, who was second in line, hit it, and up it went and back down into Gee's wheel. It chopped his fork straight off, and of course Gee went straight down and hit his bloody chest. We hadn't cut down the fork extension on his new bike – we'd said, 'Just leave this for a little while', as it was only about one centimetre high – but he got that straight into his chest and it ruptured his spleen. The one thing that I remember Geraint telling me as he got into the ambulance was, 'I feel like I need to piss, or I'm about to,' and straight away I knew something wasn't right.

It was chaos, but fortunately Shane Sutton was over there managing Great Britain at the World Cup, so he went directly to the hospital. It was pretty tense getting hold of Geraint's parents; he was in intensive care and he was pretty bad. And just to make it worse, Cav flooded the hotel. It had rained on them one day out on the road, and he decided to try and dry his shoes with a hairdryer. He left the hairdryer on with the shoes, but it set off the fire sprinklers – not just in the room, but the whole floor. The hotel staff were going bonkers. While this was going on, we were shuttling back and forwards to the hospital, and Geraint's family were coming over. Fortunately, he was fine, although he ended up with a massive scar. The poor guy was in hospital for ages, so the lads went to visit him every other day, taking him things. It was a really testing time for them, but you could see the bond they'd built up.

When Geraint did get out of hospital, we didn't send him home; he stayed with us and would come to help me every day with the coaching. He had actually been selected to ride the world Madison championship in Los Angeles with Rob Hayles; the reserve was Mark Cavendish, so Cav got the ride, but Gee flew to California with them so that he could take in the whole experience. I wasn't in LA because I came back with the others to Manchester, but that world championship was the big breakthrough: Cav and Rob won the Madison, Cav finished fourth in the scratch, and Ed Clancy rode in the team pursuit, only the qualifying round, but they won the gold. That was the moment when senior members of British Cycling started to say, 'Crikey, this is working, this is quite interesting . . . what work have you done?' I think Simon Jones had seen the progression over time, but Ed riding so well in that team pursuit was critical because this had always been the key discipline for Great Britain, and here was the evidence that we could produce riders who could earn their place and perform on the day. It had been an incredibly quick progression. Things had suddenly started to gel, for no one particular reason. The team started racing well together, the staff started working well together, the riders started to understand what we were trying to do, and it was as simple as that. That was when the whole academy idea came of age.

Those world titles gave all the lads more belief. The mindset became, 'Right, let's just get stuck into a really good year.' We started going to stage races abroad and winning: Geraint won the Flèche du Sud; Ed won a stage in the Tour of Berlin in fantastic style on his own, clipping off a group of six riders; Cav landed the points jersey in Berlin and was winning races at home willy-nilly. About then I began thinking that the only other person I had seen at that level, winning races by lengths from the rest, was Robbie McEwen, who had been a prolific stage winner at both the Tour de France and the Giro d'Italia, and had taken the green jersey in the Tour. I still stand by what I thought then: if you're going to be fast as a pro, you've got to be winning by five or six lengths as an amateur; if you're just throwing your bike at the line and nipping in by an inch, you're not going to be quick enough to beat the very best guys.

In 2005 the academy was unique, because we didn't have a whole new cohort of riders – Geraint was the only new recruit – and so we didn't have to start from scratch. It wasn't that the funding was cut; the riders weren't there. But they were about to start coming through. During the first year I had written up a junior programme to link in with the academy, because the kids who were coming through weren't good enough. They didn't have the skills. What they were doing was too individual – no group sessions, big weekends or school holidays together. So British Cycling got a Welsh coach, Darren Tudor, in to do the job. We had a good working relationship, and everything he did was based around what the academy did. At half-terms he would have what was called the academy week, because it was all about preparing them to come up to the next level. It was basically the same regime: lots of split days, with a bit of education during the middle of the day. A lot of people think that the academy was where the riders cut their teeth, but it wasn't; it was one of the stepping stones. The junior programme was a big part of it, but so was the under-16 Talent Team programme: it was all feeding off what we were doing at the top. That in turn meant that the quality of the riders coming to me at the academy was even better.

When you look at the British Cycling system, the whole idea

is that the Talent Team should keep pushing up towards the next level, with the juniors and the academy doing the same. My goal was to get the academy riders to be Olympic Podium athletes – good enough to get on the senior programme and win Olympic medals – when they moved on at whatever age. They needed to be ready to go onto the Podium programme, as the senior programme was also called, with no shocks, or ready to be pro bike riders on the road. That meant I had to look at the whole thing, ask what it should look like and break that down. That's what I was always trying to do with the Talent Team and the junior programme. The skills were a key element. A fifteen- or sixteen-year-old athlete can show potential physically, but there is only so much they can actually give you. There are some who are ridiculously good at that age, but there are a lot who perhaps don't have it yet but will grow into it eventually. What you can work on are the skills for when they get to eighteen or nineteen – that's the time when they can start working hard. At that age, you can't rely on your talent; there are lots and lots of other gifted people in your sport, so your training, physical conditioning and attitude come massively into it. If you're trying to improve physically, and at the same time still trying to learn those skills, you're not spending your time well.

The European track championships were another opportunity to integrate the programmes, because the juniors and the under-23s would always be racing together. At the Euros I always told the under-23 guys, 'You are on show here, and I want you to stand up, be proud to be part of the academy, because I want those junior lads thinking, "Look how good these academy riders are."' During the Euros I would always have a meeting with the juniors so I could get to know some of them; I'd go around their rooms, check up on them, always trying to find out, 'Are you guys on this or not? Are you guys up for this? Are you guys good enough or not?' I always did it with Darren, linking in with what he was doing; he would be working in a similar way with the Talent Team, and I was constantly feeding information up the chain in the same way to Simon Jones or Matt Parker or whoever was looking after the senior track endurance team.

With those wins behind us we started getting ready for the European track championships, knowing that we were going to perform. They were training well and riding well. I didn't really think about how quickly it had come together. I just had my head down and was constantly thinking about what was coming next. We needed to move on in some way, and I needed more numbers. I was looking at that junior programme and doing quite a lot of work and discussion with Darren, who was looking after the likes of Ben Swift, Ian Stannard, Peter Kennaugh and Jonny Bellis. We both knew that it was going to be pretty damn good when we got the next batch of kids on board as well.

I wanted to prepare the team properly for the Europeans, like the Olympic team, so that the riders would get experience of preparing for a major event. It was a big moment: as a team we'd concentrated massively on it and we turned up in a really confident state of mind. The lads would have absolutely dominated the team pursuit, but Tom White hit one of the sponges that the judges put at the bottom of the track to keep the riders from going too low; his wheel picked it up and threw it into Cav's front wheel. It stuck underneath the fork crown, and I don't know how he didn't go down. It stopped Cav dead in his tracks and split them all up; they ended up fifth by about a tenth of a second, so they didn't even get a second ride. They were absolutely gutted, but Cav took fourth in the scratch race and then won the points race. We had had a target of one gold medal and we managed it, but this was another moment when it hit home: these lads really are at world level. They were really competitive, all of them.

That took us to the summer of 2005. Cav won the national circuit race championship in Otley, and that got me thinking: 'I've got a load of young juniors coming along who are going to be good, we've got two world champions on the team, we've got a European champion, we've won stage races.' We had the space to move on now. The next step was to set them all up with teams abroad in August and September, going into October, to get them into a different world.

Cav went to Sparkasse, a German semi-pro team; Gee went to another one, Wiesenhof; and Matt Brammeier and Tom White went to France, to CC Étupes and UVC Aube. We started forging links with T-Mobile as well, through Heiko Salzwedel, who'd worked at British Cycling and was running their development side. It took a bit of time for people in the professional cycling world to understand how Cav works, however. In 2005 we had a meeting with T-Mobile at the Tour of Britain, on the morning of the criterium on the final day, and I said to their *directeur sportif* Brian Holm, 'Keep an eye out for this guy Mark Cavendish. This guy is going to win the stage today.' Brian had a look of 'seen that before, heard that before', and unfortunately Cav crashed on the final lap; he was brought down because the pros were giving the GB guys a bit of a hard time, as they sometimes do with the amateurs. If Cav had won that stage, they would possibly have taken him on as a *stagiaire* – apprentice – or looked at him for the following year.

Even when Cav did turn pro, he needed quite a lot of support, because people didn't totally believe in him. But if you look at the results from the academy, he was in everything: Madisons, team pursuits, road races. His name was in all the results, but he also brought something else: an X-factor. He was passionate about winning, and would be asking, 'How are we going to win?' He'd be looking at it and breaking it down, not scared to take it on and be the leader. He wouldn't hide behind anybody.

The academy had three riders selected for the world championships in Madrid in late September 2005. The target we had set ourselves was a rider in the top twenty, and Mark managed fourteenth, so we achieved our target, although they didn't ride that well together. Within British Cycling you could feel that things were starting to move; it was getting a bit more road focused. Max Sciandri had got involved with the GB set-up; he was an Italian pro, born in Derby and brought up in the US, who had got a bronze for GB at the 1996 Atlanta Games, pretty much off his own bat. Max had arranged for the team to have the use of the Lampre pro team bus, which was another step forward. On the women's side, Nicole Cooke had been one of the best in the world for a few years, and she got a silver medal for us. So, for the first time, we had potential contenders in all the road races.

But the key moment for me was when I sat watching the professional race on the final day. Roger Hammond was a good one-day rider who'd finished seventh in the Athens Olympics the year before and had come third in Paris–Roubaix, matching the best any Briton's ever done. There was a massive kerfuffle when Charly Wegelius and Tom Southam rode for the Italians early on in the race, basically repaying a favour or two. It was the sort of thing that happened at the pro Worlds in those days: the bigger teams might get a bit of help from a smaller one early on, and there would be a reciprocal deal somewhere else. John Herety, the road team manager, ended up taking the rap for it, and lost his job in the end.

That race was when I first thought we could do a lot better than we were at the world championships. We didn't have a big team in the pro field, but it struck me: 'Bloody hell, we're a lap out from the finish and we've still got Bradley Wiggins and Roger Hammond in this bike race.' If they had all ridden as a team   Roger, Brad, Tom and Charly, and the other riders, Steve Cummings and Rob Sharman – what could we actually have done? I was sitting there thinking, 'Charly's good enough, Brad's good enough, Roger's good enough. Why haven't these guys got the belief? What's happening? We've got some great riders, so why aren't they together and why isn't it working?'

6 : The Italian Job

It was baking hot at the European track championships in Fiorenzuola in June 2005. I was sitting in the stands with Dave Brailsford, and I said to him, 'These lads are ready to move on; the academy's ready to up sticks.'

'What do you mean?'

'I think we need to move abroad. We need to stay in Manchester this summer, but we should think about how we can go and live somewhere in Europe, how we set up out there.'

Fair play to Dave, he just turned round and said, 'Listen, you're the person who's going to do this. You go and find out where. Come back to me with a plan, and I'll back it.'

To start with I was thinking of Germany, Belgium or France. Germany appealed because they were strong on the track side, so I thought they'd understand a British national team, plus we'd already got involved in placing riders at teams like Sparkasse. I'd read about the Bundesliga: there were two hundred under-23 riders there. But I was looking at France as well because I had some connections there and I knew the racing. And there was a case for Belgium because of the volume of races you could ride there, all the *kermis*es.

But then Dave suggested something to me: Max Sciandri was now involved – I think Dave had employed him purely because he thought he might be useful somewhere – so what did I think about going to Italy with the academy? It was daunting. I had never really been to Italy. We'd had riders do well there: Jamie Burrow, who got a contract at Lance Armstrong's US Postal Service team, was one that sprang to mind; Russell Downing had been out there; and earlier on, Dave Rayner. I'd heard that the under-23 racing calendar there was something quite special. On the other hand, I'd also heard that there was a lot of cheating going on in Italy, even at the under-23 level. I'd spoken to quite a lot of people, and all they would talk about was how hard the racing was, how difficult. However, I knew the Australians were based out there and I always believed the Australian Institute of Sport's system was pretty good – they were well structured, driven hard, and their approach was similar to ours. But I didn't say yes to Dave there and then; I went home and thought to myself, 'Bloody hell, I'm quite scared about this, but what's the academy about? It's about being a bit ballsy. This is different. This is something new, so why don't we do it?' I went back to Dave and said we should go for it.

Max lived in Quarrata, a little town in Tuscany off the main road from Florence to Pistoia which looked as if it could be a handy base, so we started putting the plan for the move together. At about the same time Dave spoke to Shane Bannan, the Australian performance director, and the two of us went over to Italy to meet him. I thought it was pretty good that the guy who was in charge of our biggest rivals was prepared to meet us and help us set up down there in Italy. I think he did it because he really believed in what we were doing and felt that the more people were racing out there, the better it would be. What he said to us was, 'If you get better, we'll only get better, because you'll force us to keep moving on.' I thought that was a pretty open way of looking at it.

Shane talked us through loads of stuff: he was really good at how the system worked in terms of getting in there; how the Italians were; how you entered races; the different standards of races; what you can and can't do in Italy. It was good to go through all that. But the main thing we gleaned was just how hard it had been for them in their early days. He said they'd get into the top twenty and crack open the champers, but he also said he used to sit on the end of his bed crying because it was that tough for the young lads. It wasn't going to be straightforward.

While all that was happening, all of a sudden I had six riders to look after for 2006. Geraint Thomas was still with us, but there were five new members who joined on 17 October 2005: Andy Tennant, Ian Stannard, Ross Sander, Ben Swift and Ben Greenwood. Cav and Ed Clancy were going to ride in Germany for Sparkasse for the whole year; they would ride a few races in Italy with us but had moved on to join the senior programme. With the new lads, I began a three-month boot-camp period, a condensed version of what we had done in the first year with the same mix of split sessions of track skills, track league at Manchester, education, plenty of hours on the road, and in between, the amateur six-days. With Steve Peters I tweaked the rules and consequences, bringing in things like having to clean the GB team cars rather than more time on the bike. The rule was they had to be at the track at ten to eight waiting for me, helmets on, waiting for instructions, so that by eight o'clock we were on the track. It was pretty strict: sometimes the consequences would apply to the whole group, so that if one guy did something wrong, everyone suffered. The idea was that they would work with each other: you would get your mate out of bed rather than just leave him to suffer on his own.

At the same time we were preparing to go to Italy: finding a house out there with Max and sorting out all the equipment we would need without the British Cycling umbrella in Manchester to support us. It was a good winter in terms of results – the riders were getting up there every time in the six-days, with Swifty and Gee winning in Dortmund, and Stannard and Tennant in Stuttgart – and then we went to the Commonwealth Games in Melbourne. I'd worked with all the GB guys by now, but for the Games they were spread across all the home nations – for example, Cav was riding for the Isle of Man, Gee for Wales – and so were the coaches. I was seconded to Wales. What I did was keep the riders racing and training together; we were pretty determined to put one over on the Aussies on their home turf.

Just how determined became clear when we were planning for the scratch race. Cav would be one of the fastest, with the only real threat an Australian sprinter, Ben Kersten. I went to discuss tactics with the lads and said, with a dead straight face, 'We've been thinking about it and we think the best way to go about winning this scratch race is to take this guy out. We need to take him right out so he can't get back up. Hands up, who's up for it?' It was Geraint Thomas who raised his hand. 'I'm up for that.' 'Only flipping joking, mate . . .'

Cav's gold medal in the scratch was the first major title I saw him win. He was in a group of about five or six who gained a lap early in the race, and with only those few riders to worry about he was bound to win if he got a clear run to the line. I could hardly believe my eyes: the Aussies had none of their best riders in that group. I sat there thinking, 'Oh my God, have these guys not been watching what has been going on? Do they not realise that this guy won the World Madison last year?' I couldn't believe that they let that group go with Cav in there, but it was perfect for us. Given the rivalry we'd had with the Australians since Athens, it was quite entertaining.

That gold medal was a massive thing on the Isle of Man, and Cav was so happy, because he's so proud of where he comes from. But one thing that shone through for me was just how driven he is as an athlete. He called me that night at almost eleven thirty from the Isle of Man house: 'Oh, Rod, I don't know what to do.' The team wanted to throw a party for him and had got the champagne in, but he wanted to go to bed because it was the road race in a couple of days. He wasn't going to sit back: he'd won the gold medal, he was the Commonwealth Games scratch-race champion, but he'd already moved on.

I came home early from the Games and drove straight out to Italy with a car full of my kit for the year, leaving Jane at home. I was there a couple of weeks before the lads, in a little B&B about three kilometres out of Quarrata. It was dead quiet; every morning I'd get up and there would be no one in the house. The owners would leave me a cake and a glass of orange juice, with a flask of coffee on the side, and I would sit there thinking, 'Oh my God, what am I doing here in Italy?'

I didn't speak the language and had to rely on Max. His role was to deal with housing and language issues, help us get into the races – help us settle in, if you like. He would have a coffee with the riders but not a great deal else, although he came to the first couple of races. You can imagine the young lads moving out to Tuscany: nice weather, foreign parts – they thought they were on a bit of a jolly. But I wanted to keep the same momentum and the same standards as at the academy; that wasn't going to change. Training rides were at nine o'clock, recovery rides were at ten, and this was one of the first big clashes I had with Max: he wanted to ride with the lads, but he didn't want to get up for nine o'clock. The Italian style is that you meet in the cafe in the square, have a coffee, then you go for a ride from there, but I'm not interested in that. Maybe it's a British thing, but I'm not interested in meeting for coffee first; let's go training. Max never agreed with me on that, but we stuck to what we wanted to do. His heart was in the right place and his ambition was for us to win, but he just didn't understand how I wanted to do it. That's why we really never got on from a coaching point of view, which in turn made it a little bit difficult with the riders.

We didn't race much in that first year because it was hard to get into the races. The racing was so sparse that I'd bring in a mechanic and a carer part-time for two or three weeks, then they'd go home for a fortnight. We didn't get many results – a couple of second places for Gee was as good as it got – but we got so much hassle when we did race that it felt like going to war every time. We were always fine in Quarrata, because Max had quite a reputation in the town; he was a bit of a character, people knew who he was. I also used to work a lot on the lads about living there: 'Be careful what you're doing, be respectful to the locals. If a car gives you a load of abuse on the road, think about it before you respond, because you've got a British jersey on your back and they know who we are and they know where we are.' We had hardly any issues of that kind; it was the reception we received at the races that made it tough.

Back then, Italian races still had the old system where the

team managers can chip in on the internal radio system – normally you don't have them on for talkback – so they would all be jabbering away to the *commissaire*. On one occasion the *commissaire* had said something in English over the race radio for my benefit, and one of the *directeurs sportifs* said down the radio in English, 'Fucking English, go home.' That was the attitude towards us. Our tactics were that we would always try to win the race, even though perhaps we wouldn't succeed. Sometimes we would get on the front of the bunch and ride together to win the race, then perhaps miss out on the sprint. Some of the other teams used to go mad at us. That must have made it quite hard for Max: a lot of his mates, other ex-pros like Luca Scinto, were running these teams, and Max didn't have a great deal of input on how we raced. I think he felt embarrassed because we weren't doing very well and he had wanted us to come in and perform.

I felt confident in the guys – 'Let's just keep plugging away' – and we had to build a reputation. We were there to work hard and we could put up with all that shit – riders trying to run us off the road, the cheating that happens, particularly riders trying to hang onto cars. I wouldn't let the lads do that; it was our first rule – if I see you hanging onto a car, you are going home. I found out that the Australians had the same rule as well. In the under-23 Giro that year, Geraint Thomas went over the top of a climb just off the back of the first group, about thirty to forty seconds behind; he was racing away on his own behind a group further up the road – he could see them but he wasn't catching them. A few cars and a couple of motorbikes went past with a load of riders hanging on, and they were all shouting at him, '*Inglese!*' Geraint just said to me, 'Fucking wankers,

I'm not even English. I'm Welsh.' That used to wind Gee up: all he ever heard was '*Inglese, inglese!*' He would say, 'It's Great Britain. Does this jersey say English to you?'

There were so many times when the lads were getting bulldozed by the Italian riders. They would work against us to make sure we were never, ever going to get in any breaks. It felt as if the peloton was entirely against us, but I believed we had to earn our stripes. We were in their country, coming in to try and win their races, so I can imagine how they felt. There is one event called the Gran Premio di Capodarco, a massive race, one of the best under-23 races in the world, with forty teams of five. We were a long way off the pace when we rode there that first year. But in 2008 Peter Kennaugh won it in absolutely magnificent style; in two years we went from being a million miles away to winning several times a year. That was pretty special.

Tuscany was a hot spot for top under-23 teams; we'd see them everywhere, and they all had a similar structure: the riders live together in team houses rather than all over Italy; they train as a unit in a certain way; the *directeurs sportifs* have links with the pro teams. So when we were out training we would see them all the time. The fundamental difference was that all those teams were run like miniature pro teams. Even in the second year in Italy, when it was starting to come together, I still had only one carer and one mechanic: Andy Naylor and John Keegan. Andy had raced all over the place as an amateur and had come in from Australia to do the job; Johnny was Irish, and a real character.

To give an example of the way we worked, Johnny was never allowed to touch any of the bikes. The riders had a single bike each – they were still not allowed a race bike and training bike – but if there was a young lad who didn't know how to take the cranks off and change the bottom bracket, Johnny wouldn't say, 'Out of the way, let me do it,' he'd have to stand there and tell them how to do it. The riders had to clean the bikes when they were at home; Johnny would clean them during stage races. When we were at races, Andy was never allowed to make the lads' race food; what would happen was that we would turn up at a hotel, he'd set up a table in his room, and while he was massaging the lads they would have to come in room by room – six of them, in three pairs – and they'd make their own food for the following day. He'd show them how to do it, and they'd pack it up, wrap it in silver foil, put it in their *musettes* and make the drinks – just enough for the bikes, and Andy would make the extra ones. They always had something to do; we'd get home after a race, and on Sunday evening I would email them all the jobs for the next day. I'd take the race car round and the people carrier, and they would have to clean everything – the cars, the cool boxes, all the bottles. We weren't a professional team and we couldn't afford to bung the *bidons* away, so they would clean all the bottles, wash the bikes, then do an easy ride.

This meant that the riders didn't get total recovery. They didn't get massages all the time, even in races; once a week maybe, because it's not a necessity – it's a luxury for when you're a pro. My thinking was that when they had the chance to recover totally, they would appreciate it and their lives would change because of it. One day they would be pros with team helpers to look after them; they would appreciate what these people would be doing for them, and they would improve physically too, because for the first time they would be completely full-time bike riders, able to devote large chunks of time to resting up and letting the training and racing have an effect. The academy was just a stepping stone.

There were things we did gain immediately from the move. All of a sudden we were training on the climbs, in the heat, and the lads were acclimatising and improving. The biggest upside was that we brought in the riders at eighteen, so they'd barely raced in the UK, yet they were racing at this high level from the very start. The lads would struggle with the fact that the Italians would be cheating, hanging onto cars, but I constantly reminded them: 'Listen, guys, at the European road race championships and the Worlds they will not be able to hang on. If you keep doing what you're doing, you're going to come good one day.' The move took them out of their comfort zone, out of Manchester, making it a little bit more controlled in terms of the amount of work they could do, and it meant they had to bond together as a team because they had no other friends in the entire place.

The Italian move pushed the academy rapidly to another level. Upping sticks was at the base of all that came in the next few years. It guaranteed that we had enough British riders to put teams together at the very highest level. Back in Italy, you could see that people started to warm to us. I kept saying to the lads, 'We are going to stick to our game here. We are going to be polite. We are going into the races in the right frame of mind. We aren't going to win every race but we are going to give it our best every time, and we are going to talk to as many people as we can.' By the time I left Italy there was a massive difference. Cav was spending a lot of time in Quarrata, as he wanted to stay close to the academy – he still goes down there to train sometimes – and his growing fame helped us get accepted. Other British pros were gravitating to the area: riders like Steve Cummings moved down – he still lives there – and Gee and Ian Stannard stayed there when they got pro contracts. People wanted to know about our riders, wanted to take them on. In 2006 Mark Cavendish was a nobody, but in 2007 the whole pro cycling world began to say, 'Wow, who is this British guy?'

By 2007, as the academy went into its second year in Italy, Mark had really started to come on. He'd turned pro for T-Mobile on the road and started to win races quite early on in the season: the Scheldeprijs in Belgium and stages in the Four Days of Dunkirk and Tour of Catalonia. The management at T-Mobile started thinking, 'Bloody hell, we've got a true talent on our roster,' and Mark was on a roll – he was going for everything. He was so hungry for it. He was a young pro, not earning lots of money – I think he was on the minimum wage at the time – but he felt he was moving forwards and felt really happy with himself.

I'd made one thing clear when he turned professional. One thing I'm always afraid of from a coach's point of view is that you think you know your riders really well, but if it turns out one of them is doing something you don't know about – doping – no one would ever believe you. I remember talking to Cav just before he went off and signed his contract. I built myself up for the conversation; it wasn't an easy one to have. I said, 'Look, Cav, you'll do whatever you want to do – at the end of the day no one can stop you – but if you are ever in a situation where for whatever reason you do the wrong thing, just fucking tell me first so that I can get away from you.' I'd never worked with anyone who was a proper professional, and I was scared of that particular situation.

We had to be equally direct when it came to getting him into the Tour de France. I always think, 'If you don't ask, you never know' – and at worst, the people you ask can only ever say no. Talking to Mark that spring, the Tour kept coming up. We'd be chatting away together, and he'd be saying things like, 'You know, I don't think the team have got anybody else for the Tour. I think I could do as much as anybody else.' He was desperate to go, so I just said to him, 'Why don't you ask the guys who run the team?' 'Oh no, I daren't.'

I think he didn't feel people would listen to him. So I said to him, 'If you write them a letter, a proper letter, they will read it, of course, and wonder what all this is about.' It was exactly the same as when my grandfather made me write to the school and ask for the grant to attend the ESCA course. So he wrote a letter to the T-Mobile team managers. I remember giving him a bit of an outline of what to write: that he would like to be considered for the Tour de France, and these were the reasons why. I remember saying to Mark, 'You've got to point out that they've got nothing to lose because you will either win a stage or two or, if you don't, you're going to learn loads about the race.'

He got the OK and was absolutely ecstatic. It was the year the Tour started in London, and he went into it with massive ambitions. He wasn't going to the Tour thinking, 'Great, I'm riding the Tour.' He was absolutely cacking himself; he seriously didn't know what he was getting into and didn't take it lightly at all. But in the next breath he would say he was fast enough to win a stage.

At about that time, I was in regular contact with the T-Mobile *directeurs sportifs* Allan Peiper and Brian Holm as part of the support I still gave Mark. Allan said to me on the phone one day, 'I can't believe it, this young guy wrote a letter to the management.' My first thought was, 'Bloody hell, they really did read it, didn't they?' and I do think it got him a ride in the Tour de France.

Going into it Cav had such huge aims, so I was a bit nervous for him, but I knew how he loved these big hits. The problem is that the Tour – along with the Worlds and the biggest Classics – will always be a big step above any other bike race. I'd never been in that environment and it felt like a massive step up for the riders. But Cav wasn't the only rider from the academy among the starters in London. Geraint Thomas had found a place in the Barloworld squad for 2007; they were only a small team, but that meant he was drafted into their squad for the Tour. He was only twenty-one, the youngest rider in the race, and it was a baptism of fire for him. He really suffered on a few stages, but he got through. Being at a level where he could finish the Tour at that age was quite something.

Cav has always been one to get stuck right into any race, and the Tour was no exception. He's never been overawed by reputations. On the Tour of Britain in 2005, he took third on the stage into Blackpool, and the next day Jeremy Hunt came up to me and said, 'You need to tell that Mark Cavendish to bloody well calm down. Who does he think he is?' I just said, 'Flipping heck, Jeremy. To be honest with you, I encourage them to get stuck in; if they don't, then they're scared of you guys.' And Jeremy laughed – he had been lethal as a young rider; he would either win or fall. Cav was the same, and in that first Tour he crashed on the stage into Rochester, which he had targeted as one he really wanted to win, and he had a massive pile-up in Ghent and lost a load of skin. The effects of the crash began to get to him in the Alps and he abandoned, but I don't think it was planned that he would go all the way to Paris.

In all my time coaching Cav, that Tour was the biggest learning curve. He was pissed off with how it went, but he learnt a massive amount. We were on the phone constantly. He was trying every different way to get up there in the sprints. It looks easy when you're sitting in front of the television, but you could see he was having to make huge efforts. He realised that if you want to get in there in the sprint, from fifty kilometres out from the finish you have got to be constantly in the first twenty of the bunch. In run-of-the-mill pro racing you can move up in the last fifteen kilometres, but in the Tour it has to be fifty or else you use too much energy to get to the front at the key time. That was what he was tending to do that year – come up too late. As a youngster, if he was really going to get stuck in he needed teammates in front of him all the time, to take him right up close to the finish like a proper leader, and he hadn't quite got that yet. The team were dropping him off too early because they hadn't quite bought into him, and then he was on his own. And he needed to hit out earlier when the final sprint happened, but he still didn't have the strength to do that.

Of those three things, he'd perhaps get two of them right on any given day, but he wouldn't get the third. In the conversations we had, Cav was constantly telling me how frustrated he was. He just couldn't quite work it out and didn't want to hear where he was making mistakes, but he went away and thought about it. With the help of Chris White at the English

Institute of Sport – which is where all the performance analysis is done for the GB track team – I got him a load of footage of all the sprints on a DVD; that meant he had something to go at rather than just trying to filter it all. He learnt loads from those. Cav and Gee were at opposite sides of the spectrum: Cav was at the sharp end trying to perform; Gee was trying to get through, although he did get up there in a couple of stages. That meant I was having conversations with Cav about how to win stages, followed by talking to Geraint ten minutes later about just surviving.

That July was a fantastic time for the academy; we were in Cottbus, in Germany, at the European track championships, so we would ride in and train or race, then dart back to watch the end of the Tour stages. We had Peter Kennaugh with us; he was a junior but rode up a category in the under-23 team pursuit, which we won. Being from the Isle of Man as well, he was so excited at Cav riding the Tour. I'd always encouraged the academy lads to watch racing, but all of a sudden we weren't just watching pros on television, we were watching two lads who had come through the academy. You couldn't have asked for better: you've got two riders who started in the first year of the academy, came through it, and four years later they are in the Tour de France. There's no better motivation for young riders than to think, 'In three years that could be me.'

Gee, Cav and Ed Clancy had moved on to the professional ranks for 2007, but there were plenty of characters coming through. Ross Sander is no longer a cyclist, but he was the only rider I saw who was capable of getting round Cav on the track. Ross came from South Wales – there are some fantastic pictures of him and Geraint Thomas starting out at Maindy cycle track – and he was very, very quick. However, he seemed to have a lot of problems at home and always struggled with the discipline; it wasn't that he was trying to get himself into trouble, he just got into it, and my position would be, 'I've got to stick to the rules, Ross, and if you break the rules, there's a consequence.' I tried hard to work with him because I could see he had problems. His stepfather was a cyclist, but his real father lived in America, and when we were at a training camp in San Diego, Ross suddenly decided to go and see him, and that was it; he stayed on in America for a while and eventually joined the US Army. He sent me an email about two years ago, just saying, 'Thanks for all the help, it's served me so well. I'm finding the army quite straightforward because I understand the discipline.'

Ross was part of a group of young riders who got the team-pursuit silver medal at the Junior Worlds; another was Steven Burke, who joined the academy for 2007 and would go on to win a gold medal at London 2012. What was interesting from a coaching point of view was that when they took Ross out of the team and put Ben Swift in, the team moved on. It wasn't down to ability or physical potential; it was just that while Ross had more ability, Ben committed more. That's what we've seen all along with him. Maybe his raw ability isn't the absolute best, but he commits 100 per cent. You will always get more out of an athlete like that.

Swifty was this tiny kid with spindly legs who we used to see all the time at the track in Manchester – he'd pop over from Sheffield with his parents. Then all of a sudden he grew to six foot, and we all thought, 'Oh my God, where did that come from?' He's a great little racer. He cut his teeth in Italy with us and found his niche; he's fast, but not as fast as Mark. He's not a big bunch sprinter, but if he is in a group of twenty or thirty you would put a lot of money on Swifty winning. He has one thing in common with Mark: as young kids they weren't particularly powerful, so they had to learn to win from within the wheels; they had to stay in the pack late and learn to come around the other guys at the last minute, fighting for the wheels, pushing for position. The guys who are big and strong at thirteen, fourteen or fifteen just have to turn right, come out of the slipstream, press on the pedals and they can come round the others. They don't need skill or fluidity – it's all grunt.

Swifty had the skills, became a bigger, stronger lad, and Italian racing suited him because you'd often have a smallish group coming into the finish after a section over the climbs. So he was winning races regularly in Italy, and in 2008 he was one of the best three under-23s there.

Going to Italy in 2006 was another breakthrough for the academy, but in terms of performance on the road we hadn't stepped up. But that year we won the team pursuit at the European track championships, and you could see the progress: in 2004 and 2005 we didn't really do anything – although in 2005 we would have won but for the sandbag in their wheels. But the following year we won, and after that no one ever got near us. In 2007 the lads really started to move on in the road events, partly because we'd adapted to being in Italy, and we managed our first medal at the under-23 road Worlds in Stuttgart, thanks to Jonny Bellis.

We qualified a team of three riders, which was a bit frustrating, as we'd have liked more, but we chose Ian Stannard, Swifty and Jonny. It was a bit of a surprise to us that Jonny ended up with the medal, because actually Swifty was the one they were riding for. Here, what paid off was the way the riders had been trained to think for themselves during the race, to communicate and to be honest. Swifty's legs gave out on him in the last lap and a half, so they changed roles on the road. Swifty and Ian are good team riders; if one is going better than the other, they're happy to ride for whoever has the best chance. They were a well-knit team – it wasn't a case of all three of them going into the race thinking they were going to win. It was about the team winning, something I had homed in on all the time.

With a little bit more belief Jonny could probably have won those Worlds. He definitely had the ability – he'd won the scratch race at the European track championships that summer in real style, with absolute grunt and determination. He had massive top-end speed; he wasn't super-fast like Cav, he just had an ability to go and go and go. Jonny was always a bit wild, though; there was always something going on with him. He constantly caused me grief: going out, pushing the boundaries of the rules, and he would get other riders into trouble because he would want to do something and drag the others along with him. He won the medal, and unfortunately he switched off after that. He turned pro with the CSC team, and it's impossible to say how his career would have developed if he hadn't had a near-fatal moped crash in 2009. He has never reached those heights since.

Our first-ever world under-23 road race championship medal was a breakthrough, but Cav and I were beginning to think of aiming far higher. Cav rode at those world championships in

Stuttgart, but in the professional race. In his early years with the academy, he'd set his goals out: one day he wanted to be world road race champion, and to do that he needed to win Milan–San Remo. I don't remember when we first discussed it, but it became a regular conversation we had. At that point I thought, 'OK, that's an ambition.' All these guys dream big; they all want to be Olympic champion or win the Tour de France, and maybe there's something in it, but you've got to put a lot of work in. The idea of getting Mark a ride in Stuttgart was not that he was going to perform there; we just wanted to have a good look at the other nations, see how they moved, figure out the differences between them and us.

It was at those Worlds that we started talking about it a lot. I remember standing outside the hotel with him and discussing it: 'Yeah, you could win the World's, of course you could.' We ended up talking about it constantly. My feeling was always that the rainbow jersey is fantastic: you look at it and think, 'Wow!' I'd begun talking to the British pros more as well; every year when we did the Tour of Britain with the academy, I always had one senior pro in the team to guide the under-23s. A couple of times it was Roger Hammond. He was great with the lads, absolutely fantastic. I'd be getting him to work with these young guys, and at the same time I'd be talking to him about his experiences so far with British Cycling. I was thinking, 'Bloody hell, we could do so much more for these pros.' And Geraint and Cav were good examples of riders who had come through the academy, gone into the Podium programme, turned pro and then ridden the Tour de France in preparation for the Olympic Games in Beijing. By now we knew we could produce professional-quality riders who could fit in with the

British Cycling system. The pro Worlds wasn't my role – my brief was the under-23s – but part of my job was to work with Mark, and this was a goal for him.

In Stuttgart, I was starting to think about how the other nations build up to the race. The Italians, for example, have a whole myth around what they call *la squadra*, and I thought to myself we could create something along those lines. One of the key things for me was how the pros rode together as a team. Take the Spanish, for example: do they work for each other or not? What's the difference between the Worlds and a normal professional race? Can you build a team that actually believes in one person? Quite often you could look at the race on television and see the Belgians thinking, 'Oh, we've got three leaders,' and the Spanish thinking, 'Oh, we've got five.' There was always internal conflict within the teams; even though the Italians have this mythical *squadra* and they build this great atmosphere, they never manage to have one single voice in the team.

That was eating at me; I believe totally in having unity in a team. What I hate is if you have a team sprinting for the finish, and you end up with one rider finishing third and another ninth. To me that is total failure because it means that one rider hasn't committed to the other. If you do a proper lead-out, when the person who does the final stint drops the sprinter he should be so empty that he can't keep sprinting and be able to get fifth or sixth. Sometimes in Mark's case, particularly when he was at HTC with Mark Renshaw, he would win and his lead-out man would get second or third, but that was because they were so far ahead of the rest. If you win and get second too, great, but if you get second and eighth, that's failure.

My feeling was that if you've got someone in the team who's super-fast on the bike, then the road Worlds should be quite easy. There are only so many riders who can win a race in a sprint, so that's why it would be straightforward: all we would have to do is get the riders behind one person. In our case, that would have to be Mark. Having a proven winner who is confident in his ability and prepared to take on the leadership is an easy way of getting people together, to get belief in the team. It's much simpler to get a whole bunch of guys thinking, 'Yes, I can do this, I want to do this,' when the leader is a sprinter on a suitable course because it's obvious he has the best chance, compared to when you have several leaders and various options. I didn't know the road Worlds were going to be in Copenhagen in four years' time, but even at that point, in 2007, I thought, 'Bloody hell, if you could pull a squad of riders together riding for the fastest sprinter in the world, it would be an easy win, wouldn't it?'

7 : Beijing and Beyond

Six of the Great Britain squad at the Olympic Games in Beijing had emerged from the academy, which was astonishing. Ed Clancy and Geraint Thomas were part of the gold-medal-winning team-pursuit squad; Steven Burke figured in the individual pursuit, where he took bronze; Cav raced the Madison; and Jonny Bellis and Swifty were in the road race. It had never been a priority to get so many there, but I always knew the riders had the ability. I had just concentrated on getting as many of them to the highest level as I could, rather than fussing about how many would be ready. In British Cycling we talk a lot about focusing on the process, not the outcome, and this was an example.

We had a conference during 2007 where we began detailed planning for the Games. Staff from every area of the Olympic Podium Plan were called in; we all had to stand up and say how we were either going to be involved in the Olympics or how our work was going to impact on the Games. If you were a Talent Team coach, you would get on your feet and say, 'I'm going to be super-organised. I'm going to have my budget set well in advance, so that I don't have to bother Dave Brailsford or any of the Olympic performance team.' What I said was that I was going to run the academy in Italy, we were going to keep our heads down, we were going to keep developing as we were, and I was going to support Matt Parker – who had taken over as the men's endurance coach when Simon Jones moved on – in any way that he wanted, helping Steven, Mark, Geraint and anyone else in my orbit. Dave had made the conference a really big thing, and he was dead right: it made us all think, 'I've got to be perfectly organised for the whole year.'

I had spent a lot of time working with Matt; he had come to see us in Italy a fair few times, and we had built up a very similar working relationship to the one I enjoyed with Darren Tudor, the junior coach. That meant I was looking both below the academy and above it. I would keep an eye on the senior riders who had left the academy and were living in and around Quarrata – Cav, Gee, Steve Cummings. I was working with them regularly, but Matt was leading their training, so we would communicate constantly. When Steven Burke went the other way, from being at the academy full-time to spending long spells training on the track in Manchester in preparation for the world championships and Olympic Games, I would help Matt with him.

It's a matter of sharing knowledge. One of the things I had learnt from working with Burkie was that every night before you leave him you have to say, 'Burkie, what's on tomorrow? What do you need? Is everything ready?' Steven was a very young athlete who wasn't given to thinking ahead. So if he wasn't given a nudge, he'd wake up the next day and realise that he hadn't got a clean skinsuit or something like that. Matt was used to working with adults who had wives at home and maybe kids – riders like Paul Manning or Rob Hayles. They were well organised, and you could have adult conversations with them and be dead upfront with them. Burkie and the others were young lads who were still playing computer games, but they were now competing at the highest senior level.

By now, people were coming up to us in Italy, saying, 'God, are you guys ever going to stop winning?' Our riders were really buzzing; they could obviously sense the build-up to Beijing, and 2008 turned out to be an incredible year. The highlight was the day Peter Kennaugh won the Gran Premio di Capodarco, and Burkie got his medal in the Olympic individual pursuit behind Bradley Wiggins. Pete is another Manxman like Cav, and he'd been a solid talent from when he was an under-16 all the way through the juniors; he'd been junior world champion in the scratch and team pursuit. His win in the scratch was pretty special. He's a proper little racer, powerful for a small guy, with that real desire to win – he's the only other rider we've had who's similar to Mark Cavendish, with a real killer instinct, although he's a different character to Cav, with more endurance. He's not a sprinter, but he has a real talent for one-day races. There was no better place than Italy for him; if we had been based in Belgium or somewhere like that, it wouldn't have been quite the same. He handles the heat really well, climbs superbly, and it was obvious that one day he would ride the Tour and be successful. The GB riders in Beijing were on the track in the morning before Capodarco started. It's flat for the first sixty or seventy kilometres, so early on in the race I was giving them updates on how Burkie was doing. I was on the phone to one of the staff in Beijing, and I was radioing what I heard through to the riders – 'Burkie's two seconds up,' and so on – and then Pete went and won in the afternoon, the biggest one-day victory in all our time in Italy.

Those few weeks through July and August were a golden period, although Beijing ended up being very frustrating for Cav. He was really starting to perform on the road, winning his first stages in the Tour de France – the first one at Châteauroux was a big moment, you could see it on his face. He's always held that stage quite dear since then. He had ended up winning a total of four stages, in spite of pulling out early for the Games. Speculation about the British professional team was just starting in the background, and winning the world road race championship suddenly looked possible because Cav was looking like the fastest sprinter in the world.

That momentum built into the Beijing Olympics. Cav had been really keen to finish the Tour but he was also fully committed to the Madison after taking the world championship in March with Bradley Wiggins. That win in Manchester was a dominant one, but Beijing turned out to be a trying time. They started as favourites, but we didn't know that Bradley had been really unwell in the build-up, before they left Britain for China. But Brad being Brad, he had ridden the individual pursuit and got his gold medal, backed with a second gold in the team pursuit, and I think after that he went, 'Phew,' and lost his focus. The day after the team pursuit they had the Madison, and I remember Cav ringing me that night and saying, 'Brad's still not in' – because obviously he'd got all the press stuff and doping control and television and everything. Cav just asked me, 'Am I wasting my time?'

Cav knew, even before he got on the bike, that Bradley was wasted. Brad had been the worst one of the four when they took the gold in the team pursuit. He was swinging in that race, and Cav was thinking, 'What am I doing here? I've pulled out of the Tour de France for nothing.' At the time, I don't think anybody in British Cycling realised how big the Tour was, because our world was the Olympic Games, but that Tour could have made a big difference in the career of a young rider who could potentially have won the green jersey. I was with Mark on that; I didn't side with him but I was with him – there's a difference. I worked for British Cycling but I understood what he was talking about. Cav said that as soon as they got in the race, it was obvious that Brad was going nowhere. You can't bluff in a Madison; you need to be physically perfect, as well as highly skilled, so they were never on the pace from the word go.

Cav was really unhappy; his view was that he hadn't pulled out of the Tour de France for this, and I empathised with him a little bit. I think there were a few people who were critical of Mark and how he behaved afterwards, but he'd just pulled out of the biggest bike race in the world. With hindsight, there was a lot of evidence to say they should have changed the team, but unfortunately from a British Cycling point of view, the Madison was always on the back burner. I tended to see it the other way; I'd be thinking, 'We've got to keep driving this on,' and so I was quite frustrated too. Dave had asked me if I wanted to be there for the Madison, but I had felt that my place was in Italy with the academy lads. After the Madison disaster Cav went through a hell of a hard time. He became very anti-British Cycling, and I don't think he's ever bought back into them as wholeheartedly as he had before.

I was beginning to think about moving on. I had done all I could in terms of turning the academy into a going concern. One objective had always been that I would build it up to a point where it could carry on running after I left. One of the things I wanted to look at next was the professional cycling world. During the Tour, I had had an invitation from Bob

Stapleton at Columbia-High Road to go and visit Mark, so I had a good couple of days there seeing how it all functioned. I'd never been within a working team on the Tour before. It was an eye-opener; the enormous scale of it and the restrictions around getting anywhere near the race were the most surprising things. I was beginning to get ideas about how things could be done in a professional team. For example, I spent the day walking around the different teams at the start of the time trial, seeing how they were doing their warm-ups. I thought it looked pretty poor and could be done so much better. The riders' environment could be improved: at Columbia, they had Kim Kirchen in the yellow jersey, but during the warm-up for the time trial even Bob was going over into the pit and talking to the riders. At British Cycling we made the pit zone a performance area; the only people allowed in were the riders, the carer and the coach. The overall manager of the team – which was quite often Doug Dailey – would stand on the edge of the pit. Even riders who had finished their event would have to clear out as quickly as they could, not sit there with their head in their hands, even if they were super-disappointed, because all the riders were coming in and trying to stay in the zone.

At the Tour, Bob Stapleton offered me a job working with Columbia, either on the coaching staff or working with young riders. They were looking at having a proper development team, and he was keen to base it in Lucca, in Italy, which was only down the road from where we were living anyway. I felt it was a brilliant opportunity, but Dave Brailsford got wind of it while he was in Beijing. He called me on the morning of the Olympic women's road race – the first cycling event of the whole Games – and I remember thinking, 'Bloody hell, poor old Dave doesn't need to be dealing with this just before it really kicks off.' He said to me, 'Whatever you do, just wait till I get home before you make any decisions.'

The night after he flew back from the Games, Dave agreed to meet me in Ilkeston. I said, 'I've been offered a job, and you know I want to move on. I want to do something different.' It was then that Dave showed me a letter from Sky saying that they would sponsor a professional team for 2010. He said, 'Listen, this team's on, and I want you to stay and help me do it. Are you up for that?' I didn't hesitate. We agreed there and then. Dave had been talking about it for a while, and I think he had always had that as a goal. In fact, when you read the original document by Peter Keen setting out his aims for the World Class Performance Plan, it's in there: Britain would be the world's number-one cycling nation in 2012, and to do that you'd have to have a road programme and a team. I think even Peter Keen realised that the most important part of world cycling, in terms of public interest, media and money, is road racing, far more so than all the others – BMX, mountain bike, track, cycle-cross – put together.

Dave loves road cycling; it's always been a passion of his, and the team is what he wanted to do – he'd begun talking to the press about it as early as 2003. But it was only from summer 2008 that he was able to say to people that he had the commitment from Sky; quite smartly, Dave held back and made sure he'd got them signed up before he started to ask people like me if they would commit to it. He was happy for me to move on from the academy; I think they felt that in Max Sciandri they'd found someone who could take over, and Max was pushing to do that – I think he thought he could do a better job than I did in running it.

I was massively disappointed that I was never really involved in deciding who took over. We'd built something pretty big, but I was told to stay out of it. Once I did leave, I wasn't given the opportunity to consult on it or help mould it. Max didn't want anything to do with me; he said he didn't want me living in the town because the lads would keep turning to me. That was a massive gut-wrencher. At the time, Dave and Shane Sutton backed him, so I had no option but to leave Italy at the close of the 2008 season. I packed up, went home and took on a new role: I became part of the senior endurance track team, working alongside Matt Parker. Matt was focused on the team pursuit, in which the guys had smashed the world record on the way to gold in Beijing; my brief was to look after the distance races, where we had taken only a bronze in China, and after the nightmare with Cav and Brad, there was to be a massive drive on the Madison.

We had moved on quickly after Beijing, but that wasn't surprising – the London Games had been in the back of our minds for three years. On 5 July 2005 we were at a training camp in Grantham, getting ready for the European track championships; I'd taken them there for some training and racing on different roads. I went into one of the lads' rooms to hear the announcement of the venue for the 2012 Games; they were all in there – Geraint Thomas, Ed Clancy, Matt Brammaier, Mark Cavendish, Tom White – and when London was announced they all jumped up, shouting. They assumed that was going to be their first Olympics; I don't think they thought Beijing would be within their grasp. It was a really nice moment in that pokey little room.

The rumours about the course for the road race in London began almost immediately after that. We were getting word that it wasn't too hilly; to begin with we thought it would be in central London. In 2006 the Tour of Britain ran a stage on closed roads through north London, taking in Primrose Hill. That, everyone imagined, was a blueprint for a possible Olympic road-race course. Cav's immediate thought, of course, was, 'I can win there.' We had also heard that Copenhagen would be hosting the world road championships in 2011. I'd been talking to Brian Holm about it, and he was certain it would be a flat course. My first thought was, 'We're on our way here.' After that, the next question was: how do we actually do it? Nobody told me to do so, but at the end of 2008 I wrote up a four-year plan to win the road race in London with Mark Cavendish. The four-year timeline had three big hits in it: Milan–San Remo, the world road championships and the Games themselves. What became known as the Worlds project was up and running, but it was an Olympic project too.

Great Britain had never approached the elite men's world road race – as the pro race was now known – with any structure. Historically, it had always been open to whoever wanted to ride, with selection based on who was available. In 1965, the year Simpson won it in San Sebastián, he had paid for the other riders to back him up, but that was a complete one-off. Sometimes there had been a rider capable of getting a medal – like Robert Millar in the mid-1980s or Max Sciandri ten years later – but the team was never built around them, mainly because there was no core of riders capable of performing. The debacle in Madrid in 2005 summed up where GB was at the time: the squad was highly organised and brilliantly focused when it came to track racing, but the professional, or elite, side was completely informal, an add-on to the track. The root of the problem was that no one had any belief.

For the first year, I began with this thought: 'What do we need to know?' We knew when the world championships were and we knew the date of the Olympics. We knew where the Worlds would be. I began by thinking about Italy, the team everyone in cycling regarded as the best at riding the world championship – they'd won it for the last three years and seemed to get a medal most years. So what do they do? How did they build up? How did they get the team racing together? They used the whole of August, when there was a programme of one-day races where the head coach would be watching the riders. The Australians used to do a training camp, all of them together in Varese, Italy, where the AIS under-23 team was based; that seemed a good idea. The Aussies always had that base in Europe where their pros would come if they needed something; if they had an injury, for example, they could go there to get treated. The way we worked in British Cycling was that there was a tightly knit group of riders within the team, and then there were those who were just affiliated. We had a good number of pros, but the ones who hadn't started out with British Cycling had no way in. I thought we needed to follow the Australians' example and open up a little bit. In his time as road manager, John Herety had always tried to help and support the pros, but we had to go one step further.

The first goal on the timeline was that by September 2009 we needed to be travelling to the Worlds – which were in Mendrisio, in the southern part of Switzerland – for the pro race as a proper team, which was something Great Britain had never done before. I didn't care if we performed, but we'd go there as a unit, with all the riders feeling that they were included. At least I knew we had a leader. Every single rider in the UK, every single rider in the world was looking at Mark Cavendish and thinking, 'Bloody hell, this guy is unbeatable, he is so much faster than the rest.' We were lucky that Cav is a natural leader – I wouldn't have to persuade anybody to get behind him. It was obvious that if this guy was in the right place with 300 metres to go, he was going to win the bike race – you'd put a hell of a lot of money on it. So it would be easy to get the riders to buy in.

I went all the way back to basics and listed the riders who could be a part of that group, all the way to London in 2012. There were about thirty; I was thinking that there were some who weren't pros at that point, but they would be soon – academy riders like Peter Kennaugh and Alex Dowsett. There was Bradley Wiggins: he was already working with British Cycling because of his long involvement on the track, but we would still need to talk to him. There would be no issues with the lads I'd worked with, but there was a host of riders who we'd never really had very much to do with: David Millar, Roger Hammond, Jeremy Hunt, Dan Lloyd, Dan Fleeman, Russ Downing, and so on. They had to be included in this; everyone had to be on side, all thinking the same thing.

On the one hand, we had a really young group who knew how to work with British Cycling; on the other, we had this bunch of experienced guys who had never really got that involved, who had always felt that they were on the outside. I thought, 'Bloody hell, if you put them together we could use them really well.' I had already tried to do this a bit by getting Roger Hammond to help out the young lads at the Tour of Britain, and I'd had the odd word with Jeremy Hunt – 'If you're racing against Geraint Thomas and he's doing something wrong, take an interest in him.' But there was more we could do: if they had injury problems, we might be able to help them out; if there were things they needed with their bikes when they were in the UK, we could sort it out for them.

It was a three-stage process to begin with. First, I had to call them and see how interested they were; then I would have to meet them and explain face to face what we were trying to do; after that, I needed to start getting these guys in one place and bring the groups together. For that, I drew up a training-camp programme for when we could do this: the national road race championship in June, because most of the riders would be in the area to compete in that in any case; Mendrisio in August for a look at the world championship circuit; and then the race itself in late September. These would have to be organised as well as I could manage, so these guys would think, 'Bloody hell, I want to be part of this.'

At British Cycling there were a few people – Shane Sutton in particular – who were against me doing this. I think Shane felt that if we did all this for the lads, we would have to do it for the women, but I told him that wasn't my problem; I was trying to get this group together to win the world championships and Olympic Games, and that was all. There were some people in British Cycling who felt that we should keep our distance from the professional side because of the knowledge – particularly when the original plan was put together by Peter Keen – that doping was so prevalent in European pro racing. But as I saw it, it was simple: British Cycling had clear-cut doping policies, and the riders adhered to those policies. If they didn't, they would have to leave and they would have no input.

The project got moving at the end of 2008, when I got all the lads, including Bradley Wiggins, together for a session on some of the circuits I'd used with the academy around Jodrell Bank. I split the riders into two groups to do some lead-outs. It was what I'd been doing with the academy for years, but this was the first real senior session. At this stage we were doing two or three rides on the road every week as a team; we had two rides when we met at Manchester velodrome before or after a track session, with rides over the weekends as well. I was inviting all the academy guys and as many of the senior riders as could get there; it was like going out with a big club and meant all the riders were getting together. Cav was coming over from the Isle of Man for a track session to keep his speed up, and then going out on the road with them. We even had Jason Queally – the kilometre rider who had won the first GB gold medal of the Lottery-funded era, at Sydney in 2000 – out on the road a few times as well, which was interesting. Jason didn't like riding in a group because he'd had a horrendous injury in a sprint at Manchester, so he would sit ten lengths off the back of the group. But he'd get round with no problems at the end of four-hour rides, and I couldn't help thinking, 'Bloody hell, this guy's got some ability, hasn't he?'

There was a third project I was involved in by the end of 2008 and into early 2009. The move to get the professional team going was rumbling along. I began to spend quite a few long evenings with Fran Millar and Dave in Dave's office in

Manchester. It was a massive brain dump in which we listed all the jobs we had to do to get this up and running: how the hell do we get this team off the ground? What does it look like? What does a race programme look like? What vehicles do we need? We didn't have a clue, but we wrote everything down. With Team Sky beginning to happen, that was another side to the Worlds project – having British riders in a British professional team at a time when we were trying to win the Worlds and the Games would be beautiful.

Part of the world championship and Olympic road race plan dealt with the question of how we would get enough riders to qualify; we needed to make sure that we got five riders into the Olympics, and qualification was decided using the same ranking system as the Worlds. Both use a complicated formula based on world ranking and the number of riders who have scored those ranking points; having British riders racing for a British pro team would help us get those points and get them with the maximum number of riders.

At that point, of course, Dave was starting to think about which riders to sign for Sky – experienced guys like Dan Lloyd, Roger Hammond and Jeremy Hunt, for example – but we realised it would be healthy to have British riders in other teams as well. If British guys were riding for Cervélo or BMC, you would have more chance of British riders scoring points in more events. Not having all the British riders in Team Sky had to become part of the strategy.

My initial phone calls to these riders were key moments in the project. I spoke to them all: 'What do you feel about the thought of winning the world championships? What's been your experience so far of British Cycling?' In the timeline I'd given myself a deadline of the end of March 2009 to speak to them all initially. I had to meet them face to face by the end of May, because the first training camp would be in June. The things I heard were amazing. Bradley Wiggins was an easy one; he was up for it, and I never really heard much more from him, but that's Brad and that was fine. Roger Hammond said, 'Yeah, I'm in, but I'd like a bit more support from British Cycling.'

'OK, what are your experiences?'

'Well, you don't know if you're getting selected or not. You don't know. Nobody ever really calls. Nobody takes an interest.'

Dan Lloyd was even more critical: 'You find out that you weren't selected on the internet. Nobody ever rings and says, "You haven't got the ride in the Worlds." If you were going to the Worlds, the travel and everything was always a bit disorganised. You didn't really know what you needed, you didn't know when you were going, you didn't know if you were racing together or not.'

Talking to the riders so early on in the process was absolutely invaluable. It was clear there were fundamental things we would have to do to get people involved. We would have to get the selection right. We had to get the communication right. When I met them face to face, it was another opportunity, this time to show them something of the plan I had and give them an idea of how we were going to manage it all. I went on my own and showed them the outline plans that I'd written, talked to them about the academy, explained about the young lads. I thought guys like Dan Lloyd and Roger Hammond would be really into all this.

David Millar was already buying in, but he'd had more contact with British Cycling than most of the other experienced

Finishing fourth in the individual pursuit (racing Rob Hayles for bronze), national track championships, August 1988

The national hill climb championships, Widecombe in the Moor, Devon, 1990

With Glenn Holmes, in our Team Continental kit, 1994, realising we were a long way from where we thought we were in the sport. One of my best friends still, I met him racing when we were both fourteen

Caltex team, 1994: (L–R) Chris Lillywhite, Simon Lillistone, Jeremy Hunt, Glenn Holmes and me

Bondi Beach, Sydney, 2005, the day after Gee came out of hospital

Manchester track, 08:00 hrs session

Pinning on race numbers, Bendigo International criterium, 2005

With Bradley Wiggins, Stuttgart, 2007

Looking at the route, with Matt Parker, road Worlds at Mendrisio, 23
September, 2009

The night before the race

With Cav, after the scratch race at the world track championships, 2009

With Dave Brailsford and the team before a training ride to Box Hill for the London-Surrey Olympic test event, 2011, which Cav won. Cav's on his green-accented Venge, having just won the green jersey in the Tour de France

Job done – on the bus with the rainbow jersey

In the car with Sean Yates, Tour de France 2010

With Dave Brailsford, Tour de France 2013

pros; he'd been friendly with Dave Brailsford for years, and had got close to riding for the Olympic track team in 2004 before he was busted for doping. And when he came back after his two-year ban, he had help with his return to racing from British Cycling. He's a thinking bike rider, so it wasn't that much of a surprise that after our conversation he sent me a long email, listing all the points that he thought would make this work. One suggestion which I followed, and which worked really well, was that the selection process had to be super-clear. He also wrote something which I felt was hugely powerful: 'British Cycling does not understand the demands that are made of us as professional cyclists.'

Dave felt that we needed to understand that the travelling the pros did meant that they couldn't just be anywhere and everywhere; they were on the road for 360 days a year, so they needed flexibility in what was asked of them. There were some more concrete questions: would they get funding or not, would there be a payout if we did win? As David Millar was saying, they were professional athletes, so what would happen if they were injured? Could they call on British Cycling and get help from the doctors and physios? These were simple things that he felt were holding this group back, or that he had seen in the past. I used many of his suggestions to help me mould the project. I didn't see myself as the guy who was going to get the credit for whatever we ended up with; I was the person who was going to sit between everything and hold it all together.

The only British professional rider I never talked to was Charly Wegelius. He was one of the most seasoned pros we had, one of the best team riders in the business, but he'd been banned from racing for Great Britain ever again after the episode at the world road race championships in Madrid in 2005, where he had ridden for the Italians. That meant there wasn't a great deal of point in approaching him. Personally, it was a difficult one for me because I'd got to know Charly well in my last years as a rider, though we definitely went our different ways a little. I didn't really feel it was my job to reconcile him with British Cycling; Dave Brailsford had taken the stance on it and it was his issue. My personal opinion was that it was such a shame because we could have used Charly so well, and he would have loved to have been part of it.

From the start of 2009 I began sending the riders monthly newsletters. Initially, they were headed 'GB World Road Race Project'; a few months in, the title became more specific: 'Road Worlds Project 2011'. They weren't great works of literature – they were written in my style, with my passion behind them. But that was the point: I wanted to show them that I felt really strongly about this. I didn't want the win more than them, but I was as patriotic about the GB jersey, and about GB being the best team in the world, as anybody in this country. I still am. And I wanted the riders to feel that coming from me; if you are working with somebody who gets out of bed in the morning and clearly wants to support you, you're more likely going to go with them.

The newsletter was an obvious way to keep them all in touch and bring them together; every month they got an email which had updates on what we were aiming to do and gave the outline structure of what it was all about. I started saying to them early on that such-and-such was going to be the date when they would know if they were selected or not. It was important to keep them up to date with where we were in the selection rankings. For example, it was important that they knew that if we qualified nine riders to start, it would mean we could name twelve on the start list; that in turn meant that the three reserves – riders ten, eleven and twelve – would need to stay fit because they could be called in the day before the race started. Every step of the way it was about getting these guys to remember the one goal. The objective was theirs – it was up to them to go out there and pedal their bikes, to win the race. So there was the goal, but how would we achieve it? My job was to answer that.

Getting them to absorb that sort of information was key; so was the simple fact of keeping them in touch with each other, creating a group spirit. I would write a general introduction – 'This is how we are doing in terms of qualification . . . So-and-so has broken his wrist, so give him a call if you can . . .' In the early newsletters I even put that I wasn't going to select the team; they were going to select it themselves, but the selection process was going to start in June 2009. They were going to write the rules about how they would get selected. I gave them all the dates, plus all the travel dates for the Worlds, all the basic details, early on in 2009, but I said the heart of it – the selection criteria – was something they were going to work out in June.

2009 was the critical year for me, because in order to qualify all the riders we needed, we had to get them thinking about how they would qualify for each year's Worlds. I'd give them a breakdown: 'This is where we currently are in the rankings; this is our score in points; for those of you going to this race or that race, these are the last opportunities to score points.' What I could do then was call those riders and say, 'Listen, if you can pick up a point or two here or there, that would help – can you speak to your *directeur sportif*?' I'd encourage them to put their hands up and go for a sprint or something like that. But the biggest thing for me was if I could get Jeremy Hunt talking to Ben Swift, with the common denominator between them the world road race championships. If that happened, it was bingo! – job done.

8 : Our Leader Steps Up

Through the 2008 and 2009 seasons Mark Cavendish went from being a promising sprinter to the best in the world: that Milan–San Remo victory was the cherry on the cake as he landed ten stages in the Tour de France. By now he was winning around twenty races a year. Those two seasons were when he really broke through. If I had to put my finger on one key factor that helped him move on, it was when he moved from Belgium – where he was living with Roger Hammond – to Italy. It was a big move for him. There were people around him, like his *directeur sportif* at Columbia, Brian Holm, who had concerns. I'm a big supporter of Brian and his relationship with Cav is very good, but Brian was brought up in the Belgian cycling world; he likes the hard work, hard weather, rolling your sleeves up and cracking on. He had an issue with Mark going to Italy because of the people who might be around him, but I said to Brian, 'Look, I'll be there too. It'll be fine.' We knew Cav would have to be kept working hard or he might get drawn into the life down there – he likes to live the good life, go out for dinner – but I'd take care of that. He ended up with a really good routine in his life. My idea was that Cav would train with the academy guys, because he liked that whole scene and he would have a masseur and mechanic at the academy; he was a pro, but British Cycling was still supporting him at this time.

Compared to his debut in 2007, the biggest difference in Cav's sprinting when he rode his second Tour de France in 2008, something that massively changed his racing, was that he became capable of going full-on from 250 or 300 metres out in a sprint finish. It was the major thing he had learnt in 2007. During the first week of the Tour that year he was unsure when to make his move, so he tried different things: he put a fifty-four-tooth chain ring on so he had a bigger gear, then came back down; he was wondering whether he had enough power, whether different length cranks would make a difference or not; he was trying to figure out why he was getting caught up in the crashes. My answer was that the level of competition at the Tour was higher compared to other races; he was hesitating, not coming out early enough when the sprint happened. We concluded that he had to jump earlier. We had to try training him to sprint for a little bit longer so that he would be confident enough to hit out early. A lot of riders didn't have the nerve to do that; they tended to wait for the 200-metres-to-go marker, and often someone else would get the jump on them.

We didn't do specific training for that, but we did do longer sprints. It was pretty simple, but for Cav it was more a mental thing, just getting it into his head: 'Yeah, I've got to go out from 300, and I can.' Then his style of sprinting did the rest: punch, bang, create a big gap – because people can't hold him when he comes off the wheel – then he would cruise a little bit, then he would go again. In 2008 that was his key thing; that was why he won so many stages. He would consciously wait for the other riders to start catching him up, and then he'd put his foot down again. It's not very often that you see Cav do a long sprint, flat out from the point he emerges to the point where he crosses the line. The only time is on the Champs Elysées, where he hits 300 or 350 metres out and goes; he doesn't look back, he just goes and goes and goes, and he wins by flipping lengths. The reason why he always wins by so much there is that it's one of the only sprints where he absolutely empties the tank.

The move to Italy led to a massive shift in Cav's professional development. I knew that for him to win Milan–San Remo he was going to have to go over the climbs better. How are you going to do that? There's no point being based in Belgium. If you live in Italy, you can't avoid decent-sized climbs, so even on your rest days, when you do an easy ride, you're still going up a five- or six-kilometre ascent. That in turn means that all of a sudden your idea of what makes a hard climb changes; you don't worry about the smaller ones. So suddenly he believed he could start getting over decent climbs, and he learnt how to do it.

I was doing hours and hours with him, sometimes six to seven hours with him behind the motorbike. We'd have a coffee stop and I'd have to have a couple of fuel stops, but we used to go over the climbs pretty bloody quick and I'd put him on the rack every single day. We'd do different things: sometimes he'd do four hours, then I'd meet him so he could spend two hours behind the motorbike; sometimes I'd just meet him on a finishing circuit and do that as if we were racing; other times it would be an hour with one big climb, or perhaps the whole ride behind the motorbike. The crucial thing about training behind the motorbike is that you can have the pressure on, put the speed up when you're training, and because you are in the slipstream you're working at race speed. It's not something you can do on your own; it's the only way of replicating race pressure when you're training. Whatever we did we'd always finish with a big sprint – nine times out of ten when he is training Mark finishes with a big sprint because he's a sprinter, and that's as extensive as his training for sprinting gets on the road.

The classic climb that we used all the time was San Baronto, which is up behind Quarrata. You have no option but to go over it if you're coming back into the town from the west, and there are several different ways up it. There's another climb called Vinci – close to the village where Leonardo came from – which we did loads of times. It's about twelve kilometres long, but the average gradient is only about 4 per cent, maybe not even that; that means it's a climb you can go up on the big chain ring, a fast one. I used to put him through the mill all the time up there, so he'd build himself up for it as if it was a race finish. It was a brutal climb to work on with the motorbike because it had corners, so I'd be on the motorbike, the corners would be a bit too fast, and I'd be taking silly risks to get round them, with Cav spinning away behind.

The other element in Cav's training was work at the velodrome in Manchester, again behind the motorbike, just as we did in the academy days; that was general speed rather than specific sprint work, although he'd finish each block of work with a sprint. That was one of the key sessions before he won Milan–San Remo: he'd go out on the road in the morning, then come in and do a track session. We'd put a 52 × 15 gear on and he'd ride his UKSI bike, the carbon-fibre one made by the UK Sports Institute that he'd ride at an Olympic Games or world championship. He liked that; it made it a bit of a special session. It was just me and him, one on one, and we'd try and do about an hour and a half in blocks of fifteen to twenty minutes; we'd try and average about 130 rpm for the session, and then he'd finish each block with a sprint, getting up to 150 rpm or more. I remember him saying after he won Milan–San Remo, where the first two hours had been covered at an average of fifty-two kilometres an hour, 'I was sat there thinking, "Bloody hell, I've been doing two hours at fifty-five kilometres an hour at 130 rpm. I can cope with this speed. It's nothing for me."' When a rider feeds that back to you after a race, you think, 'Job done there.'

The other training we made sure we did for Milan–San Remo was to vary the speed and intensity on the climbs, to replicate how it would be in a race. This was something I could never understand with the other teams when they were racing against Cav: if you want to get rid of him on a climb, you have to do lots of accelerations, not just ride at one tempo; if you ride at one tempo, if he's got enough fitness, drive and momentum, he'll hold the wheel, because he's great at that. That comes back to a lot of those motorbike sessions, where he's just sitting there, on the edge for a long time. You can't just burn him off with speed. We saw that on the stage into Aubenas in the 2009 Tour, where there was a long second-category climb before the finish: they took it at a sustained speed, Cav hung on up there when most of the peloton got spat out, and then he was all over it at the finish and won by a street.

If you look at the way the riders race on the Cipressa and the Poggio, the two critical climbs close to the end of Milan–San Remo, the pace is very much on–off, on–off, so we did some sessions like that up the climbs. It was pretty simple: sometimes twenty seconds on, forty seconds off; at other times I just randomly accelerated and decelerated, time after time. We would do that in the fifth or sixth hour of training rides to replicate roughly the time at which he would have to do that in the race itself. The critical thing with Cave is that the finish of his race isn't the final hundred metres; it could be fifty or a hundred kilometres before, on a climb. This was something he got into, something I always said to him: 'You could be absolutely empty at this given point, on your knees, completely wasted, but nobody is going to drop you on the descent which comes after the climb, or this lumpy road here into the town where the race finishes – and you've won.' So his personal finish line might come at 150 kilometres. He'd be quite nervous going into races, so you'd break it down. It's a Steve Peters thing – what's the biggest challenge, the biggest obstacle? Well, it's this climb here. OK, what does it take to get over that climb? When are you going to eat? Where in the bunch do you want to start the climb? Before the climb, where do you move up through the bunch so that you are in that position?

For Milan–San Remo, we'd gone through how to ride in the bunch as well, the need to be sitting right up the backside of somebody all day – it was Bernie Eisel or Thomas Löfkvist, as it turned out. It was the old sugar-lump principle, which I had learnt from John Herety: you see yourself as a big lump of sugar, and every time you make an effort you're knocking bits off. You're going to whittle away at it, but you want to get there with as much sugar left as possible. With each pedal revolution you're chipping away, so it comes down to how hard you press on the pedals. If you brake too hard here and you have to press on the pedals a bit harder there, you're going to use some. If you go forwards up the side of the bunch on your own rather than using someone else for shelter, you will use some. If you go up the outside of the peloton rather than up the soft spot in the middle, you use more. I always talked about that. So in Milan–San Remo he had to sit behind a teammate, as low as he could on the bike, and save every ounce of strength, because he was going to need every bit of energy for those final climbs.

Cav and I constantly went through scenarios like that. At the 2009 Tour de France, which started in Monaco, I challenged him over the first road-race stage, because he'd never come into a major Tour and won the first stage. I felt that might be down to a slight lack of training over the last day or two, or just a little disrespect for his fellow competitors. That first day in Monaco was quite a hard stage, with a couple of little obstacles, and Cav was super-nervous. I was staying down there, because Dave Brailsford, Carsten Jeppesen – our Head of Operations at Team Sky – and I had gone down to talk to riders we were looking to sign for the team. I would talk to Mark on the phone; we would go through the profile of the stage, and I would get him to explain what he was concerned about. The conversation might go: 'What's bugging you?'

'This climb here, it's after 120 kilometres.'

'Are you fit enough to do it?'

'Yes, I am.'

'Well, that's good. How long's the climb? What's it like – has it got corners in, is it straight up?'

'I don't know.'

'Well, go and find out. Who are you going to ask?'

'I'll ask Brian.'

'Well, give us a ring when you've done it.'

That was the kind of stuff we were looking at. In that 2008–9 period I was working well with Brian Holm, Rolf Aldag and Allan Peiper, the *directeurs sportifs* at Columbia – or

HTC, as it became in 2009. I would give them ideas to talk to Cav about, and they would consult me over working with him – 'Cav's just said this. What do you think?' – so I'd explain how he is, about calming him down, getting him to concentrate on something, trying to get him to invest in cycling, little things like that.

In 2009 he won a stage in every stage race that he rode. He was just buzzing. He'd come into the main square in Quarrata, and you could feel the energy radiating off him. That's the other thing with Cav: as well as the talent he has on his bike, the energy he has is pretty phenomenal, whether positive or negative. Sometimes he rubs people up the wrong way, because he's opinionated and can act like a bit of a prick at times.

He bounces around deliberately to wind people up on occasion. He turns it on and off when he wants to. There was an interview in one of the cycling magazines in 2007, an article titled 'Cool Britannia' which featured Gee, Swifty and Cav, with clothing by Paul Smith. I was trying to arrange the whole photo shoot, as it was a good story about the development of those three academy lads, but Cav was really against the whole thing and didn't want to try the clothes on. Ironically enough, he has a good relationship with Paul Smith now. I spotted him afterwards; he came bounding into the dining hall in the hotel where we were staying and said to me, 'Thanks for pushing me to do it. We had a great laugh.' I said, 'You looked happy coming into the dining room.' And he said, 'Yeah, yeah, I did that on purpose, bounded in to make sure that everybody saw me.' I thought, 'You cheeky sod' – he was this new kid on the block at that point, but that's how he was. Sometimes he deliberately walks into a room with his head held high, with a real swagger to make people go, 'Shit, that's Mark Cavendish.' It can get him into trouble occasionally, but that's his way.

My relationship with Cav is definitely the closest I've had with an athlete. You could point to a few reasons: Cav believed in the discipline side and the structure which I was building into the academy; also, at that point in his life, he was obviously looking for someone to lead him. Another way in which we got on was that Cav loves to hear about the history behind the sport, and that was something we had in common. I think the moment on Gun Hill, when he had that crisis I described earlier on, must have been influential in the relationship. He's a sensitive guy; he's not super-strong in his self-control, he's not a big, tough chap. At times you have to put your arm round him and support him, and I think that's what he appreciated with me. I'd be tough with him; I'd tell him when he'd done well, but also when he'd not done well.

I deal with him in a similar way when he's ill. He doesn't cope with that too well. When he's not winning, he struggles to come to terms with it. There are times, when he's ill or it's not happening in the bike races, when you have to bring him back to basics: 'Right, what's going to make the difference? How are you going to do this? What are you going to do tomorrow?' He'll have the answers, although you have to guide him: 'I need to go and speak to the doctor. I need some medication because I'm sick.' 'What does that mean?' 'I can't train too hard.' 'Right, let's not train too hard; let's be patient.' That's the sort of stuff he needs, not the 'Go and do twenty efforts of this, or ride at this intensity.' It's more quite basic life stuff with Cav.

Other people could coach Mark Cavendish and get the

same results; if ten other coaches had begun coaching him at the same time I did, at least nine of them would have ended up with something similar. It was about me being in the right place at the right time. In terms of coaching his cycling, I've never made a massive difference to anything he would have done; it's the coaching around his bike, keeping him on the straight and narrow when he was younger, getting him organised, pulling him back to focusing on certain things. Mark constantly has ideas; he's always thinking about what's next – he finishes one thing and is straight on to the next before he's even taken breath. Sometimes you have to say, 'Hang on, let's look at what you did. Why did that happen?' I don't think he's a great reviewer of occasions when things have gone wrong. He looks to blame other factors quite a lot. It's at those times that you say, 'Hang on, did you do this? Did you look at that?' If it was other people telling him to do that, he might tell them to piss off, but that was where my relationship with him had grown, to a point where he wouldn't. So sometimes I'd suggest things, and he'd say he didn't agree, and occasionally I'd be right.

One thing I've learnt massively with Cav is this: don't tell him what to do. The skill is to get him to say what he is going to do off his own bat. Sometimes it will take two or three months for him to come round to telling you what you were thinking about. Then you think, 'Bingo, you're on it. We're there.' Sometimes I've been six months or so ahead of Cav, putting little ideas into his head here and there, so that he will then say, 'I'm on this one, I've thought about this.' If you were an ego-driven person, you'd be in trouble; you've got to be prepared to sit back and say, 'OK, guys, this is your programme.' That was the way I approached the road Worlds, but it was something I always did with Cav.

With Cav one example would be when he first rode the Tour de France. I thought he was ready to ride it, but I wouldn't actually say, 'You're ready to do the Tour'; it was a matter of getting him to tell me, 'I'm ready.'

Then I could ask, 'Why? How come you're able to?'

'I know I've got this. I was training well here. I was going up these climbs faster than I've ever done before, so I can cope with the climbing. I'm definitely working the sprints out better than before. I'm definitely more consistent.'

Those are the answers I'd be looking for.

We've had our share of funny moments. The amount of crashes he had at the academy was horrendous, unbelievable, but sometimes they were just hilarious. We were over in Cronulla in Australia just before he won the World Madison championship in 2005; it was just after Gee had had his bad accident and lost his spleen, so my nerves were a bit on edge. The lads would go out at six in the morning to do three hours or so, while I'd be sat in my room. One morning there was a knock on the door. It was a guy I didn't know from Adam with one of our bikes, but straight away I recognised it: it was Cav's. He said, 'Are you Rod?' He was in cycling kit, a local Aussie bike rider, and he said Mark had told him where I was – he'd been knocked off his bike and taken to hospital.

I thought, 'Shit', and raced to the hospital, thinking it was going to be really bad. What had happened was that a car had pulled out in front of them, and Cav had ploughed into the side of it and gone over the bonnet. I was quite concerned after the business with Gee, so I went racing through this hospital, asking people where he was. As I got closer and closer to the ward all I could hear was Cav going, 'Quack, quack, quack,' and laughing and joking. Straight away I was pissed off: I'd come racing down there in a panic, and all I could hear was Cav giving it large. I drew the curtains back, and there he was, with this nurse talking to him. He was in clover.

'Are you all right?'

'Yeah, there's nothing wrong with me, but they insisted on putting me in the ambulance.'

'Come on, let's go home.'

He was full of it – 'I had a great time in the hospital, all these lovely nurses looking after me' – and I was so pissed off. Now I just laugh about it.

As to why Mark crashed so often, technically I don't think he's that good. He's not always super-balanced on the bike. To be in there to win those sprints you have to put yourself on the edge at times, and he's not scared. He would never hold back. He would always push to win. Until recently, he'd very rarely actually crashed in a sprint – it had always happened while he was getting there. He would take risks, race really hard; he gets away with it because when he does have a collision, he has so much speed that he stays upright half the time. Even when he's not going well, he still races as if he's at his best; sometimes he doesn't quite have the condition, and when you're on the edge you're likely to get into trouble.

The funniest one I had ever had with Cav was when he got a splinter. It's one we all still talk about now, partly because for Cav and the other lads the academy was such a massive shared experience. They still say things like, 'You didn't have it as hard as I did,' 'Yeah, but you did this,' 'Yeah, but Rod was super-hard on us,' and so on. We were doing a Madison session behind the motorbike, practising changes; it was Ross Sander who I was worried about, because he was just coming back from a broken wrist. I'd been looking at the track by the start and finish line and thinking, 'Oh my God, it's all broken up where they wheel the start gate up and down time after time.' The wood was all worn; you could feel the splinters standing out as you rubbed your fingers along the boards. I had a clear view in the wing mirror. I spotted Ross coming down the track for a change, and my gut feeling was, 'Whoa, they've got this wrong.' We were going at a decent rate of knots when Ross and Cav got hold of each other, touched their front wheels and flew over the bars. And they both fell straight onto their chests on that bit of track at over 50 kilometres per hour and slid along.

I was worried, but as always on the motorbike I didn't come to a sudden stop because I had the other riders lined up behind me. By the time I realised what had happened I had gone round the next two turns on the opposite side of the track. Ross was up, Cav was rolling around a bit, and they were both a bit shaken. They both got back on their bikes and said they thought they were OK, so I said to ride round for a little while – 'Good for them that they got back on their bikes,' I felt. The next thing Cav rolled off the track, and he was looking at me, quite concerned. He parked up, and I finished the session and went to stand on the green part in the middle of the track. Cav had his skinsuit on and he was walking a bit bent over, a bit awkward. He had this face on him, laughing slightly but in pain. He opened his skinsuit and there were splinters all over his chest. There were a couple of long ones, not in very deep, so he was pulling them out. He said, 'But that's not the worst thing,' and he pulled his skinsuit down and there was this splinter right through his penis. I'm dead squeamish about anything like that, so I sent him off to our then doctor, Roger Palfreeman. Twenty minutes or so later Cav came bounding into the track centre with the splinter in a little bag, waving it proudly in the air. I've no idea what he did with it.

He had another accident in 2004, a few days before we were going to race the amateur criterium at the last stage of the Tour of Britain in London, with £1,000 on the line. Cav had won a good few races by this time, and the academy lads had really started to knit together as a little unit. The race was on the Sunday, and on the Wednesday or Thursday they were out training around Manchester way when I got a phone call. They were panicking like mad: 'Cav's in hospital, he's smashed up big time.' He and Tom White were out near Hatton Park and had tangled their handlebars when they were messing around. They went down, and Cav fell straight on his face. I went to pick him up. They thought he might have broken his cheek – he had massive cuts to his face, a ripped lip and was really bruised. He was in a right state. Roger Palfreeman was adamant: 'This guy can't race at the weekend.' We were all massively disappointed, because these guys were all set to do well for themselves and they wanted to earn a bit of cash.

Cav was pleading with me: 'Rod, you've got to let me race, you've got to let me race.' It was one of those moments when I did go against the doctor's orders. I was looking at him and thinking, 'He's absolutely fine,' but Roger's issue was that if he fell again on his face, he would be in trouble. I ended up saying, 'He'll be all right, he's a tough lad.' So Cav won the race. But what struck me at this one wasn't his determination to race; it was his recall in the sprint. Afterwards he went through the entire final kilometre with me as if he'd been going at fifteen kilometres per hour: 'I came up here. I noticed the lads skipping up a drain cover here, so as I was going up the gutter I went slightly to the left of it. I sensed someone coming here, so I just moved a little bit this way. I pressed on at this moment, with 100 metres to go.'

I can't remember the exact details, but I remember what I thought: 'Bloody hell.' It was the first time I'd seen that in any bike racer: this guy could recall the sprint finish as if it was in slow motion. He could go through what happened on every corner; he knew which team was where and had such incredible awareness of what was going on around him. It goes back to the question of how he got to Manchester for the interview to enter the academy: 'I took the M56 to this place, and then I got the number 10 bus going to somewhere else.' His awareness of what he's doing is quite special. It's a skill that some people have. I don't think it's something that you learn.

In the same way, as a sprinter you either have that speed or you don't. Has he worked on it? Perhaps as a young lad, but he's just got that ability. I remember having conversations with him: 'Have you always believed you could sprint?' 'Oh yeah, I've always known.' 'When did you realise?' 'When I was a little kid riding BMX. I was always fast.' I remember him saying, 'Even when I'm knackered I can sprint.' And he always sprints home. Physically, he has so much going for him: you look at his muscle quality, how he lies over the bike when he's sprinting – he's small and much more aerodynamic than someone like André Greipel. Cav can always get himself into a good position in the bunch, which may partly be down to his upbringing in bike racing. As a young lad he had relatively little strength and endurance; to compete he had to learn to scuttle around people. Ben Swift is exactly the same. Cav also has incredible leg speed when he is sprinting out of the saddle. In 2009 we did a complete analysis on all the sprinters: Cav was spinning on average at about 105 or 110 rpm when he was out of the saddle turning a 53 × 11 gear; most of his competitors were at about 90 rpm. If you assume they are mostly using the same gear, they're not going to get anywhere near him because their legs simply don't spin fast enough. Seated, Cav will turn the pedals comfortably at 130 rpm.

One year I managed to get hold of the overhead footage of all the stage finishes Cav went for in the Tour; with the shots from the helicopter you get a fantastic view of the movement in the bunch. We were looking at how other teams worked. At the time I was saying to Mark, 'One day somebody else is going to challenge you here, so we need to start looking at other teams, what they are doing differently. Are any guys doing things that could work for you?' What we noticed in the overhead footage was exactly how he moves. He's skilful; he doesn't sit right behind the rider who is in front of him. He's not straight behind their back wheel; he sits slightly to one side. It's as if he was riding an elimination race on the track, so he's got room to move out. That means he creates space for himself all the time; he's got room to come back and get onto the wheel if he knows it's his teammate's and he wants to get it; he can latch onto the wheel of a rival if he's coming past, or he can just bluff by constantly moving from one side of the wheel to another.

For me, bike racing isn't all about the scientific side, and that's one area where we saw eye to eye early on. Cav is the sort of guy who will say, 'I don't care if I can produce this number of watts in training if I can't scratch my arse in the bike race or I can't get over that climb.' It wasn't about the data you put out on your power meter or in rig tests, but that was what was drilled into him as a junior – the numbers, the numbers, the numbers. In the end his attitude was, 'I just can't be bothered about the numbers.' We used to do rig tests and so on at the academy, and we'd use some numbers, but not in quite the same way as the rest of the GB team. I remember that he didn't want to do his first rig test after joining the academy – it was a ramp test, where you constantly increase the power until you crack, and he said, 'I don't want to do it.' My answer was, 'Well, you don't have a choice, you're doing it.' In the first year of the academy they did one every three months, and it was quite a key thing. I got him to come round to it by saying I didn't care how he compared with Matt Brammeier or Ed Clancy; what I cared about was how Mark Cavendish on 1 January compared to Mark Cavendish on 1 April. What we wanted to know was whether he had moved on, whether he was fitter. When he understood that, he didn't mind doing the test.

All the bike riders have different attitudes here. Geraint Thomas is half and half: he likes to use the numbers to train with, but sometimes likes just to ride his bike. Bradley Wiggins is about the numbers. Although he has all the cycling knowledge and history at his fingertips because of that amazing memory he has, he really buys into the numbers for training and racing. Cav got more into the numbers in the run-in to the London Olympics because he could see that, delivered in the right way, they can be useful. I would say to anybody that if

you're having a conversation with Cav, you always have to finish with 'in the bike race this is what happens' – you always
relate it back to bike racing, rather than just referring to data. If
you don't bring it back to the racing, you lose him.

The quality that has made Cav special over the years hasn't
left him. Even now, when he earns good money, he's still as
passionate about winning races as he was when I first met him.
It's not money that drives him. He likes earning it – and why
shouldn't he? – but if he was earning £10 a week he'd still have
the same drive to win bike races. That's just how he is. He constantly wants to win, and he gets frustrated when he doesn't.
It's not that he's selfish. When he wins, he sees it as winning
for the team – he's very genuine when he says thanks to his
teammates. He's always been like that – he would always be
very opinionated on how they were going to win races. In the
early days of the academy, I remember it got to a point when
I began to think, 'Bloody hell, he actually does know how to
race. This guy has got a good racing head on him.' We didn't
always agree on race tactics, but I always tried to encourage the
lads to speak up, because they won't go to the line understanding what they're doing if they don't discuss it first. Mark would
always come up with pretty good ideas for how to win races.

The other thing I've learnt with Mark is that what you see
is what you get. When you hear him being interviewed after a
stage of the Tour, he will come out with something, and you
know that's really him saying it. It's not a front. I agree when
Brian Holm says, 'I like him talking' – and Bob Stapleton said
the same thing in the HTC days. But when Mark was at Team
Sky I think people were trying to control him and what he

was saying, and I didn't like that. It became a bit robotic. You can't squash Mark Cavendish. You can't keep him in a box. He needs to be a bit more flamboyant, be himself, not just give the regular answers.

Cav has more ambition than any cyclist I've ever known. He certainly has more than Brad, but in a completely different way – comparing those two is like comparing Usain Bolt to Mo Farah. It's a different mental attitude. I think Cav is really good for Brad – Brad feeds off Cav's desire to win in a very positive way. The ambition is not in Brad in the same way. He wants it badly enough, but he's not this outspoken character saying, 'Right, we're going to get out there and win today.' But when Cav is alongside him he really believes in him, and Cav believes in Brad. There is a good balance there. Cav has never changed. He is his own person: always streetwise, always ahead of the game in his thinking. I've only rarely got on the phone with him and found him down. He had a few problems with his girlfriend in the past, some real down moments, but those are about the only times when he wouldn't be talking to me about ideas, about moving forward, about the next thing and the one after that. Normally, you get him into a cycling conversation, and it's 'I want to do this, I'm looking at that, do you think I could win this race?' He's always thinking ahead.

A key part of drawing up that world championships plan was getting Cav involved right from the very start. I guided him through every step of it, because he was the managing director, the boss. It was through him that the other riders would get involved. I had to point out to him, 'Listen, Cav, you can't miss a trick here. Every single training camp, every single time you talk to these riders, you've got to be talking to them about the Worlds.' And Cav was chipping in with ideas, particularly about who he wanted to be involved. For example, he was very much behind having Jeremy Hunt in there.

By the start of 2009 we had begun working on the next step in the process: if he wanted to win the Worlds as a stepping stone to the Olympics, he would have to win that year's Milan–San Remo as part of the build-up to the Worlds. To win it he would have to move to Italy; at the back end of 2007 he'd made the move. When Milan–San Remo was on, I was in the velodrome at Manchester getting ready to travel to the track Worlds. I watched the race in the office and ended up on the phone to Matt Parker – who'd already arrived in Poland and had called in – shouting at the telly. I couldn't fucking believe it when he won that race, just millimetres in it from Heinrich Haussler, who led the sprint out.

It was a massive shock: 'Has Mark just won Milan–San Remo? Oh my God, he has.' I texted him, as I always do when he wins: 'Well done, good job.' That night I was over the moon. I thought over and over again, 'Wow, the world championship is really on now.' I was a little worried, though. Cav had committed to ride the world track championships with Peter Kennaugh – he had been talking about how he wanted to win the Madison for the third time – and now he had just won Milan–San Remo – were he and the whole team going to go out on the piss? I was staying in the Holiday Inn in Manchester, due to fly out the next morning, and it was about eleven thirty at night when I got the phone call. It was Cav.

'Hey up, Cav, how are you? Well done. Where are you?'

'Oh, I'm in Gatwick. I'm on my own.'

He was booked on a flight in there before flying out to Poland. He had won Milan–San Remo and there were people desperate for him to stay and go out to celebrate, but instead he was thinking about the Track Worlds. It reminded me of what had happened when he won the scratch-race gold medal at the Commonwealth Games in 2006: his attitude wasn't that he'd made it, but that he'd moved on. Immediately after that medal, he was thinking about the road race, and this time he was already moving on to the world track championships.

We both knew that this was a defining moment, but it wasn't the end result that mattered; it was the bigger picture. It was very powerful. I had told everybody that he needed to win Milan–San Remo before 2011. It was a key part of winning over the other riders, who would think, 'Oh my God, it's really on.' It wasn't just them: suddenly, we were getting even more backing from within British Cycling than before; people could start to see what we were doing as a team and how it was building. As for how strongly Mark felt about it, the first thing he said to me when I picked up the phone that Saturday night in the Holiday Inn was: 'I can win the Worlds now. I am going to be world champion one day.' When he eventually got to Poland, he could hardly get his head through the door, but he had every reason to be so pleased with himself.

9 : The Stripes in the Frame

That evening in late June 2009, in the Holiday Inn in Cwmbran, we hung up the jersey in a picture frame, in a corner of the meeting room. It wasn't just any jersey. This was *the* jersey, Tom Simpson's jersey, nearly forty-four years old, the only one won by any British professional in the road Worlds: thick wool, rainbow stripes on the chest and the neck a little faded now against the white fabric, a small handwritten plaque on one side of the frame.

This was the first time the riders who might make up the team for the 2011 world championships would be together, and I wanted to make a bit of an impact. I needed something that would get the project truly under way, that would pull the lads together. What could be better than this piece of cycling history? It was so long since Simpson had outsprinted Rudi Altig to win that jersey in San Sebastián: just seeing it there, a real rainbow jersey rather than just a photograph, would make the riders understand the historic scale of what we were trying to achieve.

I wanted to get the riders under one roof three times in 2009; this was the first camp, forty-eight hours before the national road race championships in Abergavenny. I like the idea of everyone in a team being in a room together, so that you can explain in one fell swoop exactly what you are aiming to do. It's about going to the start line and being so clear about your job, so clear about your form, so clear about what your mate is doing next to you that there are no discussions; you just have the same understanding. It all comes back to the Steve Peters principle: 'Get in a room and tell them.' I had to get them to understand, bring up the challenges and the things that might hold us back. I had done quite a lot of my stuff with Steve beforehand, so I felt quite confident. I knew this was going to work. If bringing this group together was the pinnacle of my cycling career so far, I'd done my apprenticeship at the academy. And that's where I was fortunate: I had worked with 80 per cent of the group, so they believed in what I was doing. Steve would say, 'Target one guy and get him to buy in, because he will lead the others.' While Cav was the obvious leader, the one I felt I had to win over was David Millar. Dave's a bit of a talker; he lobbies for things. He had the perfect credentials as road captain, the guy who would orchestrate tactics on the road: he was massively experienced, very articulate and not afraid to stick his neck out and say what he thought.

What I wanted to do here was to kick-start the entire project. I had to make sure Dave Brailsford was at the meeting because he gives an event like this that stamp of authority which he has. I also wanted something more than that, something that would capture the imagination of all the lads. It was Tom Simpson's nephew, the writer Chris Sidwells, who went and got the jersey out of the museum. I kept everybody out of the room beforehand, and when they came in, the jersey was hanging in the corner. I didn't say anything; they didn't look at it. All I said was, 'Welcome, guys,' then – bang! – the lights went off and I played the archive footage from the 1965 Worlds of Simpson and Rudi Altig fighting it out in the sprint finish and Simpson pulling on the jersey on the podium, with David Saunders's commentary playing flat out on the big speakers I'd put in the room.

Chris White at the English Institute of Sport had found a short video clip of every single rider who was going to be at the meeting, and up they came, one by one: Dave Millar, Ben Swift, Ian Stannard, Geraint Thomas, Roger Hammond, Jeremy Hunt, Chris Froome, Brad – actually he wasn't at the meeting because he didn't turn up – and Cav. Some of the clips weren't great, but that didn't matter: I really wasn't interested in the flashy side, in it looking all showbiz. It was just plain and simple, a roll-your-sleeves-up-and-go presentation. Then I wanted to go straight to the heart of it: right, how are we going to win the rainbow jersey again?

When the lights came back on, I pointed out the jersey in its picture frame in the corner: 'This is the prize we are all going for; this is the jersey we are trying to win.' They couldn't believe that they were seeing the jersey, the one worn by the legendary Tommy himself. All of them were open-mouthed, but I got the best reactions out of Cav and Dave Millar, the two guys I was particularly looking to tie in. We were on our way.

The difference between trying to win the Worlds and running the academy was that before I had been working with athletes at a formative stage in their sporting lives. For the Worlds I was dealing with mature athletes, most of them in their physical prime, and most of them hugely experienced. It called for a different approach. The academy was very much a regime; some people called it a dictatorship. It was a matter of 'do or don't do'; do and survive, or don't do and don't survive. Dave

Brailsford had said to me, 'Look, Rod, you've got to change your coaching philosophy'; obviously I appreciated him telling me, but I was aware of it. All of a sudden I would have to be in a support role, the guy behind the riders rather than the guy telling them what to do.

What I had learnt from the academy was this: how to get athletes to buy into an idea. What counted was getting the riders to work towards one goal and getting the message across to them. And even if I didn't have an intimate knowledge of the professional cycling world, I was fortunate that I did have respect from a lot of the riders for the hard work I did. They understood that we were pushing hard to win something big and they knew I would support them. When we began talking about the whole project, there was no question with Cav: he knew I was going to bust my balls to make this happen. He knew that even in his darkest hours – when he was ill or had crashed or whatever – I would always be behind him and supporting him. And all the other lads knew that as well. They knew I was always going to be there.

I didn't have any sophisticated objectives for this get-together. These guys aren't used to sitting in classrooms, listening to people lecturing them. This was completely new; there was nothing from the past to go on. A road team always went to the Worlds every year and to the Olympics every four years, but there was no real drive, there was no clarity of vision, and there was no leadership in terms of getting a group together and making it a focused programme. So I had a clean slate to work from. I wanted to get the lads feeling, 'Here we go, this is the project.' I wanted them to come up with their own selection criteria, and now they needed to start talking about how we would win

– what would the whole strategy look like? The idea was to understand where we were, to put together some general ideas about what we were trying to do and how we could make it work. I also wanted to set out our standards and principles.

The official programme targets were: 2009 Worlds, top ten; 2010 Worlds, top ten; 2011 Worlds, top three; 2012 Olympic Games, top three. But in fact the goal was simple: to win the professional world road race championship in 2011. Note that: to win it. In spite of those official goals, there was no 'Let's try and get on the podium,' no 'Medal or nothing,' which was the Olympic track team principle; this was about the gold medal and the rainbow jersey, and nothing else. When you've got someone like Cav, you've just got to win. He was never happy with second or third, so why should we be? We had to win. And we never took our eyes off that objective, which was symbolised by that jersey hanging in the corner.

During the rest of the meeting, I made a big point of looking time and again at that jersey, to make sure that the riders' eyes would be directed to those rainbow stripes. I made a huge thing of something else: each time I said the phrase 'to *win* the world road race championship', I would pause after I'd said it and leave a gap of four or five seconds before I moved on to the next point. I would look at each and every single one of the riders, right in the eye. And every single one of them was listening.

I had been quite nervous about this meeting; putting a team together in this way for the road Worlds was a completely new thing for Britain. I had taken a couple of ideas from Sir Clive Woodward – my girlfriend Jane had bought an audiobook about his campaign to win the Rugby World Cup in 2003 – and one aspect that was helpful was the way he had broken the whole thing down into different parts. Another was injury prevention: injuries can cripple a team, so what we did before and after training and racing would be important. Another inspiration was a British Lions DVD I'd been given by Richard Wooles, a GB *soigneur* who ended up running Canada's track programme; that got us talking about team building and what a team stands for. Someone else put me onto Gordon Ramsay's *Kitchen Nightmares* – where that helped was in finding out the good and bad characters to have in a close-knit body of people.

We went through the Great Britain principles. It was quite straightforward: we don't cheat. That meant in every way – no hanging onto cars, no doing anything that broke the rules. I made no bones about it: the riders had to agree to the GB anti-doping policy, and that was that. If anyone didn't agree with it, they wouldn't even be getting a start. They were all professional bike riders, riding for different teams for the rest of the year, but riding for GB means riding for GB. I had to make this a big point: they had to feel proud putting on a British jersey, they had to feel honoured – 'Let's not take this lightly, you are riding for your country.'

Honesty was another key thing I talked about; in the end, it was one of the key factors at the Worlds. Eventually, I was getting riders ringing me up during the selection process and telling me, 'Don't choose me because I'm not fit enough.' Adam Blythe, Jeremy Hunt and Dan Lloyd were the three I remember very well at various times in the years the project ran – and I really appreciated their honesty. This wasn't about any single individual; this was about a group of riders going to the start line and trying to win a bike race, and the example of those three really made that point. And when it came to the race, they had to buy into the roles and responsibilities of the team – each and every single one of them.

There were other things, starting with the financial side. These guys were professional cyclists and they raced for a living. If we won, what did they want? What were people's expectations? Dave Brailsford stood up to explain that Lottery funding was not going to cover all of them, but on the other hand we appreciated that the winner would do well out of it, so they would need to be rewarded. Getting Dave to stand up and explain gave it that gravitas: they were hearing it from the man at the top. And he had to explain a bit about Team Sky, because this was June of 2009 and it was very much in the making, and Dave and I were bloody busy at the time; it was full on throughout, so I was pretty knackered. So Dave stood up and gave a bit of an update on where Team Sky was, which wasn't easy, given that not everybody in the room was going to be signed up to ride for them.

The gist of what I had to tell the riders was this: last year at the Worlds there had been no goal and no plan, and that had been the case in the years before. That was just how it was, but now that we had the riders, we could build the team together with a long-term plan. So I went through it, pushed the new ideas and looked at the detail. A major point I wanted to make was that the plan would be based on understanding the life of a pro cyclist. That was a big point that Dave Millar wanted to make – 'Nobody understands what we do, how many days we spend on the road.' So I gave this undertaking: no camp was compulsory. If someone didn't turn up to one, he would not be ruled out. It was about putting the best nine riders on the road, and that was all. For example, Bradley Wiggins never came to any of the camps, but I could tell he had been reading the information. He clearly understood the history of it and what we were trying to achieve. The only person who I said had to go to every single camp was Cav – he had to buy into every one we did. I made that clear to him before we even started. To make that work I had to fix the dates around him, because he was the key person in all of this.

I told the riders, 'You're the ones who can make this happen.' They were a good mix of old and developing talent, established professionals like Cav and Dave Millar alongside younger team members who might come on board in future – the likes of Peter Kennaugh and Alex Dowsett. I went through the events we would ride in over the next few years – a hilly Worlds in Mendrisio, a rolling one in Melbourne, the Olympic test event in London, a mainly flat Worlds in Copenhagen and a pretty flat Olympic Games. I'd heard a little whisper that maybe the Worlds would be in Britain in 2013, so I added that in as a bit of a teaser.

We went through the potential riders for these events, what the team might look like, how many riders could qualify, possible team tactics. I'd also got them printouts of the qualification rules from the UCI: what do you have to do? What events count? How many riders need to qualify? That was pretty straightforward because it was there in black and white, but just explaining it in front of them helped, rather than letting the lads end up with their own interpretation. And they all seemed to sort of remember it. That was the key thing – they seemed to get into it a little bit.

I had looked at the Italians' way of working, and all they seemed to do was have a race calendar that was quite helpful:

they go to a series of one-day races leading up to the Worlds, and the pros come together as a national team on a couple of those occasions. Whoever the manager was – Paolo Bettini at the time, Franco Ballerini before him – would go round those races, and you'd see pictures of them stood by the team cars with their shades on. What I thought was, 'What are they actually doing?' They were going round all the riders and selecting them for races, which is all fair enough, but I always thought to myself, 'We can do a better job than that.' One problem with the Italian system is that getting in the team is so important, so prestigious, that the riders fight all summer to get selected. You can't help thinking there must be an element of 'Phew, job done, I've got in the team,' which actually damages the way they compete when the race itself comes around. They get so much publicity – even when they get in the Worlds, they have motorbikes following them with cameras and so on – but it seems to be all show.

Selection was the key one: we split the riders up into groups and left them for about twenty minutes to come up with ideas. The principle was this: 'Tell us what you want as a selection policy. How do you want to be selected?' That way you're giving them the cards. It's the way we had operated at Great Britain for a while – it's a Steve Peters thing. They have their say, but usually they don't want to make the call, so they come back and say, 'Tell us how you want to do it.' It always happens like this.

They wanted clearly predefined dates. My view was, 'Perfect, we've got that.' They wanted a personal phone call, which was one of the things that had come up when I first spoke to them; they didn't want to find out any other way. They wanted complete and utter openness and clarity in terms of why they didn't get selected. It was all pretty straightforward stuff really. One of the other questions was who would be selecting. I'd actually put down 'Selection Panel' as a heading, so we went through it: Steve Peters, Dave Brailsford, Shane Sutton, Chris Boardman. We would take the results from 1 January to 1 August, I would give my recommendations as the person heading this part of the programme, and then the panel would select from my recommendations.

Why wouldn't I be on the panel? We never do it like that. It's the same for all the coaches in British Cycling: before any major event we write down our recommendations, and the panel goes through them. The idea is that the coach can keep that distance; if a particular rider isn't selected, he doesn't feel it's the coach being personal with him. It's not me doing the selection; I'm simply recommending. I was trying to be dead honest with them and say, 'Guys, you know I totally appreciate you all want to be part of this. It's not an easy decision. I will have to make some hard decisions, but it's not personal. It's not about me; it's all about getting the best team on the line.'

I've worked according to what we agreed at that meeting for the last two or three years. I always do a long list, so if it's nine riders, I want to bring it down to a group of twelve by a certain date – 'OK, you're in the pre-selection, so knuckle down to work.' Nine times out of ten, that sort of selection is done quite easily, because there are always one or two who are sick or have an injury or a crash or whatever. They know that the final cut will be made on a particular date, and I make sure that once I have that information, Abby Burton, the GB press officer, sends out a press release. But she isn't allowed to send it until I've contacted all the reserves and riders who have made it. We've always stuck to that, so riders don't end up seeing the news on the internet or having journalists ringing up saying, 'Hey, I've heard you've been selected for the Worlds!' or 'How do you feel at missing out?'

We had quite a lot of discussion over one question: what challenges do we face? Getting the buy-in from the riders, all aiming for one goal, was pretty straightforward; so too was bonding the team together, in spite of the fact that they all rode for different pro teams. The history between us was a big one. You might have Dave Millar and Cav spitting at each other because when Dave is leading out his team's sprinter, Tyler Farrar, they might all clash. Cav hates Farrar for a while, and he hates Cav, then Dave ends up in the middle because it's his team. I made quite a big thing of us putting all that to one side and working as a unit.

There were specific issues that might come up on the day of the race, little things that I had heard over the years, such as 'the end of season blues' – the fact that the race takes place at the end of September, when some of the guys have been putting numbers on their backs for eight months. There's a fair bit of mental fatigue out there. A lot of people complain about the Worlds being at the end of September and want it back in August like it used to be. So I turned that on its head and said the date was what makes the Worlds special – riding there means you're a pro who is capable of racing and earning money all year.

Another one they brought up was that the Worlds were on a circuit, lap after lap. When you think about it, pro riders very rarely race that kind of event. More often they are competing in a place-to-place event, whether it's a Classic or a stage of a race.

On a circuit it's easy to get off when you're having a hard day, because you're going past the team pits every lap, maybe seeing other guys who have abandoned because they haven't got the legs. Then there is the fact that the Worlds are a big occasion: a team can get a little bit too excited about that and push too hard too early.

Compared to how they usually race, at the Worlds the riders have to adapt to different tactics. Normally it's one professional team against another; here it's nation versus nation. Some nations can have teams within teams – maybe the Belgians aren't quite together, or the Italian team manager can't make the call, so they have two leaders – and that can dilute everything. The *directeurs sportifs* giving them the race information aren't the ones they usually work with. A national team will have different staff, different race food, different food at the hotels and different kit, which is a massive one. They ride in a certain pair of shorts all season, then they rock up at the Worlds and for one day in their life they ride in different shorts and think, 'Oh my God, this chamois is cutting me in two!' I remember saying, 'There's no option here, guys. We're riding skinsuits, and we'll try and ride the best kit that we can.' Wearing skinsuits for a long road race rather than the conventional jersey and shorts was just coming in at the time – it was Rob Hayles who began it – and there's an advantage there, so we had to follow suit.

I didn't know exactly how many camps we would have before Copenhagen, because we were having to fit them around the demands the professional teams made on the riders. The national road race was an obvious time because most of the riders would come back from Europe for that, so it became our regular camp. In 2010 that was the only one we did; in 2011 we had a second hit, the Olympic test event in London. The key issue at the camps was to overcome the fact that most of them had different employers; getting them to feel like a team, racing alongside each other and building some common ground was what we needed to do.

We met again in Mendrisio in early August, about a couple of weeks after the Tour de France. We had a big turnout: Ian Stannard, Chris Froome, Jeremy Hunt, Roger Hammond, Jonny Bellis, Ben Swift, Dan Fleeman, Geraint Thomas, Steve Cummings, Mark Cavendish, Russell Downing, Daniel Lloyd. We flew them out there and made sure all the GB vehicles were there, although I was doing it off a bloody small budget. I think I had about £15,000 for the whole year – to do the two camps, the rooms, the flights. It was done for nothing really. In Mendrisio we did a couple of days with a training ride of about a hundred kilometres. They wanted a cafe stop, and I was a bit pissed off, so I just sat in the car waiting for them. I think Cav knew I was a bit unhappy about it, because we didn't have much time, and there were a lot of staff there: Dave Brailsford, Shane Sutton, Nigel Mitchell, the nutritionist, and Dan Hunt, who was working with the track endurance riders.

The question of making attendance compulsory came up here because a couple of people got quite shirty about it. They were a little bit upset that certain people hadn't made it to the camp. Dave Millar had had a stag do the day before, so he missed his flight, and nobody knew where he was. There were a few people who were a bit disappointed about that, saying, 'Should he get selected?'

The minutes say, 'Much discussion followed. Most riders

expressed their opinions and it was felt that a show of commitment to the team from the riders was appreciated . . . the commitment of Bradley Wiggins and Dave Millar was questioned, and the subject raised considerable debate. The riders felt that they had committed, travelled and given up free time, and given that they were talking about riding for Dave Millar and Bradley Wiggins, it was felt that the commitment was not matched by those missing.'

I did discuss it later with Dave and Brad. But at the meeting I hit back at the riders: 'Guys, we agreed from the very outset you don't have to be here. So yeah, OK, Dave Millar's been on the piss, what do you want us to do? You talk to them as well, tell them how disappointed you are.' People were more pissed off about Dave than Brad, because I think with Brad everyone said, 'Yeah, you know . . .' We can all get frustrated, but we're never going to change people. Brad does buy in when it comes down to it. I knew Dave was totally behind the idea, but as with Brad, he had bought in in his own way. It wasn't in the same way as Mark Cavendish or I, but he was 100 per cent committed on his terms.

I'm glad I made it clear from the outset that attendance at training camps wasn't compulsory, because I think I would have been in trouble otherwise. A lot of teams in various different sports do get themselves into trouble by creating rigid rules. I remember one year with British Cycling, the winner of the national road race earned automatic selection for the Olympics. That meant if you had a freak winner, an outsider, or one of the best guys punctured or crashed, you were going to leave one of your best riders at home while someone else went off to have a good holiday.

*

Mendrisio in September 2009 was our first world championships as a team. We had qualified nine riders, the most ever in any Great Britain team, because Brad had just finished fourth in the Tour and Cav had won a heap of stages – and the UCI had yet to bring in the ruling that to qualify nine riders you had to have the riders get the points between them. That came in because Luxembourg fielded nine riders in Mendrisio – the Schleck brothers had ridden well in the Tour and scored highly – but they didn't actually have nine pros, so they had to fill the team up with amateurs.

The selection brief I sent to the GB management beforehand began like this: 'The goal is to race the best any GB elite team has ever ridden at the Worlds. Every rider will go to the line with a goal/job; two riders will be delivered ready to race with four laps to go (fifty-five kilometres). All of the riders will support these two with several different jobs.' After that, I went into an overview of the race, with the jobs the riders would be expected to do: 'Dave Millar – 234 to 262 kilometres, lead rider, waits until the final moves with two laps to go; needs to be patient and sit tight all race.' And so on down the list: 'Geraint Thomas – his job comes in between 179 and 234 kilometres, sits with Steve Cummings all the race, but starts to work with him after 179 kilometres. The rest of the time he sits and waits and leaves the jobs to the others.' The idea was to make it quite clear who was doing what, but it didn't end up like this because Dave had been quite sick, and although he did start, he felt bad.

Mark wasn't selected because immediately before the Worlds Jonny Bellis had his horrendous moped crash in Quarrata; he was close to death, in intensive care in hospital in Italy, and Mark was with him, supporting him and his parents. So Mark didn't have to be in Mendrisio, and I wasn't expecting him to be there, but he called me up and said he was going to drive up, because he knew that more than the result on the road, this Worlds was about the camp and being together as a group. One of his friends was in hospital, nearly dying – it was a huge thing for Cav to turn up at all.

As far as the results in Mendrisio went, Steve Cummings wasn't far off the top twenty, and the lads raced quite well as a team. It wasn't a bad start, but we didn't really do anything. I was fine with that. The old GB saying – 'Process not outcome' – really applied here. I remember thinking, 'We've had three good hits this year; we've brought the group together.' The biggest thing for me was that I had integrated the riders who weren't usually backed by Great Britain – Jeremy Hunt, Roger Hammond, Dan Lloyd, Dave Millar. They were all in. That was quite a big thing for me.

But there was one other major development which made a big difference: the Madison and the points race were pulled out of the Olympic track programme. For Cav, this was quite a big thing, and he was super-disappointed. He loved the Madison. His original target for London had been to win two gold medals – the road race and the Madison. And you wouldn't have put it past him. A lot of the riders, including Cav, totally changed their way of thinking about 2012 – mainly the riders who had come up through the track programme, like Ben Swift, Peter Kennaugh, Geraint Thomas and Brad. Some of them kept going with their eyes on the team pursuit, but all of them became focused more towards the road.

10 : Growing Pains

I really didn't enjoy Team Sky's first season in cycling. I wouldn't ever want to have to go through the stress of 2010 again. We'd said to a lot of riders that Sky could be a great outfit and we'd given them an idea of what we felt we could do, so I felt quite a lot of weight on my shoulders. But we underestimated how big a deal setting up Team Sky was, and how much it was going to take out of everybody. Part of the trouble that we encountered that year stemmed from the fact that we were entering the final two years before the Olympics. London was such a big deal, and Dave was trying to concentrate on getting Team Sky up and running while at the same time keeping his eye on the Olympic programme. How the hell he did it, I don't know; the guy just gets through so much work.

My initial role at Sky was Race Coach – not a title that had been used before in pro cycling. My brief was to deal with anything to do with the performance side, moving that along, learning and capturing things: how do we race? What training do we need to do to get better at racing? The point is, I'm not a physical trainer, so it wasn't so much 'Here are the numbers you need to hit in training.' It was also partly linked to the role of *directeur sportif*: the idea was that I would be out there coaching people through the races, while the DSs dealt with tactics and logistics on race day. It was a massive learning curve, because no one had ever tried to split up the jobs before: traditionally, the *directeurs sportifs* had tended to deal with everything, while riders might have personal trainers employed privately who had no input into the racing.

There were so many teething troubles. Dave had employed Scott Sunderland, an Australian former pro who had worked at CSC with Bjarne Riis and who had set up the Cervélo Test Team; the thinking was that Scott could come and run Team Sky, but it didn't work out. The bottom line is that Dave is the boss – Sky own the team, but Dave runs it and has the ultimate say in everything – and I don't think that Scott quite understood that.

Part of my job was to set up training camps. I was confident we could do it better than any team had ever done it, and I think we do now. I was sitting and listening to the current pros, the lads I worked with, to find out what their camps were like, what worked and what didn't. I tried to capture all this and I presented it all to Dave the year before the team started – even down to some of the detail with the hotel rooms. For example, the size of the bathrooms was important because if you have a decent-sized bathroom with a big shower and so on, you relax more after your ride, and that means you will train better the next day. We were looking at little things like that.

We wondered whether to stick with what we knew, which was Majorca, or find something else. Scott said he'd found a really nice place in Valencia, and they would do us a good deal and so on. I went there with Scott to look at it. Chris White at the English Institute of Sport had done a weather analysis to find the best place to train between December and February. The Algarve was the best, then Valencia, then South Africa, which is in the same time zone. So we thought, 'Wow, Valencia is one of the best places; that's another good reason to go.' But I didn't have a great feeling about the roads, and it ended up being quite difficult because as soon as we got there with the riders it snowed – for the first time in twenty-five years – and we couldn't go over the climbs. Dave was not happy.

I set it all up in terms of the training. The main thing for me was to change the training style, keep the groups quite small – not have one big group but split them into two or three smaller ones, which was something that other pro teams weren't doing. I had to fight against all the *directeurs sportifs*, and Scott as well – 'Oh no, the riders all need to go out together.' There was no particular reason, but obviously it was easier for the management. The camps were a disaster partly because of the weather, but also because the climbs weren't long enough and there weren't enough roads to train on with any variety. That came early on, and it got us off to a bad start – a lot of the responsibility for that was put on me.

I had already realised I would have to change my way of working after going from coaching academy riders to guys who, in some cases, have been pros for many years. In those conversations I had about my coaching style – after beginning the Worlds project – it became clear that you have to involve the riders a lot more, let them take the lead. And if you don't know something, you have to go and find out. Don't try and tell them if you don't know. I tried some new things, like getting the riders training for sprint finishes. I had thought, 'How many times does a pro bike rider actually sprint if they're not a sprinter? But how many times do you finish a race on your own? Not often.' For example, I asked a rider like Juan Antonio Flecha, 'Are you going to finish Paris–Roubaix on your own?'

It wasn't very likely, so he needed to practise his sprint. It was a simple way of making things happen, but a lot of pros don't do the simple things. At first there was a little bit of resistance, but people got it eventually.

There were lots of things that were hard work. Take race planning: the traditional way was get to the race, then plan for it once you are on site. You had a rough outline; you would turn up and the *directeurs sportifs* would get on with it. Then they'd get back to the hotel and say, 'Right, what's on tomorrow?' At British Cycling we were more used to finding out what the race was and having a look at it, not just in terms of performance but also logistics. At Sky we've changed that over the years: we're now looking in detail two to three months ahead. For a race like the Giro d'Italia we will have briefing notes several months out, containing all the things we need to know for every stage – route, timetable, accommodation. That was a challenge because people hadn't worked in that way before.

What surprised me most was the lack of ability of some of the riders, given that we have always had the idea that professional racing is the pinnacle of the sport. I was surprised to find guys who had made a career as a pro, who had been out there for a long time, but who actually weren't that good physically. They had all sorts of excuses all the time, were all earning reasonable money and living a bit of a life, I thought, not really buying in. I didn't like it at all, but that gave me a lot of confidence about what we were doing at British Cycling and about the guys coming through from the academy: I realised, 'Bloody hell, these guys are better than we thought they were – they are super-competitive.'

I knew the British lads were hungry for success, perhaps

because of their age as well as their basic attitude. They were ready to go and had a lot in front of them, whereas at Team Sky we had other riders who we didn't know. We thought they were good, but they weren't at the standard we'd been told they were at, and we were stuck with them for two years.

We tried to use the philosophy that we'd adopted at British Cycling from Steve Peters, but people just didn't get the jargon – the chimp model, athletes as kings and queens. They got that wrong – the riders are the kings in that they can do what they want, but some took it literally. In fact, what Steve says is that there have to be rules and consequences – as we had at the academy – although the athletes take the lead. One of the things that we try to do is put the riders first – it's very much the British Cycling way. We constantly ask them for feedback, and I think the pros who came to Sky became frustrated because they weren't used to that. It was part of the riders being the key people in the team, but they would say, 'Stop asking us what we think, just put an extra carer on the race,' because we'd got the staffing model wrong. There were little incidents like that constantly.

I had a really difficult time because I'd not been a professional bike rider in a European team. The pro cycling world was – and still is – dominated by a lot of former pros, and I'm totally against the idea that that is the ideal model. You need a balance in what you're doing, and we've moved towards that within Team Sky. I was always being belaboured with, 'What the fuck do you know?' This was coming from riders and staff – carers, mechanics, *directeurs sportifs*. It was a major issue with Scott Sunderland – and as far as he was concerned, why shouldn't he say that? What did I know? All I had done – and he would say this – is work on the track and with the under-23 group. I didn't know a lot.

Like everyone else, I'd had the impression that professional cycling was the pinnacle of the sport, in the same way that Formula One is the cutting edge of motor racing, but it's not that simple. Olympic cycling is purely performance orientated – for example, the thirty years that the Australian Institute of Sport has been developing sports science, or the way the German track team has moved bike design forward, all with an Olympic focus. For years in professional cycling, on the other hand, it would be a matter of someone getting some money and putting a team on the road. The riders tended to be left to do what they wanted, some managers got more involved with training them, some got into running doping programmes, but all in all there wasn't much of an eye on improving things. For example, Manolo Saiz brought in team buses when he was running the ONCE team in the 1990s, but no one thought about how to make buses better; they just bought buses as well.

I was surprised by what I found. It still shocks me how disorganised teams are about travel. You find riders flying places, with no one there to pick them up. I've got the impression that the riders never come first for a lot of the teams; the sport got in the state it did because riders were just expected to turn up on the start line and be healthy. Doing it right involves hard work and thought. If you think about after a race, getting the riders to recover without cheating involves plenty of time and effort for the staff. For example, in the Giro one year we had the riders eating dinner on the team bus during the longer transfers, which really helps, but involves a lot of work for the chef.

*

I moved back to Italy in late 2009 to set up a base in Quarrata for Team Sky. The idea was that it would combine a service course with a training base and support facility for the riders which would run alongside the academy, replicating the hub I had created when the British pros moved there. It was intended to be similar to what we had at Manchester with British Cycling. But we were a bit premature with that idea, and it was eventually shelved.

Scott left in April 2010, when we were barely into the season, and left a massive void; we were missing our lead *directeur sportif*, and I had to pick up a lot of the slack. That meant I spent a lot more time away from home than I had expected, and personally that made it quite a difficult time, with Jane stuck on her own in Italy. I was doing something which I'd always said I'd never do: working as a *directeur sportif* at a World Tour professional team. I don't have sufficient experience to be a DS; I'm not a true race tactician. We can all sit there in front of the television and have a good old rant – 'Oh, they should have done this and should have done that' – but that's about as far as I get. I can have a good go at managing a team on the road, though, so I had no choice but to take it on. What I'm happy to do is to stand in front of any of the world's best bike riders and ask, 'How are we going to win this bike race tomorrow?' and then help the group break things down. I'm always up for that, but I don't enjoy driving around the peloton.

Sean Yates and some of the other *directeurs* love being in cars, and they seem to live for darting around the back of the peloton. I don't think I'm a bad driver, but it's a dangerous game. It's ludicrous when you think about how close to the riders you are, the road furniture everywhere, the competition for space between the cars, the way you have to multitask. You really need experience. I can do it – I drove in the Tour that year on the cobbled stage, which was the most intense of the lot. But I don't look forward to doing it, and I told Dave it wasn't my best area.

At Sky we had our heads down all that year, learning as we went along. One of the biggest differences was that all of a sudden I was working with foreign cyclists. Since I'd started at British Cycling I'd only ever worked with British riders; I had never had anything to do with foreign ones. Some of the riders at Sky couldn't speak English, and if they didn't have French I found it hard to communicate with them. We'd talked about it beforehand, but until you experience it you can't understand what it's going to be like. Personally, that was a big shock for me.

There was a very clearly defined culture which had built up in British Cycling over the years. At British Cycling we'd get the odd team member joining from outside Britain – the sprint trainer Jan Van Eijden from Germany, our Belgian carer Luc de Wilde – but they were joining a British team with a British culture. So there were sixty of us at British Cycling who were influencing one or two people coming from outside. But at Sky we were trying to run a British team with the same British ways, but out of perhaps eighty people only ten of us had that British Cycling background. So we were a small minority trying to influence a big group of people who were very set in a historic way of working. That was a constant bind.

For example, at British Cycling we have always used performance plans. When a team is travelling to a race, you set your stall out before it starts – you communicate as a group of people, so before everyone gets there they have an idea of what they are doing. The idea is that at least a week before the race the riders receive a document saying this is the goal; this is how we are going to achieve it; this is your role within the race. For example, it might avoid a situation at a road race where a rider turns up and finds out the evening before the start that he's got to work for someone else; or that he's the leader, but he's been sick for two weeks and has told his coach he just wants to stay in the wheels. We developed that by giving it out to the staff so that everyone could see what we were trying to do as a team. Traditionally in professional cycling you don't do it like that, and there were people who were resistant; trying to get the idea across to the ones with that sort of mentality was frustrating. And that in turn creates personality clashes. The issue was getting them to take it on board and actually do it. This was where Sean Yates was particularly good: even though he'd been in the sport for forty years and had always worked in that traditional way and wasn't particularly computer literate, he took it on board pretty well. It was fortunate for us, because where he led, the others followed.

There were so many examples where we were trying to do things differently and had to change people's mindsets. Just calling the carers 'carers' and not '*soigneurs*' was a cultural change for the traditionalists: they would go, 'Carers, humph. What does the word mean?' And then there was the work we expected our carers to do – for example, dealing with food and hydration for the riders on the bus after every race. They generally worked in the same old way or were left to their own devices without a lot of direction, but we are more regimented: the carers make up drinks for each rider – cherry juice, pineapple juice or whatever

– and they are left in the fridge. But that is extra work for them. You'd have a carer from another team who'd say, 'We don't do that. I've never had to do that before.' We worked with a bedding company to produce mattresses and pillows for each rider that would be taken on stage races, so that they would have the feeling of being in the same bed every night, get more sleep and recover more quickly. They're heavy and unwieldy, so it's a big job to lug them around. When they were asked to move them, some people's attitude was, 'You are fucking joking,' but now it's part of the routine and they feel proud to be doing it our way. Other classic ones included meetings: we had a few issues about those, so it became clear we had to calm down on them. We like our meetings, but people don't need them; they just need good information so they know what to do the next day.

One massive bone of contention was the time trial set-up. It was a classic example of us coming in from outside pro cycling, trying to do something new and drawing a lot of flak. We looked at what we did on the track and what we had developed at British Cycling over the years. If you look at the team pens at a major track event, there are people in there left, right and centre, such as mechanics, who waltz through as the riders are trying to get in the zone for racing, and people from other teams, who come in and ask, 'Hey up, mate, how's it going?' So at British Cycling we brought in a protocol that the only people allowed in the pen are the carers, coaches and riders. No one else can go in – not even mechanics, which is why they set up outside the pen. It's a performance environment. So we know that works. And on the gate there is a pit manager who looks after the timings for everything. As a coach I could come into the velodrome with my riders, go to the pit manager and ask where we are on the programme; he'd have the full list in front of him and say, 'We're here. You're about thirty minutes behind schedule because you've had three false starts or something like that.' 'Perfect, thank you very much.'

Over the years I'd gone round the pro teams and looked at their time trial set-ups. My first thought was, 'This is so bad' – you'd get everybody in and out, talking to each other, someone slapping someone else on the back, but the guy next to you might be in the yellow jersey, trying to perform. Most teams put out the tensa barriers, arrange the turbo trainers on the floor, pavement or whatever it might be, then off they go and that's it. The turbos will be put anywhere, with the spectators half a metre from the riders' faces, taking pictures, trying to talk to them. So we thought, 'How can we do this better at Team Sky?' And I spoke to Brad a lot in 2009 as we were putting the team together to get his thoughts on what our set-up might be like. Brad likes to get in his zone, get his headphones on, feel like he's on his own and have no hassle.

We came up with a whole strategy based on the need to pen the riders off a bit, but we got it wrong at the beginning. We wanted to create a bit more space, so we put up what looked like a carbon-fibre box – we wanted to make it look quite good – but it went down really badly; even the race organisers and so on were asking, 'What's all this about?' We changed it pretty quickly, learnt our lesson. The point was that we'd come from an environment which was about pure performance rather than a circus. Basically, a pro team is about showing your riders to the public and displaying the team sponsors' logos. We'd come from an environment where you don't have to give a monkey's about sponsors or media – we didn't have to advertise anything, we just had to perform. The Olympic medals were the advert.

The carbon-fibre box wasn't the only thing that drew comment. The Sky time trial set-up has black foam flooring which we put down every day, so wherever we are – a gravelly car park, a field in the countryside, a wet pavement – the environment will always be exactly the same, and the riders can get used to it. It also means they're not slipping around on their cleats. We have screening, which means the spectators and media can see in but the riders can't see out easily – it's about two metres high at one end, then goes down to normal barrier height across the front of the bus. That creates a private area where you can put your key rider, but the crowd can still see plenty because they can see through the screen; they can come to the part where the barrier is low, but the rider doesn't see out and get affected by the people staring in from the other side. Putting the flooring down is an operation, on the same scale as moving the mattresses; it takes about an hour from start to finish to set up for a time trial. I swear on my life we had other teams laughing at us because they would turn up and – boom! – in ten minutes they would be done. We would be installing the flooring, putting the screens up, putting the clocks up, making everything look nice and tidy. The other teams thought it was hilarious – especially when we were underperforming in the first year – but we were getting good feedback from the riders straight away – they liked the environment. I had to keep saying, 'I don't care. We're going to stick to our standards, and we know this works.'

It wasn't easy getting people to come round to the idea of the pit manager restricting entry. If the rider wants something, he calls someone in. You can imagine the first year, having to tell staff who were used to going everywhere, 'You're not allowed in here – I'm the pit manager.' It was one of the biggest things. Now you look at it and the riders think it's great.

The first thing the pit manager does on the morning of a time trial is ride down to the start, then set the clock in the pit to the official start time. I still have a Casio watch which Matt Parker bought me in 2010 – it cost him five euros, and I swear it's hardly lost a second. You come back and set all the clocks on the bus to that time, so we're all running off that. We have TV screens displaying it as well, because you can't afford to get it wrong or you could be in big trouble. We do the same thing every time: the night before I go round the riders: 'When do you want to eat? What do you want to eat? When do you want to leave the hotel? When do you want to warm up?' Rather than a printed sheet of paper, for every time trial we give the riders a credit-card-sized piece of card to put in a plastic sleeve, with all their timings for the day, so when they go out for their ride in the morning they can just put it in their jersey pocket. It's details like that that make a difference.

The 2010 Tour was horrendous from start to finish. There had been so much hype about the team beforehand, because Brad had finished fourth the year before; the assumption was that having joined Sky he would be bound to improve. I remember thinking, 'Oh my God, why is everyone so excited about what we're doing?' Dave had said a few things too; he wasn't wrong, because we've done everything he said we would, but I think everyone thought we would just come straight in and domi-nate, and of course when we didn't, all we got was slander. Brad was in a difficult place. He was struggling to take the whole thing on. He'd made comments – like Sky being Manchester

United and Garmin being the equivalent of Wigan – which obviously fuelled the fire, although I don't think he was wrong at the time in fact.

It was inevitable that we would underperform in the Tour. Brad wasn't fit enough, and the team wasn't ready for it. It was obvious from early on that Brad wasn't going to perform. You could tell that things weren't ideal at the training camp in the Alps before the race. The camp was well organised, it came at a good time, the number of people out there was small and nothing went wrong. It was exactly what the riders needed – but the atmosphere wasn't there, and it didn't feel right.

I was working with Brad because there wasn't really anyone else to do it, and that wasn't ideal. In hindsight, it was never going to happen. I'd known Brad for quite a long time; he knew me, and I don't think he ever really believed in my coaching. I think he understood what I'd done with the academy and he always backed that. But when it came to getting him to perform, he's very much a numbers person and I'm not, so it wasn't going to work. Having also raced together when he was a youngster, we were almost too close – why should he believe me?

And I may have given him too much rope. I had come from a system where I was telling these lads at the academy what to do, and all of a sudden I was faced with something different – working with professional athletes who I needed to have more open discussions with. Perhaps I took that too far and was not strict enough or on the ball. Inside I'd be thinking, 'How's this going to work? Why should this guy who's finished fourth in the Tour listen to me? All I've done is coach a few under-23s.' I felt that pressure all along.

I took a lot of flak. I felt I was in the firing line because I was on the road with the team a lot – Dave wasn't there so much due to his work for British Cycling – and I was trying to hold up what I believed was the British Cycling side. We were fortunate to have Sean Yates, who stepped into the breach as lead *directeur sportif* after Scott left. He believed in the way that British Cycling had worked in recent years, even though his career as a pro went back as far as the early 1980s. He struggled with the British Cycling ideas at times, and some-times he didn't get it, but eventually he revelled in it. He'd always come round to our way of thinking – for an older guy who'd always been so traditional he was very open to ideas. But Sean is young in his head – the way he dresses, the way he is around people.

Another issue that year was that Brad and Sean's relationship was constantly up and down. It was a challenge for both of them. Sean was expecting a lot, and Brad wasn't dealing very well with all the pressure of expectation. I ended up in between them and felt quite uncomfortable. I'd turn one way and hear something, then turn the other and try to pass the message on. I'd be trying to get them to communicate, to understand each other. The problem for Sean was that he was in a situa-tion where he was having to coach the lads through the races. Sometimes we were the last car in the convoy: it's decided on your overall position, and on a few races we were twenty-first out of twenty-one teams. Sean said once that he had never, ever been last car in a stage race. He wasn't very good at coach-ing somebody through a difficult situation; what he was excel-lent at was when you had a rider in the yellow jersey and you were defending that jersey. He was absolutely world class at the strategies, the tactics; that's why he was so successful with

Brad in 2012. But when Brad needed coaching through a race, needed an arm around him, Sean wasn't that sort of person. That meant they clashed a lot and wouldn't talk to each other, and being in between them wasn't a nice place to be.

Matt Parker was involved in Brad's training as well, and was trying to bring new ideas into the team. The trouble was that we weren't quite ready for recovery ideas like ice baths, compression boots, and so on. We were doing a lot of stuff like that; perhaps we were putting more energy into it than into the lads' training. All along I wanted to keep things simple, but the expectation around the team was too big for that. For many teams, getting round their first Tour with two riders in the first twenty-five and some decent performances here and there would have been fine. The problem was that the hype around the team and around Brad set us up for a fall.

I believed that Sky would need one year in which we would have to learn, plus a second in which we would get on top of things and really understand what we were doing. By the third year we would be up and running. That's pretty much what happened. The big change was that by the end of 2010 Tim Kerrison, the Australian physiologist we had brought in from swimming, started to get more involved as he acquired more understanding of what was needed. He was a cycling novice at the start of the year, but it didn't take him long to learn because he's a smart guy. He didn't get the flak I took early on because he was helping out, following and observing, so he was fairly well protected from it.

I did feel quite isolated that first year, with the responsibility for coaching all twenty-nine riders as best as I could. Somehow I had to manage what they were doing, and then suddenly I was thrown into working as a *directeur sportif* far more than I had wanted. All the time I was trying to keep the Worlds project on the road – and the Worlds was going to be in Australia, so it wasn't simple. On top of that, I was getting calls from riders in the academy telling me how unhappy they were, but I had to stay out of it and let it run its course. I was thinking, 'Fuck, I've done all this work on building it up and now it's going out the window.'

It was generally just a bloody hard year. I constantly felt up against it. I was thinking, 'We've just got to get through this.' In fact, the entire year and the way we struggled through the Tour were the best things that ever happened to Sky. You learn through failure, and we are an ambitious group, all wanting to be successful. There were a few times when my relationship with Dave was teetering on the edge because I felt under pressure and Dave had high expectations of me. Perhaps I was reading more into it than was actually the case, but when you're in there you can't see out. It would have been easy to say Team Sky wasn't for me and I was leaving, but I never thought of stopping, not once. I hated it at the time, but I wasn't going to bail out.

We went through the mill in 2010, but I don't think we'd ever have imagined quite how bad it would get. The Vuelta a España was where we hit our absolute lowest point. We didn't have a particularly strong team, but from a development point of view we had some good young lads in there: Peter Kennaugh, Ben Swift, Ian Stannard. I flew in on the Monday before the race began in Seville, and our *soigneur* Txema González picked me up. We went out that night, rolled in at 4 a.m., doing things the Spanish way, and then a few of us messed about in the swimming pool. The following evening I took a call from Sean Yates, who was going to be our lead *directeur sportif* at the race. He was on his way down, but had checked himself into hospital in Bordeaux with a heart problem. There was no way he could do the race; the only option was for me to stay on as second DS to Marcus Ljungquist, who would be stepping in for Sean.

I'd been away so much more than I was used to already that season. I was absolutely knackered, and it wasn't good calling Jane and telling her I was off for another six weeks – which is what it would be by the time I'd got back from the world championships two weeks after the Vuelta – but there was no option. That was a personal blow and a major worry. Sean ended up having a pacemaker fitted, and that was his season over. We got through the first stage, a team time trial, and that evening Txema started feeling a little bit ropey. The next day he felt quite sick, really under the weather, so he told us he would stay at the hotel and rejoin us when he improved. It's something that happens on a long stage race from time to time.

It was burning hot – over forty degrees – and suddenly the team started falling apart with stomach trouble. Ben Swift went first, then Tim Kerrison – we had to leave him in a hotel the same way we had left Txema – then more riders: John-Lee Augustyn, Peter Kennaugh and Simon Gerrans, all of them throwing up within the first half hour of the stage. I was feeling rotten as well, and Marcus was having to stop the car to keep throwing up. We were all sick, and we assumed that was what had hit Txema; we heard that he had taken himself to hospital and had been discharged because the doctors knew we were all poorly and assumed he had the same thing.

Then came the phone call from Steve Peters, the Great Britain team psychiatrist, who was head of all things medical at Sky; he was telling me, 'This is really serious with Txema; he's got septicaemia. He's not going to make it.' By this time Juan Antonio Flecha had fallen ill; we got really worried about him, so we took him to hospital at two o'clock in the morning. We were four or five days into the race and I hadn't been sleeping at all, and then we were told there was nothing wrong with Flecha, but what was weird was that his symptoms were similar to what Txema had: sickness, high fever, and so on.

The call saying that Txema had died came on the Friday. Apparently he had got a little cut on his leg and that was how the infection got in; once it gets hold of your organs you never get rid of it, and that was it. It was an immense shock. He was so healthy; he was always good fun, even though he had ended up with a lot of work put on him because he was one of those guys who actually cared about his job. He took it seriously and was prepared to do the little extras we were adding to the carer's role; we used to get frustrated because there were other carers who didn't want to take all that on. It was unbelievable to think he could die from a little cut on his leg, and then we began thinking, 'Bloody hell, when did he get that cut? Did he get it messing around in the swimming pool with us?' You just don't know.

The phone call came on the Friday; we still had about twenty kilometres to go in the race. It was weird because within the peloton everyone had heard about it; we weren't going to tell the riders until afterwards, but there were so many people in cycling who were good friends with Txema that the word got out and went through the peloton. By the time we finished the stage the media was going mad around our bus. We crammed on there. Nobody said anything. It was horrendous. By now Dave Brailsford was on his way; he arrived that evening and asked how we were. The answer was, 'Everybody's fucked. We can't carry on, we just cannot carry on. We've lost half the team, we don't know what's happened; everyone has been so sick and people are still feeling a bit ropey.' We were put into quarantine at the hotel where we were staying; a local hospital sent staff in to take swabs and blood samples from us all, and we had to stay there until we got the results.

His poor wife and kids; you can't imagine what it was like for them. What struck us was that she wanted the team to be at his funeral, to turn up on the bus. We had to get that across to the young lads and make it clear they should stay and go to his funeral. It was a long trip up to Vitoria, in the Basque Country, where he lived, but I think when they look back they will be glad they stayed on. We took every vehicle we had up there, and on the day of the funeral we had a police escort from the hotel – the whole team in convoy – and we pulled up outside the church, all in team kit. It was only then that I realised how into this team the guy had been; his widow let us know how proud he had been to be part of it.

Txema had been around cycling a long time. There were some we had brought in who hadn't bought into the way we were going about things, but he seemed to really enjoy what we were doing. He was massively popular among the riders, quietly spoken like a lot of people from the Basque Country, really good at his job – all the lads wanted him to massage them. His death changed Sky. It was the first time I had sensed the team was a bit of a family. There is a different feeling within a professional team compared to a national squad because you spend so much of the year on the road. When you do a Grand Tour together, you get to the end of those three weeks and feel you've been through this massive voyage of experience. You do actually get quite close to people, and we'd experienced that with Txema. I'd been through the Tour and the Giro and all the other stage races with him; you just end up with that feeling that a team are like family. His death was a catastrophic end to a really hard year, but it brought us together in that way.

We still talk about Txema a lot at Sky. At the end of the year we have different awards in our review of the season; the one for most outstanding staff member was named the Txema González Award. There are staff at the team still who were really good friends with him before he came to us, so he's not forgotten. The team wear black armbands on the anniversary of his death; there was a stage in his home town on the 2012 Vuelta, and something was organised around that. There are still photographs of him on people's computers; in one of Brad's books there is a picture of him massaging Brad's legs at the 2010 Tour, and we've got that hung up on the wall in the office. He is still part of the team.

The Worlds project was what kept me alive through 2010. Sky wasn't enjoyable; it consisted of a lot of things that I couldn't control with a lot of people I didn't know and involved a lot of situations coming out of nowhere that I had to firefight. On the other hand, the Worlds project was familiar territory and was something that I could do on my terms. That year it hinged on the national road race championship in Lancashire, which was the main training camp of the year, and the world championship itself in Geelong, near Melbourne. That camp and the Worlds were the only things that I enjoyed in 2010.

At the Nationals Sky took the first three places, with Gee winning. We had a great camp – really good fun, a good training ride the day before, four hours on Friday, a couple of hours on Saturday. What really struck me was their morale – the lads were happy to be together. They'd all come in from different teams but were having a good time together. They enjoyed it and they were all upbeat. I felt we were moving the Worlds project along nicely. The riders had a good understanding of where we were headed; they knew what we wanted to do.

Cav trained for a couple of hours behind the car on the Saturday, and then they all rode the national road race on the Sunday, on a super-tough circuit, which put most of the field out of contention in the early kilometres after Gee, Peter Kennaugh and Ian Stannard broke away. Cav had been doing his normal programme – the Giro, the Tour of Switzerland – and we always used the national road race as a final hit out before the Tour. So within a few laps who was on the side of the road? Cav. I purposely drove up next to him, stopped the car, looked and didn't say a word. I just kept on driving. He knew what I was thinking – 'What the fuck are you doing sitting on your arse? There are still groups going around, so why aren't you with them? You're not trying to win these Nationals but you need the work before the Tour.' So he went out on his bike again.

I was still coaching Cav; some people had made comments about a possible conflict of interest given my involvement with Team Sky. I'd said from the beginning that if it became an issue, I'd have to decide one way or the other, but it was squashed pretty quickly. Dave was supportive there, because I was still working for British Cycling as well as Sky, and the Worlds project was a big objective. Brad, Gee and Swifty were all on the Olympic track programme, Peter Kennaugh soon would be, and Cav was part of that group even though he wasn't with Sky.

Although I'd been coaching Cav through his earlier years as a pro – in 2007, 2008 and 2009 – I'd not been to many races, so I'd met up with him when he was back home in Manchester or Quarrata. All of a sudden, in 2010, I was working at a lot of races which Cav was riding, so our contact was in a different environment, which was pretty refreshing for us. We didn't do anything different. Cav had a decent year and came good at the Tour, where he won five stages and was just eleven points from winning the green jersey. He was ticking over. One of the big things was that he had said he wanted to be in good form at the end of the year. That was always going to be the plan, to rehearse the transition from the Vuelta to the Worlds themselves. That was what we would do in 2011, so we had to find out what it involved, what were the potential pitfalls.

At Geelong what mattered was the process: finish the Vuelta, go training, race the Worlds. It was an easy one when it came to getting fit – Cav just had to go and finish the Vuelta, and he would be in whatever shape he was when he came out of it. There wasn't a lot we could do, there wasn't a lot we could control – but with Cav, nine times out of ten it's a matter of working him well, working him hard, making sure he's riding his bike every day, and he's going to get pretty fit. And coming into the Worlds Cav won the points jersey in the Vuelta – the points jersey in one of the three big Tours had been one of his career goals, so that was a big thing for him.

For Melbourne in 2010 I wanted to practise the run-in from the Vuelta to the Worlds: what training do you do? How much, how little? What's the mindset of the team? What do you do when you're on site? That was where Mark was really good. He paid for himself and the other two riders, Dave Millar and Jeremy Hunt – we had only qualified three – to go business class or first class. Dave was very critical of the training that we did beforehand. He's the kind of rider who likes a big hit of training and then to rest up, stop cycling. That's different from what I've seen with Cav over the years: you need the right balance, you need to keep him working. We aimed for the top ten, and although I don't think he would have medalled, I believe Cav had the form for a top-ten placing, if we'd got it right leading into the race. There were three reasons why he didn't perform: he finished the Vuelta on his knees because he was fighting for the points jersey all the way, and that took quite a lot out of him. On top of that, I think he kept panicking in his training, and I didn't rein him in. I didn't say 'no' when I should have done. It wasn't every day, but he did a couple of big sessions where I was thinking, 'Ouch, I'm not sure you needed to do that.'

The other factor was that Cav didn't settle down. He hardly sat still for the whole time we were there. He was constantly up and about, shopping, going for a coffee, walking around the hotel talking to people. It was just stuff the guys tend to do, but I was really frustrated about it. There were other distractions: Dave knew a few people around the place; Jeremy had lived in Melbourne and his wife was around all the time. So we got all that wrong, but I think we learnt a lot from it. So a year later in Copenhagen it was, 'Right, Cav, sit on your arse, don't do more than absolutely necessary.' These were all little things that we were learning as we went along; they all add up.

Not one of the riders finished in Geelong, so on paper the result looked horrendous, but I walked away thinking, 'OK, I'm all right with that.' Looking at the long-term picture, I wasn't really bothered, and I said so to Cav. I don't mind when we lose as long as we are moving forward. Sometimes you have to take a step back to progress, and I knew we'd learnt some more. We'd gone through the process again. I like working on long-term projects because you have to work hard to get somewhere. I like the problem-solving, although I get frustrated when I read stuff slagging you off for not performing. I'm prepared to sit there and go through with it as long as I can see the way forward clearly in my head. And that was what the Worlds project and Team Sky had in common: goals like winning the Worlds with a British cyclist or being a Tour de France-winning team or winning the Classics are massive objectives. These are the biggest cycle races in the world to win and it doesn't just happen overnight.

11 : Turning Points

There is a stage in the formation of every team when the teething period ends, the message has clearly got through, and it is as if a switch has been flicked. Suddenly the whole thing starts to move forward. Morale improves and momentum sets in. It happens in this order: good results, morale, momentum. You get results and then, as Dave Brailsford says, people get in the right seats on the bus. Everyone has their place, and they find it. In a team everyone has an ego; people protect their ground, some have to lead, some want to follow, some rub each other up the wrong way. That was certainly how it was at Sky, where no one knew each other.

I'd seen it at the academy, with the Worlds squad in 2010. With the academy there was no real staffing change; it was a matter of the work ethic among the riders. At Sky it was a matter of clarity among the whole group. Suddenly everyone got in line, and we went forward. It happened in May 2011, at the Bayern Rundfahrt. Geraint Thomas won the overall title, Brad took Fabian Cancellara's scalp in the time trial, and almost overnight there were happy faces and a sense of momentum. Winning breeds success. You get the results, people start smiling, and then you want more.

It was not as if 2010 had been a complete disaster: we'd taken twenty-two wins, including the prologue of the Giro d'Italia with Brad and the Het Nieuwsblad Classic with Juan Antonio

Flecha, which is far better than many professional teams achieve. But we are an ambitious bunch; we had big goals, and there were prominent races such as the Tour de France and Tour of Britain where things didn't work out. Personally, I never thought we were off course; I was able to keep my eyes on the bigger picture. I was quite prepared for a bit of a struggle early on, which is why it never even crossed my mind to leave. I did wonder at times about whether I was good enough to do the job, but just upping sticks and leaving was never an option. It was a challenge – working with the pros was a whole new world to me – but I didn't feel quite as vulnerable as I did early on when I started working for British Cycling; by the time I started at Sky I knew that the under-23s had been successful, so that was always going to be there for me.

Sky turned around quickly enough. All of a sudden the staff started to work well together, the performance team started to gel, and the riders started to enjoy being around each other. I remember having a conversation in 2010 with David Fernández, one of the mechanics, and he was saying, 'Why do we do all this work? We are the last team up at night working on the bikes, and we still don't win races. What is going on?' It was as if overnight all these guys started to walk around with smiles on their faces and we were getting places. In June 2011 Brad won the Dauphiné Libéré, the biggest stage win of his career, and that put him where everybody knew he could be.

Brad doesn't lead a team in the same way that Cav does. Mark sets an example on the bike and he also heads it up around the dinner table and on the bus, quite often pushing his ideas. Brad leads purely with his legs, and he was doing a bloody good job by now. He and Tim Kerrison were starting to build a really good relationship; Brad identified well with Tim, realised his training style was working for him. Tim is very thoughtful; he looks at detail far more than me, and Brad really identifies with the way he works. Personally, Brad had turned a corner; he'd had a good talking to during the winter. Dave had a new principle of compliance: as trainers we can set the training, but the question was, how much of that do they actually do? So it became our job to make them comply, actually do the training, rather than just give them the programme and trust them to get on with it.

It helped that we finally got the training camps nailed; that laid the foundations for the whole year. In that winter of 2010–11 we decided to go back to Majorca, use the same hotel we stayed at with British Cycling and run it to the same format – as a drop-in centre. It was a radical departure from the usual professional-cycling training camp. The idea is you have several weeks in which you take over the hotel, with all your equipment there. You invite riders in for certain periods of time, but they can also drop in whenever the weather is bad at home, so they know that there are staff there and other people to train with. My idea was to invite them for a week at most and make them short, hard weeks. Then we would find that they wanted to stay for a few more days, so we would get more out of them because they were staying of their own accord. It worked so well; in the six or seven weeks we had there through 2010–11 I remember only one or two days of rain. It was a massive difference to the year before; the riders had a better winter and were getting better results from the start of the season.

Most importantly of all, the staff began to settle down. When you first start an enterprise of that size, with sixty-five people being brought in from all over, all the egos get going: you are trying to fight your ground, prove your point, make people aware that you're worth employing. And we had got rid of a lot of people: not many riders – they were pretty much the same group as in 2010 – but perhaps eight to ten staff who didn't buy into our ways, bringing in other staff who potentially did. So that completely changed the balance.

That winter we really started to put systems in place to make the team function smoothly. As soon as we got back from the Worlds, it was full gas: Tim and I spent every single day together coming up with ideas, and we were constantly selling them to Dave. I came up with this little phrase: 'We have got to make Team Sky's world smaller.' The problem was that we weren't all working from one location – everyone involved with the team was split up around the world, particularly once the season got going. That winter Dave introduced conference-call systems, and, together with Olly Cookson, who is in charge of a lot of the team's admin, Tim and I set up a drop-box system. It's a live online structure where you can pick up information. It's where all the information on Team Sky is stored: insurance, cars, contacts, how to do your expenses, how to find people, race programmes, training camps, all the information on the riders. It's an incredibly useful tool. So if one of the staff wants to know what a particular rider has been doing, what he is going to be doing, how he is coming back from injury perhaps, they can just go straight in there and look.

After each race you have a report written by the *directeurs sportifs*, and the coaches take that information and give feedback to the riders. They write a weekly training report on each rider, and the DSs come up with a performance plan for the next race, using the information from the race and coaches' reports, plus a medical report. That ensures that at any race all our DSs have the information they need about every rider. For example, at the Scheldeprijs in 2013, my plan for Ian Stannard was that he was not going to race hard, because the next day I wanted him to be fresh for a training session which would be an important part of his build-up to Paris–Roubaix. In the coach's report, it would be there: Ian Stannard will just ride around at the Scheldeprijs without going for the win.

We also have a conference call every Monday morning where these sort of things get discussed; there is an agenda which any of the coaches and DSs can add to, so we can talk it through without all having to be in the same place. This way, everyone is completely informed of what is going on across the team. It cuts out a lot of the risk that the right hand might not know what the left hand is doing. In year one Scott Sunderland and I had a race programme, and once Scott left I looked after it, but I just used to send it out to everybody on a weekly basis.

The point about the race programme is that it is constantly changing because riders get injured and fall ill. So you'll have a provisional line-up perhaps three months before a race, but that will mutate constantly. I look at the race programme every single day of my life; it's still a constant. But the difference compared to Sky's first year is that now I can make those changes, and anyone can look at the latest version immediately; there is only one copy in the drop box and people only have to go to one place.

What isn't always obvious to outsiders is the complexity of the logistics involved in a professional team. For example, in spring 2012 we had a set of vehicles going to Tirreno–Adriatico in central Italy, then on to the Tour of Catalonia, and at the same time we had a training camp for Milan–San Remo and a week or two later the Criterium International in Corsica. It's a matter of making sure that the right bikes go in the right team vehicle for the right race. There is a lot of kit circulating, so the staff have to know what is going where. If you are, say, running the team at the Criterium International, you want to know when the riders are flying in so you can send people to pick them up. It's all there in the drop box, and if anything changes it gets updated straight away – every race, every training camp, all the travel. For example, if one of the staff has a car accident, they can find the insurance documents on their phone at once.

The performance plans written by the *directeurs sportifs* for each race are on there as well: this is what we need to do, stages to target, priorities, support available, roles for each rider, details of each stage, the challenges each day, official race information, all the profiles. That means I can be sat in my home in England and follow everything that's happening. It's the information that will be presented to the riders on the bus at the team meeting before each race or stage; if need be, I can take a look the night before and suggest something. Having all that information in there well in advance means that the DSs don't have to do any of the set-up; they will just go through what the weather is like, the terrain – key points for the day's race. Everything should be in there. There's the staff planner as well – what races they are doing, how many races they are at in a given year – and a list of performance impact areas, performance support and nutrition.

All the work on communication made us function more smoothly, but getting these systems in place also freed up time and mental space. It eliminated a lot of the firefighting that goes on in a big organisation if you haven't got everyone on the same page. Get rid of the firefighting and crisis management and you immediately have more space to talk to the riders and think about what makes them function more effectively.

The philosophy which underpins Team Sky, the thought constantly in the back of our minds, is that you have got to put the bike riders first. I think we listen to our riders more than any other team – not just the one or two big hitters but every rider. What we try to achieve is make it all completely seamless for them, whether they are going to a race, going home, going to a training camp or going to a media session. They shouldn't notice anything; we could be paddling like hell underneath, but there should be nothing on the surface to make them aware of that. We want them to be left to get on with training, looking after themselves and competing. We began coming up with different mottoes: ready to train, ready to race, ready to inspire. That sums up who does what: the riders have a responsibility to be ready to get on their bikes and do the work, not eat like pigs and be as fat as anything; to get them ready for racing is down to the coaches; and being 'ready to inspire' is the function of the DSs. Racing well is what inspires those who follow the team: if you think of the way Ian Stannard competed in Milan–San Remo in 2012, getting in front in the finale, putting the British national champion's jersey out there, with fans jumping out of their seats in front of their TVs and shouting at him with two kilometres to go, as I was – that's uplifting.

I felt like we weren't doing a very good job running the team in 2010, but many of the Sky riders were still saying that it was better than anything they had experienced before. Guys like Juan Antonio Flecha, Matt Hayman, Thomas Löfkvist and Mike Barry had been around a lot of different teams and seemed happy with what they had found. Kurt Asle Arvesen had been around the block and was close to the end of his career, and he said he could feel from the outset that something interesting was happening under the surface, even if we weren't quite getting the results we wanted.

Everything settled down in 2011. Tim had started to get going and he began to add input on the training, with some good new ideas, which was a massive relief to me because it wasn't just me having to think about it. We started working with the Training Peaks computer programme, which interprets power output and other factors to give an assessment of a rider's training and racing workload, and Tim being Tim he really got into it. We expanded the training group as well by bringing Bobby Julich on board. Bobby was an American former pro who had been around for fifteen years, and he came in to help on the time-trial side. That relieved the pressure on Tim and me, and so did the expansion of the *directeur sportif* group to five, although we only had one who was an experienced DS, which was Sean Yates, so we were trying to develop guys like Nicolas Portal, who had been one of our riders, as new DSs. At the time Sean and I had responsibility for the race programme, and Sean being Sean, he always spoke his mind and never sat back on anything. We all challenged each other; at times it was a little bit edgy, but in general it went well. Bobby took responsibility for a group of riders, and it was there that the relationship between him and Chris Froome really started to grow; what was happening was that Tim was spreading his training knowledge and ideas through myself and Bobby, and in 2011 all of a sudden Chris started to perform.

That was another breakthrough. Chris really started to buy into the training and the idea of having a good coach alongside him, and Bobby lived near him, which was a massive help. Bobby is quite an intense person, but what came with that was an attention to detail: he never let anything go. If we agreed on how we were going to do something, he would completely get his teeth into it. He was perfect for Chris because he really kept him on the ball. The culmination for Sky was the Vuelta, where both Brad and Chris were going for the overall win. We made some massive mistakes there with gearing – we just didn't have low enough gears up the Angliru. That climb was where the Vuelta was decided because of the time Brad lost after getting dropped and the time Chris lost waiting to help him. That was what cost us the race, but it kept us hungry. You learn from your mistakes; it was a massive learning curve for Tim as well, who was looking at how the riders perform through a Grand Tour. We really worked on hydration and nutrition before and after the stages, making sure that the riders were getting enough fluids in them and not just leaving it to chance, really badgering them. This was where Brad was particularly good; he agrees with the marginal-gains side. After a stage you never see him without a recovery drink in his hand.

I would estimate that 80 per cent of the practices we have now were put in place that winter, after that first year of learning. In terms of performance we went back to the old principle: 'Let's do the simple things really, really well.' By 'simple things' I mean hydration, logistics, fuelling, training, communication with the riders. We had to make sure they turned up at a race and knew what their role was. If they receive a performance plan a week before and, for example, one guy doesn't want to sit on the front and work because he feels he's ready to go for the win, he can ring up and say, 'Listen, I want my opportunity.' Whatever the outcome, at least he's got the chance to speak his mind. And the egos settled down; there were no issues in terms of who did what in the system – we all accept Dave as the boss, the man with the ultimate say. He is all over everything.

Team Sky wasn't really at the forefront of my mind once we got through the winter and the 2011 season got under way. By then I was almost completely focused on the world championships, trying to build the momentum for the riders without it being energy-sapping over the course of the season. I had to make them gradually more and more aware of what we were getting into, and at the same time be wary of the end-of-season blues. The time that really mattered was the last week in September; there is a lot of racing before then, so my focus on Cav was quite intense. I didn't want Mark to switch off in any way, but there was a lot going on with him which could potentially take his mind off one of the biggest goals of his career. He was falling out with his team, and there was immense speculation about whether he would end up at Team Sky. There was a constant dialogue with him all year, and I was the go-between, stuck in the middle: Cav would talk to me, I'd talk to Dave, Dave would talk to me, I'd go back to Cav.

The riders were given a DVD of the 2011 Worlds route at our last training camp, the national road race championships in north-east England in June. There the riders were split into groups and asked to detail what tactics they would use to ensure a bunch sprint would happen for Cav. I wanted to nail down how we would race. Cav was vocal about two things: he wanted the team to take on the race, and he wanted to be kept out of trouble, with someone to shepherd him all day. Mark's view was that if a team takes control on his behalf, it puts pressure on him to deliver, and that is how he likes it. That was how the team would have to ride, and that came through as what they all wanted at the meetings when we discussed ways of winning. When I put up the tactical plan on the Friday before the race, they weren't my tactics, they were the riders'.

That in turn drove the selection: they said they needed certain riders to do this particular job. The biggest challenge was numbers. The best way to guarantee a win for Mark was by controlling the race. To control the race, we needed a big team; if we were in the same boat as in 2010, when we only qualified three, it would be tough: we'd be guessing about the outcome, hoping all day that the race would come back together for a bunch sprint rather than being able to make it happen. So we went through all their races from mid-July to the ranking cut-off date in mid-August – who was where and whether they might get a point or two. It wasn't new; we were just making sure everyone knew what we were pushing for and where we were in terms of ranking and rider numbers.

Through July and early August I was constantly on to every rider in the squad about where Great Britain was sitting in the world rankings. The difference from 2010 was that the UCI had added a new rule: to get a full team of nine a nation needed to have at least nine riders scoring points, although you could select who you liked within your quota. We hadn't got nine riders who had scored points; for most of the year it was five, which was nail-biting. We were comfortably in the top ten in the world rankings, because although Brad had pulled out of the Tour, he had scored well by winning the Dauphiné; Cav had picked up lots of points as usual, Swifty had been winning races as well and David Millar had been scoring. But when it came down to the final qualifying event, the Tour of Poland, a week before the final deadline of 15 August, we were still looking at a team of five, because that was how many riders had scored points.

I had begun planning around five riders. It would have been flying by the seat of our pants, but we had to work around whatever we ended up with. But the lads did really well at the death: the final ones were Adam Blythe, who scored a point in the Tour of Poland, while Peter Kennaugh and Steve Cummings got high up overall. So all of a sudden we went from five to eight riders, which gave us a massive boost. Adam, Swifty and Pete didn't even get to ride the Worlds, but their contribution in qualifying was massive.

I'd had a long-term strategy here, and it had worked. I'd kept chipping away at the riders since we began the project two years earlier. I'd kept the issue alive in their minds with the newsletters, constantly reminding them of the need to score, keeping their eyes on where they were. It was a big step on the way to Copenhagen, and it could have been the full nine: Ian Stannard finished sixth in the bunch sprint on the final stage in Poland, and if he had come in fifth, that would have been a single point, which would have given us nine points scorers. But Cav and I were happy with eight.

In mid-August we had a chance to try out the London Olympics road-race course, in the test event on the Box Hill circuit, with the finish on the Mall. It was also a chance for me to put the riders in contention for the 2011 Worlds team through their paces. We stayed at the same hotel as we would for the Olympics, which was critical because the Games came so soon after the 2012 Tour de France. We already knew we were going to fly most of the Olympic team back to London on the night the Tour finished in Paris, and I wanted the lads to know the hotel they were going back to, and our staff needed to know it to ensure there would be no surprises. For the staff, it makes a difference if you don't have to find out where you're going, where you store stuff, where to park the cars, where you eat. If you know what issues you are going to have before you go into something, you can deal with them a lot better. When you are a cyclist coming off the back of the Tour, you are so tired that you just want to be able to go somewhere familiar. You can't beat understanding and knowledge.

We had two teams of five riders in the test event, under the Great Britain and England banners, but they were one team as far as the Worlds were concerned. Beforehand, Cav didn't want the stress of leading the team. He had just won the points jersey in the Tour and felt he had been under pressure for three weeks. The night before the race he was saying, 'No, guys, don't race for me,' but almost the minute they rolled off the start line he changed his mind. After that it was a matter of controlling the race, then leading him out. As a Great Britain team, we'd never taken a race by the scruff of the neck and controlled it all the way. It ended up being a dry run for what we were going to do at the Worlds, but it wasn't particularly planned like that. I was more interested in the way that the group had come together and that we had another weekend building the team.

What struck me over those few days in Surrey was the commitment from everyone. It's like players coming together for the England soccer or rugby team after kicking seven bells out of each other in the Premiership week in, week out. All of a sudden they are having to shout to each other and work as a team; here we had riders from several different professional teams now having to work together as a unit. But that had been one of the key things when we were talking about the Worlds in the first place back in 2009, and having Team Sky was only going to ensure that the team would be closer anyway. A lot of the riders at the test event and at the Worlds were coming in from Sky, so working as a team wasn't new for them.

Once we knew how many riders we had, the next question was selection. It was pretty simple: for what we wanted to do you need a good road captain and people to ride hard at the front of the bunch, big engines who are capable of doing the work. After that it was a matter of who was on form. Froomie and Brad were in pole position because they would have just come out of the Vuelta. I was a bit concerned about Brad. He had had a big year: he had been aiming for the Tour, which went belly up after his crash, but then he got himself back on the ball and went for the Vuelta. He had had a long, long season, and Sky had asked a lot of him. But he had turned himself around, complied with his training and been more cooperative with the media, and he was potentially a key character. Then again, he had never turned up to any of the training camps, so I had to ask myself, 'Is he going to buy in?' Against that, I knew that he and Cav have a really good relationship. I was banking on that.

On the other hand, Jeremy Hunt, Ian Stannard, David

Millar, Geraint Thomas and Steve Cummings had been totally in on the idea from the start. The selection was relatively easy, because younger riders like Ben Swift, Peter Kennaugh and Alex Dowsett hadn't quite performed at that level of racing, or not to the extent that you could be certain they were still going to be there and doing the job after 250 kilometres of racing. One major thing right from the outset had been that there were never, ever going to be any development spots at these Worlds. It was only ever going to be the best team we could put on the line. We weren't going to test anybody and we weren't going to give anybody a bit of an opportunity. That had been a constant message. So that was quite an easy one to rule on when the time came.

Adam Blythe took himself out of selection quite early on. I'd spoken about honesty, and this was a good example: he was saying, 'Actually, Rod, if you had picked me, it would have been quite obvious you didn't know what you were doing.' Roger Hammond was a big call, because he so wanted to do it. I felt a bit sorry for him because he had really bought into it. He really did like the British angle I had been constantly pushing: 'We are out there fighting, we are the British team and we are going to put a British team on the podium. It's about us as a team pulling that jersey on and feeling proud.' It was a really hard call, phoning him up and saying he had not been selected, but Roger didn't have the form and he hadn't been going that well all year. Daniel Lloyd was another hard one: he too was very much on side, and at the Tour of Britain he had really good form – he was in the top ten overall – but the thing with Dan was that he had only just hit that form.

We'd already gone through two selection cycles before this,

so the riders knew the criteria, and I never missed a beat in terms of phoning each and every single one of them on each of the selection dates so they would know exactly where they were. This was another benefit of coming in with a long-term plan: we'd nailed the administration side, all the nitty-gritty things where people had slipped up in the past. With selection dates, selection criteria, training camps and rider numbers fixed in people's minds from day one, when the time came all we had to focus on was the performance side: getting the qualification points and deciding which riders we were going to put in.

It was so hard to leave any of them out, but Dan was our first reserve. One of the other things I had worked on over the previous two years was the need for the reserves to keep in form. I made a real plea to them: 'Please keep training because twenty-four hours beforehand you could be called up if one of these guys crashes or is sick. Anything can happen, so keep yourselves on the ball, guys.' To be fair to Dan, he kept himself going. The selection was quite easy; who was going to do what and when was left until the last few days.

By the end of August I had a pretty good idea of the team line-up and I'd issued a massively detailed guide to the entire world championships. The idea was that there should be no excuse for them not knowing something. With that in place, I set off for Colorado to negotiate the Colombian Sergio Henao's transfer to Sky; I took Tim Harris with me, as he knew Sergio from spending time in Colombia, and he can speak good Spanish. We were in Brussels airport waiting for the flight to New York, when we caught sight of stage four of the Vuelta on a TV in the terminal. It was a hot and hilly stage through south-ern Spain, and the first thing we spotted was Cav, struggling at the back of the peloton. By the time I got to the TV, Cav was already out of the back of the peloton; the group had just gone over this little climb towards the end of the stage, with a team driving on at the front. My first thought was that he must have punctured, but then I saw the way he was pedalling. He was in a right state. And so was I: 'Flipping heck, we've got five weeks before the Worlds. Oh shit.'

There was nothing I could do. I had to get on the plane with Tim and sit there for five hours, not knowing what was up with Cav. To fray my nerves a little bit more, our landing in New York wasn't a happy one. We were well into our descent to JFK, when the plane went back up again. We were circling around New York for ages before the captain came over the tannoy: 'Hello, guys, we are really sorry to tell you we are unable to land at JFK; there's been an earthquake in New York.' People started getting a little concerned at that, but then the pilot added, 'We've got a bit of a dilemma: we have only thirty minutes' worth of fuel left, and they're shutting all the airports on the east coast of America, so we may have to head for a military airbase. We need to make the decision soon or we won't be able to make it.' Then it was near panic: the other passengers started being sick around us. And all that time I was worrying about Cav, sitting there thinking, 'Fuck it, I just want to get on the phone and ring people about Cav. He must be ill.'

When they did open the airport and we eventually landed at JFK, it was chaos because of all the flights coming in at once: people and bags everywhere, everyone trying to figure out where they were going. In the midst of all that, I finally got through to Cav, several hours after the event. He was in pieces, all over the place, with no idea what to do. On we went to the Tour of Colorado to meet Sergio Henao, but though my business was in Aspen, my mind was back in Europe. I bumped into Brian Holm, and he told me the doctor had said there was nothing wrong with Cav, although another report said that the doctor's view was that 'He was so tired that he could sleep in the team car.' At that I lost my temper: 'What do you mean, there's nothing wrong with the guy? Why on earth would he pull out of the Vuelta when he is meant to be going for the Worlds in five weeks' time and he knows he needs to finish it to have the fitness?'

All the while I was thinking, 'Fuck, the whole thing could go belly up.' The question was: how sick was he?

12 : Rainbow in the Air

My first thought when I put the phone down was: 'I need to commit to Mark here.' I rang Dave Brailsford straight away. There were races I was still scheduled to do with Team Sky, but they were going to have to go by the board.

'Have you seen that Cav is out of the Vuelta?'

'Yes.'

'Dave, I'm going to have to go and deal with this.'

'Down tools, drop everything, go and do what you have to do.'

The significance of Dave's decision can't be underestimated. Earlier, in 2010, he had been on the receiving end of a fair bit of adverse comment regarding the balance between British Cycling and Team Sky, and a review had been commissioned from Deloitte by UK Sport to assess the impact of the pro team on the Olympic side of what we did. I had a role at both organisations, but there was no question which would be the priority for Dave when a decision had to be made as rapidly as this one did, with a world title on the line. His view was that I had no option but to put the Worlds first and that I needed to support Cav.

I believe that you can be sick five weeks out from a major event and still come good, but on the other hand, if Cav had something really wrong with him, it would all be over. I knew Mark didn't have to be at his best to win the Worlds; he had to be fast but he didn't have to be at his best in terms of fitness, so we had a little bit to play with, if you like. Tim Kerrison would be able to put it into numbers, but with me it is a matter of gut feeling, and my instincts were telling me Mark only needed to be 80 per cent fit to win those Worlds. As it turned out, he wasn't at his absolute peak. Over the season I was more concerned about the other riders who might be in the team, because they would be the ones who would be sitting at the front and driving the peloton along; they would have to be super-fit for that job.

What Cav told me was that he had felt really poorly, lifeless, with nowhere to go. He said he had got to the point where he felt that if he carried on, he would end up doing more damage to himself, so he would be better off stopping, getting better and then starting again. The first thing was to reassure him: 'Don't worry, you have done exactly the right thing. Don't fret about the Worlds, we'll put a plan together. Just go and rest up for two or three days. I'll get home and then we'll go from there.' It dawned on me that the tension within the HTC team had come to a bit of a head, and ultimately Cav didn't want to be in the race. These are the moments with Mark when you just have to settle him, tell him, 'Stay put, don't worry, chill out.' At those times you have to forget what is coming up in four or five weeks' time and hone in on the here and now.

It doesn't matter how many times they get sick, all athletes panic when it happens. They all think it is the end of the world. That is how you are as an athlete. It's why I say to any lads I coach, 'If you wake up any morning and feel a little bit under the weather, and you don't know what to do, ring me. It doesn't matter what time it is – seven o'clock, six o'clock, five o'clock – ring me because I can help you make the right decision. I am not a doctor, but I can help you decide whether to get your ass out of bed and get to the doctor's or go out for a little steady spin because you're only feeling a bit groggy.'

I would have to live with Mark for that final month. Fortunately, there was nothing majorly wrong with him; he just had no energy and had picked up a little bit of a bug. First up, he took three or four days off completely to get his strength back. By then I'd put a bit of a plan together for the next few weeks, and it was clear that he had plenty of time to get in decent shape, if we did enough work. Firstly he went to stay in Girona, where a lot of the Garmin riders are based, because David Millar was there and Jeremy Hunt was around as well. I flew over with a bit of equipment, put myself in a hotel in the outskirts of the town, hired a car and said, 'Right, we are going to train for a week.' We didn't do a huge amount, but he rode his bike with the lads every day. I followed them, they did a little bit of motor pacing behind the car, and we had a nice week getting him back into the rhythm of training.

Critically, we had managed to wangle a start for Cav in the Tour of Britain. It was a bit of an operation; a professional cyclist can't be entered into two events at the same time, but if you pull out of one, you can race another as long as you have a letter from the organiser of the first event to the UCI saying that they are happy for you to ride another race. Cav's team, HTC, had got through to the Vuelta organisers and explained the situation, and they were fine. Britain isn't the Vuelta in terms of the quality of the field or the toughness of the course, but it was eight days of racing, which would get some competition into

Cav's legs and give him the chance for some morale-boosting wins. With that in mind, he came back from Girona to his home to Essex. Alex Dowsett – who had turned professional with Sky that season – was there as well because he lived in the area; he would be company on the bike. That was where Mark put in a lot of the work, replicating the overload he was missing out on because he wasn't at the Vuelta.

We were doing 240- or 260-kilometre days, back to back – two three-day blocks of that kind – and every day he rode the last hundred kilometres behind the car, which was unmarked to avoid attracting too much attention. Because I didn't know the roads too well, we did the same hundred kilometres every day. We stopped at the same cafe, had a quick cup of tea and then did the hundred kilometres behind the car, finishing with a big sprint.

There were no problems with the traffic, apart from one massive run-in with a road-sweeping lorry. We were going along a dead quiet, dead straight road, it was pissing down with rain, and this lorry began sitting half a metre off the back of Cav's wheel; there we were at a steady sixty-four kilometres per hour, me in the car, Cav a few inches off the back bumper, and this lorry right up his backside. Cav didn't know he was there, and I was thinking, 'My God, if Cav hits a pothole or has any problem, this guy will run over him.' We got to a roundabout and I accelerated away; the lorry came round Cav, cut him up and – boom! – nearly ran him off the road. We then came into a little town where there were some roadworks, so the lorry had to stop. Cav came flying past and began giving the lorry a load of abuse, and this great big driver got out. My dad had come down for a couple of days to watch Cav training, and he is a bit feisty, so he got out of the car and told the lorry driver, 'You'd better get back in your cab, mate, 'cos you are going nowhere.' I told Cav he'd better be on his way.

It was the only hiccup, although the weather was a mixture. There was one day when Cav and Alex were both behind the car and it was chucking it down. The two of them were laughing their heads off, and I was looking at them and chuckling as well. It was really foul, rain bouncing off the tarmac, and they were killing themselves laughing because it was so ridiculously bad. So we had a good time, but Mark did a lot of work. It was a nice set-up: he was at home with his missus, I was just down the road, and we would go and meet Alex at the same time every day, because he knew all the roads. We did similar routes on each ride, so Mark knew what work he was going to be doing. It was just the routine he needed: work hard, rest well, eat well, get up and do the same thing the next day.

Mark and I had to make quite a big commitment at that point, but my argument was that he should have been doing all that work at the Vuelta. There were a couple of times in Essex when he began asking me, 'Do I have to do this?' For example, one day we had split sessions, morning and afternoon, and in the plan he had to do five-minute capacity efforts on the flat – five minutes as hard as you can go – and it was raining. He was supposed to be doing three of them, but he really didn't want to, so I had to tell him firmly, 'No, you've got to do this work.' He did them and afterwards thanked me for making him do those efforts. It's a subtle difference, but there it is: if I had given him a training programme and hadn't been on the spot, he wouldn't have done that work. That justified my taking such a big chunk of time away from home. There are times when the riders need that support; you can't beat that face-to-face contact, and I think that is what Cav always appreciated.

The Tour of Britain is eight days long; for the first five we had planned that Mark would finish each day's stage and then ride an hour or an hour and a half back to his hotel behind the car; if it was too far, he would ride for the same length of time and then get in the car, and I would take him to his hotel. We didn't tell anybody; it was kept really quiet so that Cav's potential opponents wouldn't believe anything out of the ordinary was going on. On the first day we didn't manage it because the weather was foul and Cav won the stage; he had the presentation and everything else to do, and it was really cold, so it felt as if we should just get him to his hotel. We then did three sessions, until a stage in northern England where it was crazily windy and the race was cancelled for the day. Cav got a little bit panicky at that point, saying to me, 'Bloody hell, should we go out and train?' My view was that if the wind was that dangerous, he had no option but to stay put. We lost another day there, and we hadn't planned to do the extra hours on the last three days, but by then it felt as if he'd done enough work. He raced well and won the last stage, a criterium in London on the Sunday, and he won it by coming from miles back in the bunch. I thought, 'Job done.'

There were two fundamentals when it came to getting the Worlds right. We had to get the best riders we had to the start line, and we had to get them there in the best shape possible. But there was a host of other factors that might make or break us, aspects of putting a performance together that we'd been looking at since the project first got under way. We'd already laid out plans for how we would communicate with the team during the race. The UCI had ruled that teams had to stop using helmet radios at the world championships and Olympics, so we would have to give the riders basic instructions from the roadside. I had seen the Aussies using a whiteboard with their under-23 teams at the Worlds. I'd been trying to emulate them by holding up bits of A4, but the lads would say they hadn't seen anything – they were going too fast and the paper was too small. The whiteboard was clearly the way to go. We tried it out at the 2010 Worlds, but we didn't have the staff in Geelong to do it properly. In Copenhagen we selected the place for the sign carefully. It had to be on a quiet bit of the course, where the riders could see it from a distance. It would be set up about seven or eight kilometres from the finish line, so that if something was happening on the last lap, the team would have time to act. There would be two boards: one with information about the race situation, the other with a brief instruction for them.

Setting all that up was where Chris White and the performance analysts at the English Institute of Sport came into their own. They needed a television feed and a race radio to get information from, because there was no point in them being stood blind on the side of the road. We had a TV in the team cars, and I had an iPad with a television feed so that if anything went wrong, I could still stream images of the race from the internet. The plan was I would send texts to the guys on the side of the road with any messages that should go up on the board – time gaps between the break and the bunch, and basic instructions – or we would get on the phone. On the day we stopped a couple of times to talk to Chris and his team; if you are at the back of the convoy you've got all day for a quick check before heading off again.

Since Beijing an Olympic Research and Development programme had been running in preparation for London, so we were getting ideas from Chris and Matt Parker, who had moved across to be the head of marginal gains for the Olympics. They developed a skinsuit with material that would be a little bit faster, although for the Worlds we didn't get the final product that they used in London, but a development one. Cav had quite a few fittings, and he had done a wind-tunnel test that April, just after all the Classics. He had never been in one before, but we were in there for a whole day. It was all about his road bike, nothing to do with time trials, so they looked at his road-bike position, what was aerodynamic and what wasn't. The session he really loved was a freestyle one, where there is live measurement so you can see precisely what effect everything has because it sends the scale up or down. Cav was trying all sorts of different things: jersey undone, jersey done up, elbows out, elbows in, sprinting position – just playing with it.

All this meant he could see the difference the skinsuit and the filled-in helmet made in terms of aerodynamics. His bike was his bog-standard road racing bike, a machine he had ordered from Specialized which is in a museum on the Isle of Man now, with the race number on and so on. It was plain black, but on the inside, the seat stays and the forks it was silver. Cav being Cav, he had thought about everything, ordering brand-new shoes with the same colour scheme as the bike – black with silver.

I had worked hard on managing the final week leading into the Worlds – when to bring the riders in, what training to do, how hard to work them. Melbourne in 2010 had forced us to be a bit different – because we were racing in Australia we had to be there together a bit longer than usual – so Mendrisio in 2009 was the model we used. The riders would come in on the Wednesday night, have Thursday, Friday and Saturday together, then we would race on the Sunday. It was crucial to get that week right: we'd learnt from Mendrisio and Melbourne that how much work the riders did should be decided on an individual basis because they were all coming in off different races, and some – in Copenhagen, Brad and David Millar – would be riding the time trial on the Thursday.

Everything seemed to go well: the timings for getting to events, the training sessions. It helped that we'd had dry runs, and that year in, year out it was what we had been doing; with British Cycling it was always about detailed planning and getting it right. It was a bit of a dream week. Nothing went wrong, apart from one puncture, although it wasn't completely plain sailing. Cav was incredibly nervous. I remember going into his room and asking him if he had definitely tried on his skinsuit. I made all the riders try their skinsuits on, but in particular Cav; he had had a bit of a problem because the makers had forgotten to sew pockets on the back into which he could put his energy gels, so we had had to get his skinsuit remade at the last minute. It arrived on the Thursday or Friday. When I went in to see if Cav had tried it on, he was sitting on his bed with his head in his hands, saying, 'I am so fucking nervous.' All I could say was that it was fine and completely normal: 'Flipping heck, Cav, don't worry about it, you are meant to be nervous.'

The thing is, Cav does get worked up. He'll be sat there talking with his legs going up and down, up and down, up and

down. He'll be constantly moving, and you have to tell him
to calm down. Before the Olympics it was the same, which is
surprising when you think how many races he's won on the
big stage. He gets so worked up, yet he handles it really well.
He only shows it to certain people who he thinks know him
inside out.

I was worried too, but I was trying not to let people see it. It
had been such a long build-up and now this was it, this was the
moment. The elite men's race is the last one of the championships; you spend the week watching all the other races and are
the last to go off. It's always a huge day organisationally because
you have to get people to where they have to be: into the pits,
out on the circuit doing the information board, down to the
start. Everyone had to set up early. We had the Team Sky bus
at the start of the race and had to make sure that it had time to
get to the finish, but I had planned the logistics of the day well
before – who we were working with, what staff were around
and where they had to be and when.

Most importantly the lads were happy. We were winning medals all week: Lucy Garner and Elinor Barker medalled in the
junior women's events, and Emma Pooley in the elite women's
time trial; Brad won the silver medal in the time trial and Dave
finished seventh, which put him and the pro riders on a roll.
That all helped to create a good feeling in the camp.

We had the Australians in our hotel with us, which was a
weird mix. The Aussies had Matt Goss, who was probably
the biggest challenger to Cav, who was quite openly saying he
feared Gossie more than anybody in the race; and there was
Matt Hayman, Mick Rogers and Chris Sutton, all of whom

were riding for Team Sky that year. I was coaching all three of them, and all of a sudden it was us against them. So there was a lot of good banter – all those years on the track it was always Australia versus Great Britain at the Games and Worlds. Matt White was there – I get on with him, and he is good mates with David Millar, as he was his *directeur sportif* at Garmin. The Team Sky Australians were constantly coming to our bus to get bits and pieces of equipment, with us saying, 'Oi, you're not in Team Sky this week' and so on. Plus Shane Sutton was there – he's a GB coach, but Chris Sutton is his nephew. It's a friendly rivalry, but we all pretend to hate each other, so it was quite lively around the hotel.

On Friday we had a good look at the circuit when it was shut off to traffic; the riders rode around and I was on the motorbike so that I could be in among them and discuss things as they cropped up. The idea is just to let them get the feel of the circuit. The thing to remember with the professionals is that they race every single day on open roads and come across different ones all the time. They are so used to remembering a stretch of road from one year to the next – it's their job. That means you don't have to overdo looking at a circuit – you only have to do a lap or two and they remember it really well.

Brad was quite concerned; he came to me on the motorbike and said, 'Jesus, this is like a big criterium circuit. Whatever you do, don't give me a job late on, because I'm going to be nervous; give me an early job.' He reckoned it was going to be a shitfight. The team were going round at forty kilometres an hour on the Friday, just floating round, and Brad was saying, 'God, this is so fast.' Cav just said the nature of the course made him feel even more confident; his view was that he felt flipping great. Dave Millar was looking at the course for the first time, although he had seen the video; his take on it was, 'We are going to piss this – we are going to be able to ride all day.' I just got a really good feeling from them. I had been a little bit worried about Brad because he seemed super-tired after the time trial and I didn't know whether he was going to commit. Going into the team meeting on the Friday night I still wasn't sure about him.

I absolutely had to get it right. To start with I didn't want too many people on the team bus, so there was only Dave Brailsford, Tim Kerrison, the riders and me. Olly Cookson set up all the information for the presentation, and I did the wording. We looked at the route first: the race started in Copenhagen and went around a big loop, thirty or forty kilometres, before getting onto the circuit. There were photographs of those roads just to remind the riders what it was about, then photographs of different sections of the circuit, again just as a reminder. The critical part was where we went through what we were trying to achieve – win the bike race – and how we were going to control the race. I wanted to set the Worlds up as if it was just another bike race: 'OK, it's a big occasion for us, but this is what you do day in, day out for a job. It's no different. It's a bigger playing field, but the job is the same. The way you controlled the race in the Olympic test event or the Tour of Britain is how you have to control the race in the world road race championship.'

There was a bit of discussion about who was going to be working when and who would be doing what. The first thing to establish was that if we were going to let a break go away, it had to have the right composition of riders. There were six of our lads who had to be vigilant from the first kilometre

– basically everybody except Jeremy Hunt and Cav. Jeremy was to look after Cav all day, so Cav was to sit behind him as long as he could stay up there. We chose Jeremy because he is great at moving around the peloton, and him and Cav really get on well. Cav had said he felt comfortable sitting behind Jez, so that was an important thing.

Cav was sitting there, rocking his feet up and down as he always does when he's nervous. Gee, on the other hand, takes it in his stride: he sat there confident as anything that he could do the job. Ian Stannard was his usual self, so strong but never completely confident in himself until he is in the race. Steve Cummings is a nervous character – we had our issues at Team Sky and never quite connected, although we are fairly good friends, I think. Steve had always been in on this from the start.

David Millar was our road captain because of his experience. As a bike rider, he's confident, sometimes overly so, and here his form wasn't quite as good as he thought it was. He brings a bit of panache and experience to the team, a little bit of something extra; some people argued that he didn't deserve to be on the team because of his doping issues in the past, but it wasn't my job to rule on that. Personally, I think anyone who's caught doping should be banned for life, but if he was eligible to ride, that was that.

Jeremy is solid as a rock: you know what you are going to get with him, and he doesn't beat around the bush. He and Cav had come up with a strategy which involved the two of them dropping back on the one climb to save Cav's legs, then moving gradually back up through the peloton on the rest of the lap. They said it was what they were going to do – they were very connected and they had done a little bit of it the year before in Melbourne. It was something that Dave had suggested right from the beginning. It was a tactic he remembered seeing in world championships with riders like Rolf Sørensen, who was one of the cleverest and most successful one-day riders of the 1990s. You would see it in one-day Classics: the leader gets in a really little gear, floats back through the bunch to save energy on a climb, then they have a teammate to take them back to the front. So every lap Jeremy did the same thing: he and Cav waited for the same point in the circuit where the guys who could flow through the wheels and manoeuvre well could scuttle through and back up to the front of the group.

You always want your riders to be near the front, but there was another good reason for being among the leaders in Copenhagen: the feed zone was badly managed. It's a problem every year at the Worlds: the peloton comes through the pit area, where all the teams have their boxes, and every lap riders are grabbing bottles and feed bags, with team helpers and hangers-on crowding onto the road. There were so many crashes in the feed zone in the earlier races that year, and there were more in the pro race; there were just too many people on that bit of road. But because we were at the front on every lap, that made it easier; they missed the crashes, and all the other riders would get stuck in a bottleneck as they rode into the line of helpers and would have to sprint back into position in the bunch. We had an easy flow every lap, which meant the lads saved energy.

Feed zones are a danger area in any race because there are bottles, bags and people everywhere as the riders come through. But at the Worlds they're riskier than ever because the riders go through every lap, rather than having a single feed as you do in most pro races. You never know what control there is going to be in the feed zone. They need to have a restriction and a clear line that the helpers aren't allowed to go over; if the *soigneurs* all stood back, the riders would have so much more space. We managed it by making sure that Cav would never try to grab a feed bag; it was always Jeremy who snatched them for him. We planned that Cav was never to go on the right-hand side of the road, where most of the helpers stand – he was always to stay out of trouble. In hindsight it seems so easy, the lads going over the finish line first each time to be out of trouble at the feed, but it was something else to do it on the day.

Jeremy had another key task. I had taken him and Cav to one side before the meeting to go through it with them, and then I said it in front of the whole group: 'Right, Jeremy, one of your jobs is to keep Cav calm.' I told Cav that I'd given Jeremy permission to intervene if he started gobbing off. These were my words: 'Jez, if you hear Cav gobbing off at ANYBODY, tell him to shut the fuck up! Bang him on top of the head, get him to button it!' I told everybody in the meeting, 'This is Jeremy's job: "Patience, Cav, patience, patience."'

One of the things I started working on with Mark a long time beforehand was what that last lap would feel like. Cav has this fixed idea that when you come to a bunch sprint, everybody should get out of the way and leave the road to the bunch sprinters and the sprint teams. When he is at the Tour de France and the non-sprinters get involved, he says, 'OK, I'll just deal with it because I know what they are doing.' But in any other race all you can hear is Mark Cavendish shouting, 'Get out of the way, you're not a sprinter,' and throwing his weight around. I said to him, 'Cav, every single one of the guys coming to the finish of the world championship has a right to sprint, even if they are not a sprinter.' At the time he was worked up about the French riders, who seemed to get involved all the time, so I said, 'You are bound to get some French guy coming up to you and giving you an elbow in the ribs. What are you going to do?'

'I am just going to concentrate and follow the wheel.'

'Right. OK, great.'

You have to put yourself into Mark's shoes. He feels so good as he's riding along in the bunch, but every single time he wins a race it's only the final fifteen to twenty seconds in which he has to perform. For six hours before that, in every race, he has to be so patient. He has to trust his team, guide them, concentrate on saving his strength and keeping his cool. He's so good at doing it, but sometimes when he's fired up he lets it all out. At the Worlds it was a hurdle, a major mental challenge for him. The risk was that he might lose the plot and end up tangling with somebody, and perhaps having a fall when he didn't need to. I wasn't going to just hope for the best.

We went through the roles for each of the riders. We had decided that once the break developed, we weren't going to let it get more than a four- or five-minute lead; at that point Dave Millar would make the call, and once he did so, Steve Cummings and Chris Froome were to ride at the front. They had to try to ride for as long as they possibly could, and then it was down to Jeremy and Dave and Brad and Gee and Ian. In the final lap, it was Gee and Ian to get Cav there, plus originally Dave and Brad, because it was possible that Jeremy would be gone by that point. And then Cav for the finish.

Then it was time to go through the 'what if' scenarios. It's one of the Steve Peters things: always discuss what might happen in a given situation, so that if you end up in that situation you know what do. That was where we went through what to do if Cav crashed or punctured, at this point or that point in the race. It was there that Brad stepped in. I was sat at the front of the bus, Brad was sat in the front left-hand seat and Cav was right at the back. Brad turned round – he's a big gangly thing so he had his legs crossed – and did what he always does: pointed with his fingers. 'Listen, we start as a team, we'll finish as a team. We're all here for Cav, we've all agreed to ride the road Worlds to help Cav win. If we work the whole day for Cav and he punctures on the last lap, we all stop, we all wait and we all try to get back. We'll finish as a team that way.'

There was total silence. That was the moment when I realised that, thank God, Brad was in. One of my big jobs, one of my key targets had been to make sure we ended up as one unit with one goal, and I thought, 'Fucking hell, we have done it.'

Other than getting the lads to the start line on time, I was done. I could have gone home, as I didn't make any difference on race day. Brian Holm came down after the team meeting the night before the race, and I sat down with him and talked him through the plan. He just said, 'Fine' – he was so relaxed. 'Yeah, they'll be fine, there'll be no problems. Cav is great, don't worry, don't worry.'

On the day my first job was to make sure I got the lads in the right place at the right time. There was no talk on the bus beforehand; it was a matter of 'Right, guys, stick to the game plan. Let's go.' It was quite cold but nice and dry, and the weather forecast was good. The lads were quite happy, although I could tell Cav was nervous; but they had music banging out on the bus – a Bradley mix of Paul Weller or something.

I stayed off the bus and let them get ready. I was in the car preparing my stuff because I was pretty nervous. One thing I did do was wait outside the bus to wish them all good luck. I gave Cav an arm around the shoulders and said, 'Good luck,' and off he went – it wasn't the time to do anything different; just stick to the plan. Everything was fine, the carers did a great job, and the lads looked fantastic going off to the start together. Then it was into the car, and 'Fucking hell, here we go.' It was quieter than usual at the start because of the race beginning outside Copenhagen, away from the circuit; there wasn't the usual buzz. Once the peloton had gone we couldn't do anything but be ready for every eventuality. 'Let's not piss around, let's take this seriously from the word go.' So that was it – they were gone.

After that the tension just built through the day; the steering wheel was getting squeezed as I clenched it tighter and tighter and tighter and tighter. We had TV coverage the whole time, and first up all the groups started going off the front – it was quite nerve-wracking, but I could see the guys were flowing and not doing too much. All the other teams are run by ex-pros, so they were all going alongside each other and talking, but our car was quiet because nobody knows who I am and nobody realised Brian was with me. The break didn't go as quickly as we were hoping; it went after about twenty or twenty-five kilometres and was an eleven-man group. We got out onto a coast road where you can look across the sea to Sweden, a rolling road through a wooded area, and that was where the move really formed. As always, once it had gone the race shut down, the riders all stopped for a pee, and Dave came back to the car to speak to me and Brian. It looked pretty good – there was nobody in it of any real significance. It was obviously controllable, so then it was down to Dave to get the boys riding when the gap hit four or five minutes.

We had already talked about it on Friday night, so it was a matter of sticking to the game plan. The break was OK, although it wasn't ideal because the Spanish had Pablo Lastras in there. I think a lot of nations thought they knew exactly what we were going to do, but there were some guys like Paolo Bettini, the Italian manager, who had said beforehand that the finish straight would be too hard for Cav. There had been a lot of speculation, but we were just going to do our job; we weren't too interested in what anyone else thought.

Brian looked at me when the race radio broadcast the numbers of the eleven riders in the break and we worked out who was in there: 'This is not bad at all.' We came onto the circuit, the bunch was spread across the road and the break was going away, and then all of a sudden our guys started riding. What Steve Cummings and Chris Froome did after that was absolutely insane. They rode on the front from about 190 kilometres to go until about fifty-five kilometres or so to go – about three and a half laps to the finish. They spent a hell of a lot of time at the front; it was a phenomenal effort. The Germans gave us a bit of help, thinking of André Greipel, and the Aussies and Americans put riders up there at various times, but with about four and a half laps to go there was a massive pile-up in the middle of the peloton, with Thor Hushovd, Edvald Boasson Hagen and Fabian Cancellara all involved. Greipel made it through, but quite a few of the German team didn't, including their strongest rider, Tony Martin. That changed the race for us; the guys who we thought would help us later on were gone.

There was a feeling in some quarters that we'd set to work too early; I took some calls telling me that we had got it wrong, but I had to just ignore them.

Brad got stronger lap by lap, and eventually Dave Millar said he felt he was struggling a little bit, so they swapped roles. Dave went before Brad from about two laps out, right into the final lap, and Brad did the final bit of riding after the bell to keep it all together. He said later that Dave was sitting behind him, continually saying that he had to wait, wait, wait, and without Dave keeping him on a leash he would have gone too early and ripped the race to bits. As it was, when he did go, it was a massive turn on the final lap, a good six kilometres which took us up to four kilometres out.

I'll give you two examples of how they worked on that last lap. There was a moment when Ian Stannard began elbowing Carlos Barredo of Spain with five or six kilometres to go. Barredo was trying to make some space and kept going whack, whack, whack into Ian, but Ian kept coming back at him, and that was exactly what he had to do; it was the perfect moment to shove people left and right. And right at the finish, in the final 500 metres, I saw Geraint Thomas looking around for Cav, and I knew that meant that Gee was totally committed. He could have gone for the finish himself at that point, but even that late on he was still devoted to the cause. To reinforce my point, there were three Italian and two Spanish jerseys showing up in that lead group when I looked at the TV in the finale, but they weren't helping each other. Cav always says that if you get second and fourth in a bike race you've completely and utterly failed. We always made a big thing of that at the Great Britain academy: first and third, first and tenth – great, because all that matters is winning it. Getting second and fourth doesn't mean you weren't committed to winning the bike race; it just means you haven't got it right.

The Friday before I'd stood at the bottom of the straight with Cav, and he'd said, 'I can be as far back as tenth. I'll be better coming from that far back rather than being in second or third with people behind me.' We got that from the Tour de France stage finish at Cap Fréhel, when he had come around Philippe Gilbert at the last moment. He said, 'If I'm in the same position as I was there, I can get around people, as long as the road doesn't get blocked in front of me.' Coming into the finish he lost Gee's wheel, and we were all going, 'Shit, he's lost him!' But I said, 'No, he's OK – he said he needed to be eighth or tenth on the last corner. We're flipping well in there, we're OK.'

We were all slamming the brakes on in the cars as the riders went up the straight, because we had to turn left into the team car parking where the riders went right. All the riders who had been dropped from the bunch were coming past us, and everyone was sat in their cars watching the finish on their tellys. And all the crowd were standing up on the barriers trying to look down at the TVs in the cars – it seemed like they were right in our faces. The final 400–500 metres were the first time I could take my hands off the wheel since ten o'clock that morning and watch the telly properly. When we saw Cav go, we were just shouting and shouting and shouting. He was shouted up that hill, for sure.

I looked for Mark on the TV, and waited for a gap to open for him as they went up the finish straight. I'd been watching him all day, in his black aerodynamic helmet, so he wasn't hard to spot. He had got Matt Goss's wheel through the final corner and came off the wheel on Goss's right-hand side. It was all a bit of a mess, riders going left and right, but I could see exactly where he was from the overhead television shot, and when the gap opened – it was about 300 metres out – he didn't hesitate. He had wanted to leave it a little bit later, but he didn't want to take the chance of the door shutting on him again. When he went, I knew he was going to get it. I could tell he had strength in his legs, even though Goss was coming back at him. He was looking around him all the time. I could see André Greipel coming up on his left, but he had been unable to get out early enough and had started his sprint too late.

When they got into the final metres all I could see was Cav in the right-hand gutter. I didn't see anyone else: I was focused on Cav and the line coming closer and closer. I could see him looking around him, the position he was in on the bike, and I knew he still had all his strength left. I can always tell when he's going to lose a sprint – he doesn't move the bike in the same way; you can tell he's not confident. This time he was solid as a rock, bent right down low over his bike, his head up, looking to his left – he'd still got all his upper-body strength. When he crossed the line, I went hoarse. All three of us were just screaming our heads off.

Knowing Cav, I think he would have liked to have won in the middle of the road in full view of the whole world, but he wasn't taking any risks – being in the gutter he only had to worry about being overtaken on one side. Quite often he will tell me a few days before what he's going to do when he wins, say, a stage of a big race – pretend he's on the phone or something. But there are times when it's not premeditated, it's just his arms in the air with both fists clenched – pure instinct. That's how it was that day: he wasn't going to lose that sprint – and he told me afterwards he knew he wouldn't – and you could see that all the way up the straight; the way he threw his hands up, it was clear he was desperate to get to the line. You think, 'Fucking hell, he wanted that.'

As we sat there in the car, all the fans on the barriers were going, 'Who's won? Who's won?' They must have heard it over the loudspeaker, because then they all started cheering us, which felt good. The cars started moving again as they went into the parking lot, but we didn't budge. We just stayed there, all of us in tears, all hugging each other for a few minutes. It was a moment of absolute relief more than joy. That's the difference half a wheel makes. There had been all the years of build-up, and I knew that Cav wanted it so badly, and the team had made the whole race look so easy, so simple. If we had lost, it would have been a real gut-wrencher.

Then I started to think, 'Oh my God, he's won it, I can't believe it.' Then it hits you: a real feeling of release after you've been knotted up all day. My guts had been twisting and turning even early on when we stopped for a piss, because I'd been so nervous that something might happen when we were out of the car. I'd felt under pressure all day because not everyone had agreed with our tactics; I wasn't sure everyone had bought into the lads dominating the race as they did. I'd been getting messages, people saying the commentators were questioning what we were doing. But dominating the race had been the plan. That's how Cav likes it – he likes to have the pressure of knowing that the lads have committed totally to taking control of the race and that he can't afford to fail.

So when that knotted up feeling went, I thought, 'Thank fuck for that.'

We parked up at the Great Britain team bus, and everyone was hugging each other there too. I missed seeing Cav on the podium because it was a bit of a way away and it was over by the time I got there. But I saw Gee standing there on his own watching, so I stood with him for a bit, and then he gave me a backie back down to the bus and we waited for Cav. It seemed a lifetime because he was kept there doing dope control, television interviews and the press conference, and by the time he got to the bus we'd already started on the champagne.

Perhaps I'll never have a bigger moment than that in my career. It felt surreal for ages afterwards – 'We've actually won the Worlds.' I'd never thought when I finished my racing career that I'd end up winning the world road race championship with someone I worked with, but it had been a deep-rooted desire since I started working at British Cycling. I'm proud to be British and I was proud to go out and stuff it up some nations who, when I was racing, clearly used to look down on us.

As well as Cav coming up the finish straight first, and the lads doing their job all day, and the back-up staff doing all that they did, that win was about me getting up early and staying up late, following Cav around like I'd done for all those years. I'd never dropped my standards. I didn't really have a moment when I thought it might not happen because I'd always had that goal, and all I could think was what a great opportunity it was. I'll always be part of that success. It wasn't the first time we'd won the road Worlds, of course – Tom Simpson's win in 1965 was the historic one – but when you think of the name

Tom Simpson and what it means, you think about how we started out on the project with a few of us in a room looking at the jersey he won on that day more than forty years ago. It's about that long, long build-up, but it's about other things too: getting the right television and the right guys in the team car – all those little things that make it all come together.

When he crossed the line with his arms in the air, one of the first text messages I sent was to Roger Hammond, Dan Lloyd and all the guys who hadn't made the team, thanking them for their support and for playing their part in the story. To me a team is only as good as its first reserve, and this was a team victory. We'd left some bloody good bike riders at home that year – Dan was flying, and Roger would have done a good job.

Everyone else had played their part, but it meant so much to me and Cav. We had been going on about the possibility of winning the Worlds for years and years – all those little conversations I had had with him, in race hotels and during car journeys when I picked him up from stations or airports. In every single one of my notebooks every other page seemed to have a 'Worlds' heading. It looked like a very simple thing – stick the riders on the front and they'll bring it back together to win the Worlds for Cav – but we'd been going through every single scenario, all the ups and downs, the entire plan. I'd been writing about the Worlds in my notebooks all the time, right from 2007, from that day in Stuttgart when he said he could win it – things like wheels, tyres, helmets, team line-up. What would you need? What would you ride? What's the best?

Sometimes he'd tell me to button it because I'd be talking about the Worlds a year out: he'd say, 'Shut up, you're making me nervous already.' 2012 was all about the Olympics, the year before all about the Worlds. I sometimes think that Cav and I don't have a lot to talk about now. We became fathers at the same time, April 2012, so we tend to talk about our kids. That was what made him crossing that line so special: whether it was one, two or ten bike lengths in front, or just one centimetre, it was about that shared focus, all those talks, all that planning, all the training, all those hours with him behind the car and the motorbike. I don't think there is anyone who knows what that feels like other than Cav and me.

13 : Get Me to the Mall on Time

Throughout 2012 I had a recurring nightmare: I was driving the Great Britain team to the start of the Olympic Games road race in London and we turned up late. It got to the point where I was waking up in the night, asking myself, 'What the hell am I thinking about?'

The London Olympics had been knocking on our door since 2005; all of a sudden they were right there on top of us. It made 2012 a massive twelve months, but there were other things about that year which made it very special. I turned forty and became a father, both of which are landmarks in your life. We went into that Olympic Games with a British winner of the Tour de France, Bradley Wiggins, a little bit of history in the making. There was one other thing: every day I looked at Mark Cavendish in his world championship jersey and felt bloody proud to be working with him. Not that I'd made any of the effort on the bike, but I felt like I'd contributed a fair bit towards that jersey. It was a huge year right across the board.

Cav's transfer to Sky was all sorted out by October 2011, just as he finished his season on the road. I was the intermediary; it took quite a lot of work because Mark wanted to be sure he was doing the right thing, and at Sky we wanted to be sure his move was best for us. Having him at Sky felt right at the time; it was the obvious place for Cav to be given his background with GB. It made a nice change having him back in the same team as me after six years, and it made sense having him in the same professional squad, because we were both so bound up with trying to win the Olympic Games road race.

Getting the road-race team to the start at the Mall on time was an obsession, but that reflects the reality of coaching: your biggest fear is arriving late anywhere with the team. At the Tour de France in 2011 we were behind schedule getting to the start for the time trial in Grenoble. All the teams had had to stay in l'Alpe d'Huez, and we didn't transfer down in time because we didn't realise how busy the roads were going to be. The upshot was that Swifty was late getting to the start line and Juan Antonio Flecha and Simon Gerrans had to get changed in the car as we drove down. They turned up, got out and went straight to the start line. It's stressful stuff, and you don't forget those moments because it's part of your job to get it right.

I was so obsessed with not messing up the London start that I went to extremes. We spent the few days before in the Foxhills resort in Surrey, just outside the M25 and within easy reach of the road-race circuit, and we'd decided months before that we would travel into London the night before the race. All the bikes and so on were kept in Foxhills, and the key staff – the carers, the physio and I – travelled in with the team and stayed in the city centre. In the morning all the bikes and various bits and pieces came in super-early, so that meant we didn't have to get out of bed so early – the trip was far shorter. We'd done exactly the same thing at the world road championships in Melbourne in 2010, but at the Olympic Games it was very different. In Melbourne we had been just 500 metres from the start, so the lads got on their bikes and rode there from the hotel; with the Olympics you have to go to the start along a certain route and you have to go through all the security checks to get in. I wasn't quite sure how that would work out because it was the first day of the Olympics. We all know what the traffic in London can be like, and I wasn't certain which way we were meant to be entering the starting area. I had all the maps and I knew where the entry point was, but I still wasn't 100 per cent sure. So when we got back to the hotel after Brad had rung the bell at the opening ceremony, I did two dummy runs on my own from the hotel to the entry point. I got back in at about midnight, feeling a bit clearer in my mind, which at least ensured I slept that night.

The nightmares might have had something to do with the background: in the lead-up to any Olympic Games the Great Britain team is not a comfortable place to be, with Dave Brailsford on your back twenty-four hours a day, seven days a week. Dave was driving us hard. He was onto everything. His attitude was, 'If there is anything we must get right, it's the Olympics.' All of the coaches were under the cosh, constantly. Dave is supportive, yet he's watching everything you're doing: is this rider right? Are they fit enough? Is this right? Have you got that? Have you done everything? Have you covered everything? Is the equipment right? Are the staff right? Are the logistics right? Everything, everything, everything. No stone is left unturned. Some people cope with it well, some don't. I had my ups and downs, as I think most people did, but you look back and think, 'Christ, if we didn't have Dave doing that, perhaps it wouldn't be the same.' He takes a lot of credit for what he does, but he gets the best out of you. Team GB isn't a pleasant place to be, but then you come out of an Olympic Games and think, 'Bloody hell, we did well there. Why were we successful? Well, Dave drives you hard.' The reason we've won so many medals is because he never lets up.

The big things for the London Olympic road race were exactly the same as at the world championships in 2011: getting the selection right, getting Cav into form – in this case he needed to be at his very, very best – getting people on the start line in the right frame of mind and actually getting them to the line on the day. Early in the season we had a massive concern over Mark's fitness after Milan–San Remo, which could be traced back to a fairly disrupted start to his season. His first race was the Tour of Qatar in February, where he had quite a lot of bad luck – the lead-out train never really got going for him and he crashed on the last stage. Critically, however, he was sick when he arrived. I went to meet him off the plane, and he was sitting on a bench near the baggage area, sweating like mad but feeling cold. He was seriously poorly – it had come on during the flight. For forty-eight hours he just lay in a blacked-out room because he couldn't stand the light.

I felt at the time that the doctor didn't get it right, and Cav carried that virus for most of the early season. He went on from Qatar to Oman, which is a killer trip. It's too long at that time of a bike rider's year, and the racing is so different at the two races that you can't get what you need if you do both. He came back from there and won the Belgian semi-classic Kuurne–Brussels–Kuurne, which was a big win for him in the world champion's jersey because it was one of the objectives he'd flagged up before the season started. About nine or ten days before Tirreno–Adriatico he was supposed to come to the Manchester velodrome to do a speed session behind the motorbike with me, but in the morning he called in – he didn't feel well and had a rash all over him. What we realised was that he was carrying a post-viral condition. The doctor said he had two choices: rest now and hope for the best for Milan–San Remo, or carry on with training. We decided, rightly or wrongly, to do half and half – rest for a week and still go to Tirreno–Adriatico and see how he felt. He won a stage at Tirreno but never felt great; in hindsight, though, we were kidding ourselves that he was in decent shape for Milan–San Remo.

After that Dave said to me, 'Mark's not fit enough,' but the reason was that he'd been sick. It was a bit of a kick in the teeth, but after that Dave was hot on our tails to make sure that Mark was in the right form for the Olympics. That's where Tim Kerrison got a lot more involved in terms of Cav's physical conditioning. Tim did a good job – Cav doesn't really identify with sports scientists and numbers, but this is where Tim is very smart. He presented it in a different way. He gave Cav a chart with his weight down one side, his power along the bottom, and explained that to ride up Box Hill at a certain speed – which was what he'd need to do on race day in August – he would need to be a certain weight with a certain power.

We had done a few tests up there and we had the information from the test event the previous August. Tim said, 'If you want to float around the circuit, you need to be this weight and this power.' Cav chose one of the squares on the chart – 'I want to be at that one. I'll be good enough.' He didn't quite get to it but he was only about two or three watts off. It was well presented and it gave Cav a goal to focus on, so we just went out and got on with getting him to the power and the weight he'd chosen.

Ghent–Wevelgem that April was a near miss, and a big one. It's a Classic that Cav feels he can win, and it should suit his profile because sometimes it's won by a sprinter, as long as they can get over the climbs in the middle of the race. The team messed up there; it was a case of Cav getting a bit cocky, a bit relaxed, and the race just slipped away at a crucial moment. He wasn't far off his goals at the Giro – he had a massive crash; without it he'd have won the points jersey, which he missed out on by a single point. After that we went down to Italy for ten days' training, just me, Cav and Andy Naylor, the *soigneur* who had worked with the academy. We had a great time – fantastic training, good weather, the new Olympic-issue bike to play with, and Cav had great form. He had a few days' rest and went straight into the ZLM Tour in Holland, which from the outset he said he thought he could win overall; we'd been saying for a few years that small stage races were the best way for him to progress from his sprinting. It was his first overall stage-race win as a pro – and it wouldn't have happened if he hadn't done the training he'd been doing. He was down to a good weight, which enabled him to get over the climbs. We didn't need to do a lot else before the Tour de France.

In between times, we did a few sessions on Box Hill; we used to do a fifty- to sixty-kilometre loop to get warmed up, then five or six laps around the circuit behind the motorbike, going up the climb at different speeds so that Mark could get a feel for it. That ZLM Tour was confirmation that he was climbing well and that Box Hill wouldn't be an issue – his morale was really high after that. And then we got to the Tour, where we knew as long as Brad stayed upright and raced well, he was going to have a good chance of winning overall. Cav was going to win stages there, but from a coaching point of view his focus was always on the Olympic Games.

*

We knew from the year before that we were going to be competitive in the Tour, and as early as January 2012 Tim Kerrison was very confident about Brad; from all the research he'd done through 2011 he'd learnt enough of what Brad could do from a physical point of view and what training he needed to do. What Brad did was almost exactly the same as in 2011, but with a few tweaks. One big conceptual change they made was to say, 'Right, we're going to bike races to win. We're going to learn how to win and how to hold onto a yellow jersey.' And this is where Sean Yates came into his own, because of all the experience he had working in teams that were looking to control a stage race.

We'd done a lot of planning beforehand using the experience we'd gained in 2010 and 2011. For example, we had anticipated that Brad would take the yellow jersey at the summit finish at La Planche des Belles Filles – on paper, that was the most likely place, if you assumed he would be fastest in the prologue time trial and would have a good first week. We built around that day: we had a media plan with the press officer Dario Cioni, we planned how we would do the warm-downs and we'd catered for Dario and Brad to have a separate car so that they were completely independent of the team. Every day Brad was in the yellow jersey, he needed his own cool box in that car, with his own recovery drink and food, and his race bag would always be in there. We'd even figured out four or five weeks before the race when we were going to do extra feeds and who was going to do them out on the mountain passes and so on.

Part of my job for the Tour was logistics. I would do a three-day rolling plan so that every day everyone knew where they would be, what car they were travelling to the start in, what their role was, what car they were going from the finish to the hotel in. If anyone had any problems, they had to come to me, not blurt them off somewhere else. In terms of the performance on the ground, Tim Kerrison was running the conditioning side and monitoring the riders' fitness. He would look at the SRM boxes, which measure the riders' power outputs during the stages, assess what condition each rider was in and figure out what they were capable of doing day to day in the race: could they ride at the front in the next stage? Is Brad in good form for this time trial? What strategy does he have for it?

With Cav in the race, going for the sprint stages, my job was to film the finishes and recce the final kilometres. The night before each stage I'd go to the finish, stay near by, get up in the morning, film the last five or six kilometres, edit that on the computer, put little coaching notes on it and zap it back to the bus at the start so that the information could be relayed to the riders at the briefing. After that, I'd drive back down the route as far as I could, wait until I was about half an hour or forty-five minutes in front of the peloton, then feed information back to the team car on wind direction, the road surface, its width, and so on. That info would then be relayed by Sean in the team car to the riders over their earpieces. Then I'd get to the stage finish, where it was my job to make sure everyone got out of there. I'd then go back to the hotel, make sure everything was OK, and after that I'd drive to the next day's finish. I did twelve or thirteen of those stage finishes – all the flat and uphill ones, anything tricky. So I didn't have a lot of day-to-day contact with many of the team; my job was to communicate the details and make sure everything was in place – all the communication with the riders was done by the *directeurs sportifs*. I had to make sure the DSs only worried about the bike race – I did everything else.

If you ask me what my experience was of being in a team at the Tour de France with a rider in the yellow jersey for the best part of two weeks, and eventually winning the race, I'd have to say I didn't notice for a lot of the time. I had my head down. I do look back and think, 'Shit, I wish I'd enjoyed it a bit more,' but my ultimate goal was the Olympic Games. The Tour was just part of getting to the start line in London.

So while we had Bradley Wiggins in yellow in Paris – the first Briton ever to do it – my objective, my job, was to get everyone on the evening flight to London. That was hard going – while the rest of the team went on the lap of honour around the Champs-Élysées, Carsten and I were at the bus and the truck looking after all the kit to make sure no one ran off with anything and going through it all: what's going where? Who's where? What time is the bus coming to pick us up? It was straight back into the logistics I'd been doing for the last three and a half weeks. They all had their photo up by the race finish, and you think, 'Bloody hell, I missed that moment.'

I felt a bit piggy-in-the-middle on the whole of that Tour. As we went further into the race, Brad took the lead, and the yellow jersey took over everything. Cav was feeling, 'Flipping heck, I could win more stages here,' and in hindsight he could have. We could have done things differently, but at that moment it was all about the yellow jersey. I don't think we did anything wrong, but we didn't quite appreciate how Mark was feeling in terms of what winning meant to him. Even I didn't understand what that meant for him, after all those years together.

During that Tour we went through the biggest disagreements

we've had in our time together. He said he thought the team would be going for the green jersey; in fact, he had sat in a room and said to me he thought we should go with Brad, and the green jersey wasn't the focus. It wasn't difficult to work out, because it was obvious this was the moment for Brad. Cav had even said to me that if Brad didn't win in 2012, he would never win.

The discord began when we were looking at the team line-up for the Tour and which of the riders was going to be there to help Mark out in the sprints. He wanted Juan Antonio Flecha, as well as Bernie Eisel; we went with just Bernie. I think Cav was a bit upset about that. It was a slap in the face for him, but you couldn't get away from the fact that we were going to have to put a lot of eggs into Brad's basket and not Mark's.

Maybe at the time Mark couldn't tell us how he truly felt. I think he was saying the right things, but in his heart he wanted something else. He understood that the Olympics were a massive focus, and if anything, the Tour would take second place as a goal. I definitely think in his head he knew the Olympic road race was his objective, and Brad had to win the Tour. But once in the heart of the race, when he was getting into those sprints, he couldn't help thinking differently. And when he started going for the intermediate sprints in the first few days, that was the moment when I thought, 'Shit, we're in trouble here. He's actually chasing the green jersey.' That's when I knew it wasn't going to happen. There's nothing you can do in that situation as a coach. As far as I was concerned, we'd had the conversation about it beforehand, said back in June that this was how it was going to be. It wasn't a nice situation for me. I felt very responsible for Mark's position at Team Sky because I'd been very much in favour of him joining. I felt I'd let both him and the team down because I wanted to see the best for both of them.

That was when I understood Mark a little bit more and realised how much winning means to him. I look back now and wonder why I never noticed. I think it's because we are two totally different people. I'm not a winner in the same sense. I don't have the same drive as Cav to cross that line first. I was convinced we could win yellow and green in the Tour in the same year with two British bike riders from a British team – I think it's very realistic, hard but realistic – but I never said it was going to be done in the first year. And that's where I disagree with people when they said it was all about 2012. I said it would be the second year, and I told Mark that early on. I think all of us misunderstood him. We were looking at team goals – Brad winning the Tour and Mark winning the green jersey, and being the best team in the world. But Mark needs to win and he needs to be the one performing – that's what I got wrong.

The one part of the Tour I was able to savour was the last time trial in Chartres before they rode into Paris. Everything was done and I had a bit of down time at the finish with my mate Glenn Holmes – the guy I went to Belgium with back in the early 1990s – his wife and another friend, Mark. We sat on a grass verge about 500 metres from the time-trial finish, and though we couldn't see the riders, I could hear them going past. We sat there for a few hours and I got out of the bubble for the first time. The time trial finished and we realised, 'Shit, Brad's won the Tour.' It was carnage around the team at the finish. I was staying at an overflow hotel in the town and the next morning I was supposed to drive into Paris, but I decided to go that night instead so I could have a lie-in.

As I pulled my car up outside the hotel in Chartres, there were all these lads there chanting away – 'Wiggo, Wiggo,' that kind of thing. I thought, 'Oh God, here we go.' It was about half ten at night and they were banging on the car windows. I wound mine down and asked, 'Are you all right, lads?' 'You're not going to Paris tonight, are you?' I looked at them. 'Why, what's up?' There were four of them, they were staying in Paris, the last train had left hours ago and they were looking for a lift. 'Well, lads, you're in luck. Give me five minutes and I'll be back.' They were newly into cycling and had just come over on the spur of the moment: 'Shit, Brad's winning the Tour, let's go over and look at it.' So they'd booked their tickets the day before and had had a great day.

We'd got about fifteen minutes down the motorway when I had a call from the Jaguar mechanic – we have one of their mechanics with the team on the big Tours just to look after the cars – saying he'd left his bag in the back of my car, with his passport in it. So I had to go back, with these lads sitting there a bit pissed and hoping they were going to get to Paris. I pulled up outside the team hotel and said, 'Right, lads, I've got to get out of the car for a minute. Stay here and don't make nuisances of yourselves.' They couldn't believe what they were seeing: all the team vehicles were having the yellow stickers put on them – and these guys were just wetting themselves. I gave them a lift all the way into Paris, and they couldn't get their heads round the fact that they'd asked someone from Sky, of all people, for a lift.

I woke up the next morning in Paris. It was incredible watching our team come into the circuit with a British guy in the yellow jersey and another Brit in the world champion's jersey.

We were all parked up on the Place de la Concorde, where they come out from the left, then go through the right-hander up onto the Champs-Élysées. We had the big screen in front of us and we could see Brad leading Cav out. It was an amazing sight: yellow jersey leading out rainbow jersey, both of them British, and it was a fantastic way for Brad to thank Cav, when Brad could have been expected just to sit there and savour his big moment, like most Tour winners do as they ride up the Champs-Élysées for the last time.

I was thinking, 'Cav is going to piss this.' Cav winning there with his world champion's jersey on meant so much to him – that was a massive win. We were all given T-shirts with 'Sky' on the front in yellow and all the staff's names down the back. It was a great thing to be part of; it was incredible how big it was. That definitely made the lows of 2010 worth enduring. It was a long way from chasing rats in Tim Harris's house in Belgium. Back then I'd never even imagined myself working in cycling, let alone being part of a team that had won the Tour de France.

The transition from the Tour to the Olympics was one of the things I had looked at in particular detail. The issue is that five days from your objective, you're finishing the biggest bike race in the world. You can do everything right, then at the very last moment anything can happen. You have to hand it to the riders: they saw the Tour and Olympics as one big bike race lasting five weeks, or five and a half for Brad. The trick in this situation is to keep everyone aware of what's going on, tell them what's going to happen in plenty of time. That in turn means that you have to be very much ahead of the game in your planning.

The riders knew a year before the Games that we were

planning on going to Foxhills the night after the Tour. I gave the lads two options: they could come in on the Sunday night or the Wednesday. That meant the riders who had done the Tour could go home or come in with their wives or girlfriends, but the key thing was that we would be one team from 7 p.m. on Wednesday night. These lads had been on the road for four weeks already without seeing their families, so I said to everyone that this could be an obstacle for us if we just put the riders in a hotel in Surrey, with their wives and families somewhere else.

That planning is a key part of getting people to buy in – they need to know what those five days will look like and how much work they will have to do. As it worked out, David Millar, Cav and Froomie came in on the Sunday night. They brought their families and had a nice chilled-out couple of days; whether they rode their bikes or not was not an issue, but they did a little ride every day. Brad and Ian Stannard came in on the Wednesday, at which point we became a team and the families had to go elsewhere.

Cav was absolutely flying at the Olympics. He said he felt fantastic – the effort didn't hurt him all day. Physically, he was perhaps in the best condition he's ever been and he was so focused. I felt so sorry for him that it didn't work out. Looking at that race now, we always knew that the maximum number of riders we could have was five. So there was the issue of how many riders we would qualify – it was taken from the 2011 results – and we always knew that with five it would be hard to control the race, given its style and the toughness of the course. Part of our strategy had to be that if other teams came to the race with sprinters, we would have to take a gamble that they would help us – but gambles like that are part of road racing. The bet was that if it looked like a sprint finish, they would work for that. The plan was that we would control the race until the break was sitting there in front of the bunch. At that point, the other sprinters' teams would think, 'Bloody hell, we've only got to do this bit of work now to get the break back.'

I was on my own driving back to Surrey that night after the road race, where Cav finished twenty-ninth, not even winning the bunch sprint. I was pretty angry with the other nations because I got the impression that they felt it didn't matter who won as long as we didn't. Part of the upshot of that was that we had had an appalling outcome for the sport of cycling – the worst possible, it seemed to me – with Alexander Vinokourov winning, a former blood doper who had shown no contrition and no sense of the damage he'd done to his sport.

That day the Great Britain team was a victim of its own success: when you win so much, people do turn against you – and this was something which had been in the backs of our minds beforehand, though no one had actually said it. It's not something you can account for: you can't gamble by not winning races leading up to something big, just to make people think you aren't in form. We did get some things wrong, though: looking back, the lads started riding at the front too early, and they started riding too fast. I wouldn't change the tactics, but if we'd been using radios I'd have told the team to hold back a little bit – 'Easy, easy, there's a long way to go' – but they started riding very early in the race. Froomie got it completely wrong by not taking enough drinks on board – and that was something I missed, the simple thing of saying, 'Guys, look at hydration, how are we going to go about this?' Cav has a pretty sound nutrition strategy in a race – he feeds every fifteen to twenty minutes – so I took it a little bit for granted with the other guys, and Froomie was completely wasted. He couldn't even get out of the saddle when he came off the circuit because he'd had only three bottles in all that time. The Olympic-issue skinsuits were quite thick, and that's one thing I'd change because you get a bit warmer and need more liquid as a result.

There was a key moment on the last circuit of Box Hill, when Fabian Cancellara went across from the bunch to the front group. Cav went to go with him, but David Millar told him to stop. Dave was road captain, he made the call, and we stand by that, because if Cav had stopped trying to get across and the team had pulled the lead group back, we'd have said, 'Thank God you told him to stop'; if he'd gone and won, we'd have said, 'Thank God you went.' It was Dave's gut feeling at the time, and you never know whether it was the right call or not. Cav waited, so he must also have felt it was the right thing to do. I think he could have made it to that group with Cancellara, but he still wouldn't have won, because people weren't going to ride with him.

The gap to the break at the top of Box Hill the last time around was forty-three seconds. We'd said that if there was a small group ahead, we could afford to let them have as much as three minutes. It was at this point that we needed another team or two to step in, but the Germans and the Aussies still didn't really get involved. The Germans tried but they were weak, didn't have anything in their legs.

One of the big challenges for the Games was always going to be getting certain individuals on the line as fit as they could be, and we did a pretty good job there. The guys were on fire, they had such good form – and they were totally keyed into it. Bradley Wiggins had just won the Tour de France, and he had the time trial coming up three days after the road race. That had been one of my concerns – how much would Brad buy into it? He still rode hard, all the way to about two kilometres from the line. Ian Stannard rode hard all the way to the finish, even though the race had gone. There was one final thing that didn't go our way: as Cav came over the line, he came into the pits and said, 'Feel my front wheel.' I pressed it and it was soft. He heard it go with about a kilometre and a half to go. He said afterwards, 'I'm gutted, because I wanted to win the bunch sprint at home – I was determined to do it.' He wanted to show that if it had come down to a bunch sprint, he'd have pissed it. His words were, 'It wasn't meant to be.'

So physically we got it bang on and tactically we weren't too far off, but road racing isn't an exact science – you can't always predict what the opposition will do. Our five were trying to control 135 others, so part of the strategy was the gamble that other nations would want the same outcome as us – and up until fifty kilometres to go, I thought we were in with a shout. You have to gamble sometimes in a race and hope it falls your way. We didn't want a formal plan B because that would have diluted things in the riders' minds. I actually spoke to Dave Millar about a back-up plan, but not to anyone else: if Cav turned round and told Dave he was swinging and couldn't do it, Dave was to make the call about who would step in and go for it. It wasn't a plan as such, more just making sure Dave was aware that it was down to him to make that call. Banking on Cav was a risky strategy. Would you have put money on us winning? Not as much as you would have put on Brad in the time trial or the Worlds in Copenhagen or a stage race, where you can have it go against you one day but still have a chance to put it right. But that unpredictability is the beauty of a one-day race.

The anger and disappointment I felt as I drove back to Foxhills that night made me appreciate all the more what we had achieved in Copenhagen. What makes the Olympics such a fascinating target for most coaches is that you have so few chances to get it right. A Games only comes up once every four years. You get it wrong on that one day, and you have so long to wait before you get the opportunity again. We missed out in London, and perhaps we will never have the same chance again. We applied the same planning that helped us succeed in the past, but it didn't happen; that was what made me realise what we had achieved at the road Worlds. When you think how far Cav was from winning the Olympics – he wasn't in the picture, even though so much went right. A few crucial things went wrong, and with hindsight we could probably have done some things differently.

That could have happened the year before at the Worlds: we could have come second if Matt Goss had had a better run to the finish. There could have been a crash among the first ten riders somewhere on the circuit, leaving us a thirty-second gap to bridge – that could have made all the difference. The only time I did worry in that final kilometre in Copenhagen, the only time when my heart sank a little bit, was as Cav was coming off that last corner. He clashed with somebody; he was on the underneath and he hit them on the outside, and I thought, 'God, say those pedals had been at the wrong angle, or if the other guy had just moved a little bit differently, or his handlebars had been lower and he and Cav got tangled up with each other – that would have been that.'

It was the combination of every little thing going right which made that day so special. If the Games is a once-every-four-years chance, Copenhagen could be the kind of opportunity you only get once in ten years – a flat course made for Mark Cavendish. You have got to grasp your chance and go with it, and when it works it is the most special event you can imagine.

14 : Aiming for the Stars

I didn't know exactly what I was expecting in the long term from that bunch of young lads who turned up at the velodrome in Manchester in November 2003. I had an idea in my head of what we wanted: riders capable of winning Olympic medals. At the same time, in the back of my mind was the thought that if those young lads were good enough to win medals, they might also eventually become heroes on the road, winning some big races. But I didn't have any specific goals for them.

Once we chose the lads we were going to work with, I did a little bit more homework and began to figure out their characters. I knew Mark would always speak up, but it still took me aback when he said he wanted to be world road race champion one day. I remember standing there and thinking, 'Bloody hell', but the one thing I didn't do was laugh at him. That's something Cav always says was important: I didn't react with, 'What the hell are you talking about?' – which other people might have done.

You have to remember the scale of the goal. It is a hell of an ambition from a cycling perspective to say you want to be world road race champion. There was no British model to emulate; we had a few good riders out there on the road, but the best British pros racing the European circuit, such as Sean Yates and Robert Millar in the past, still seemed so far away. There was ambition, though. These lads could see there was something happening in the UK; that is what gave them the belief. As juniors they would go to Europe and race with their chests out, because we were doing well on the track with riders like Chris Hoy, Brad and so on. But there's a big difference between an Olympic gold medal on the track and being world road race champion. That felt light years away.

That Mark was aiming so high was unique. Some of the lads around him had no idea what they wanted to achieve. They were just racing, they were enjoying it, they had done quite well among the juniors and they had been selected for the programme. The goal most of them had was to be an Olympic gold medallist, but Mark wasn't saying that: he was saying Olympic gold medallist plus world champion, which is quite a difference. I began thinking, 'Why not?' It is a Steve Peters principle: don't aim for the sky, aim for the stars. If you aim really, really high, you may not quite make it, but you will come quite close if you are dedicated enough and have got the ability. That is the kind of thinking behind the foundation of the academy: we were aiming high, but we didn't know where specifically.

It's a massive question for any coach: how do you respond when a young athlete in the formative stage of his career comes up to you and says he or she wants to be a world champion? In practical terms, if that young rider came to me now, I would start by asking some basic questions, as I did with the academy lads: what does it take to be a world champion? What does it take to win a gold medal? What do the challenges look like? How committed do you have to be? When Mark Cavendish came to me at seventeen and said he wanted to be a world champion, he had already made it into the national team; he had a bit of a pedigree – there was something there. If it had been a seventeen-year-old kid who had never done anything on a bike in his life, it would be a different story.

Peter Keen came up with a set of criteria, which we went through with the riders, scoring them out of five according to where we thought they were. How dedicated are they? How technically skilled are they? In the world rankings are they in the top ten? Top twenty? How committed are they to our programme? We scored them as coaches and the riders scored themselves, and we examined any discrepancies. For instance, if you asked, 'How committed do you have to be in order to be an Olympic champion?' most people would say ten out of ten. In reality it is about eight or nine out of ten, because you can be too committed for your own good. If it is icy out on the roads and you go out, fall and break your arm, your dedication has worked against you. You have got to be committed enough to get the work done, without going over the top. You need a lifestyle balance, and if someone doesn't have that, then potentially they might not make it.

What mattered was the difference between the scores: if the coaches put eight and the rider put ten, that was a model for discussion and you came to an agreement about what needed to be done. The classic example would be the Madison, where in terms of technical skills you might score a rider five, and they might give themselves a score of nine. You would say, 'We don't see what you are seeing,' and then you work from there. I used that as a tool with the young lads and did it every year at the academy, just a general discussion and a list of everything it takes to be the person you are aiming to be: they would say you have got to have endurance, you have got to be able to go fast, your health has got to be good . . . the list is endless.

Those questions lead you to the stepping stones that the rider needs to follow. You have to get them to identify where they need to be for their age group. For instance, a junior cyclist can't be expected to have the endurance they need to win an Olympic gold medal, but you can expect them to have the stamina appropriate for that age group. If there are twenty grades of endurance that take you to Olympic-medal stand-ard, being a junior you might only get up to block four, with another sixteen to go. This is where commitment and disci-pline come in: those qualities don't change whether you are eighteen or twenty-nine. You would also look at endurance, technical skills, tactical awareness and the ability to be part of a team. For example, Mark scored highly in tactical awareness but super-low on endurance; he was also quite disorganised. He was working out a lot of his bike racing on his own; he didn't have a lot of guidance. I said to him, 'I really don't care about your cycling – your commitment to that is a given – but your life around it is what we are going to work on.' I had exactly the same conversation at the start of 2013 with Joe Dombrowski, the American rider at Sky.

That was where the academy set-up made the difference: if those young riders had been living at home and coming into the velodrome for blocks of training, we would never have tackled their lifestyle in the same way. I am not saying Mark would never have made it as a pro without the academy, but I would agree with what he has said: it would have taken him longer to make that step up.

Another key thing is that even though a rider is just sev-enteen and seems like a young kid, they are still legally old enough to have a child and get married, and drive a car. A lot of people forget that. You have to listen to them. A lot of people feel that because those athletes are younger, you can make them do it in a certain way, but in fact that is what had been happening with Cav throughout his time as a junior: nobody was listening to him and he didn't fit the model everyone had adopted. What mattered to me was how I was going to get the best out of them, and you do that by listening to them. Some of what you hear you might throw away, but you might not want to make it clear that that was the case.

I got the balance right with those riders at the academy, but I don't think I realised what I was actually doing. I knew what I was aiming for, but I was shooting in the dark a little bit. No one told me I should have those formal sit-down sessions, that it would gain me their confidence, but that moved us a long way forwards. The riders felt that they had an opportunity to tell me about their frustrations. You have got to build trust.

Working with Steve Peters made me realise how different people are, and how you need to deal with that. You have to speak to them individually and listen to them individually. It's just a matter of using those little techniques Steve taught me: for example, ask the quiet one first, because your Mark Cavendishes will always speak up. If you just say, 'Who wants to tell us how we could do that better?' then Mark will always say what he thinks, whereas Ian Stannard or Geraint Thomas wouldn't say a great deal. If you ask them directly, however, they might come in with better answers.

You have to give some people time. They all think and react at different speeds. If you ask a group of cyclists, 'How are you going to win this race?' there are those, like Mark, who will tell you straight away, 'I am going to do this, I am going to attack the bunch here and I need to wait here,' while there are some who will panic and won't be able to answer immediately. But if you say to them, 'How do you win this race? Come back to me by tomorrow morning,' they will come back with really good answers.

Once you've gone through what it takes, it's a matter of 'Let's get out there and ride a bike.' That classic one with Mark was: 'You're unfit. You got dropped up Gun Hill, you're unfit at the "Go Till You Blow" session on the track, you get dropped at track league' – Cav was getting shot out the back in the first week of track league in Manchester – 'so you know what you have to do: keep riding your bike to get fitter, and we are going to concentrate on getting you organised and ready to race.' It's about being patient; young athletes take things on at different times. It would have been so easy to get rid of Mark, but you could see from a very early age that if you just got him fit enough, he'd win bike races. That has been the essence of his career: get him into shape, get him to the start line, and he will win. In a way, it's pretty simple with him, whereas if you take a rider like Peter Kennaugh, who is more endurance-orientated and better suited to stage races, it is a much longer process for them to start winning. Sprinters like Cav tend to start winning early because it is easy for them to win races compared to the slower guys.

Many coaches skip around unpleasant realities because they're not nice conversations to have, but one of the things I talked to Cav about early on was that as a professional cyclist he would have to get used to riding around in the back group in order to survive in a stage race. There was no point hiding from it. In the last couple of years I've watched him at the top of the climbs in the Tour; he is quite often the last one to the top and he always looks in a right state when he gets there, and then he has to chase like mad to get onto the group. I think to myself, 'I taught him that when he was at the academy at eighteen.' I felt you had to say, 'Right, what are your challenges?' Mark is never, ever going to climb the Galibier in the front group, so you may as well prepare him for that as a young lad.

It's about telling people exactly what they are facing and not skirting around any issues. Cav once said to me that one thing I always did was to paint quite a dark picture first, and then it gets better. Some people might see that as a bit of a negative attitude, but it's similar to being highly disciplined with the riders at first, then backing off. Things get better, not worse. You show them exactly what is in front of them in the bike race – 'These are the most dangerous things that can happen, these are the hardest parts' – and then you move on to the good points.

The lessons I learnt at the academy and while guiding Mark to that rainbow jersey can be translated across to most other team sports and to groups working towards any goal. In any team sport the key aspect is bringing the team together and creating that understanding between the athletes; they need to have a single mindset. It's a matter of goal-setting and identifying the challenges. I remember doing a team-building exercise with Steve Peters and the lads at the academy in which we were given a scenario and split into two groups. The group I was in was up in the mountains in Norway; we'd got stuck, we had a certain amount of equipment and we had to figure out what was going to get in our way as we tried to get down.

You can apply that to absolutely anything. For example, if I was going to ride the Étape du Tour, I would look at how far it was, the steepness and the lengths of the climbs, whether they are narrow or wide roads, and so on. First up, you would try to learn as much about the event as you could. Then you would think what kind of equipment you need, taking into account the weather, the road surfaces, etc. Next you would write down your ideals, look at how you compare with them and see what you're lacking. Then you would look at practical things: 'How am I going to get there? What time do I need to be there? Airports, travel . . . do I know anybody who lives locally? Can I hire a car?' – simple things like that. Then you look at the day of the event: 'What are we going to eat? What are we going to do, and when? Who do I need around me?' Straight away there are all your challenges; if get any one of them wrong, it could throw the whole thing out of kilter.

That is simple performance planning, and you can add a performance plan to anything you do in life. As far as I'm concerned, that is the most exciting part: the pre-planning in which you take a one-off event and ask those practical questions. You've got to know a sport to be able to apply some of the details, but you can surround yourself with people who do know and get the information out of them in order to discover what you need to do. So when you ride the Étape du Tour, you assess the challenges: have you ever ridden that distance? Have you ever ridden up climbs of that kind? Are you fit enough to do them? You can then start to train yourself: 'I need to build up. I'll take a holiday and spend time riding on the climbs.' It's similar to setting up a business: you submit a business plan to the bank to get the start-up money.

I don't quite know where Mark gets the belief and the desire from, but the key thing from a coaching point of view is that you have to follow the dreams of those young people. If they set their targets high, you have to go with them, because you never know where it will take you. That is the big thing that working closely with Mark has taught me. Here was a young lad who started out very overweight, who looked so far from being an athlete, who looked like some young guy who was at university and out on the pop every night, and who certainly didn't look like a future world champion.

Let's go back to that seventeen-year-old who wants to be a world champion. You should never just say, 'Yeah, whatever,' when a young athlete says something of that kind. You never truly know. And it could be any seventeen-year-old wanting to be anything in life – an actor, a journalist . . . You have to respect their dreams. If people want to go out and achieve something, there's nothing to stop them.

Mark Cavendish will end up in the history books as the best sprinter cycling has ever had. You can argue about whether he's there now, but what I do know is that there's more to come. He has said to me that he wants to be remembered for certain things when he stops racing, which is why in spring 2013, when he won the points jersey at the Giro d'Italia, it mattered so much – it completed the triple, in the wake of the points jerseys at the Tour de France and the Vuelta. He dreams of winning Milan–San Remo in the rainbow jersey. I think he'll win the Worlds a second time, and he could certainly win at San Remo again. He wants to smash Eddy Merckx's record for career Tour stage wins and put it on the shelf – and that's within his reach. I know he wants to wear the yellow jersey in the Tour. He's hungry enough to keep going until the age of thirty-three or thirty-four if he stays free of injuries. That need to win drives him insane sometimes, but it's part of him and it means he doesn't seem to get tired of racing. Back in 2003, who would have thought Mark Cavendish would end up doing everything that he has done – and that he still can do?

Great Britain went back to the 2012 world road championship in Valkenburg, Holland, with a defending champion, Mark Cavendish, and a Tour de France winner, Bradley Wiggins. It wasn't a course for Cav, with a steep hill to the finish, and Brad wasn't in the form he had enjoyed from March to August that year. So we went with the same mindset as at Mendrisio in 2009, at the start of the Worlds project: have a goal, and build the team behind that. We knew Jonathan Tiernan-Locke was a good little climber and would have an outside chance, although he had never raced the distance before, and the lads got him in the perfect position on the final lap. Jon didn't quite have the legs, but you couldn't help but be encouraged to see young riders like him, Luke Rowe and Ian Stannard racing with no obvious nerves in the final laps.

Cav will get his chance to win again in 2016, when the Worlds are in Qatar on another flat course. With a true champion like him all you have to do is get him – or her – to within a few kilometres of the line, and nineteen times out of twenty they will bring it home for you. The task in the meantime is to win the Worlds with riders other than Mark: both Brad and Chris Froome are capable of getting on the podium on a hilly course, but I'd like to think about other leaders for the British team as well – Geraint Thomas or Peter Kennaugh. Pete is a proper bike racer with a killer mindset like Cav's when he's on his terrain; 2015, when the race is in Richmond, Virginia, might suit him, as he'll be a mature athlete by then. Great Britain have dominated the Worlds on a flat course once; if we truly want to be seen as a cycling nation, a rainbow jersey at the end of a hilly world road championship would be a fantastic way to do it.

Index

Index

ff

Faber and Faber is one of the great independent publishing houses. We were established in 1929 by Geoffrey Faber with T. S. Eliot as one of our first editors. We are proud to publish award-winning fiction and non-fiction, as well as an unrivalled list of poets and playwrights. Among our list of writers we have five Booker Prize winners and twelve Nobel Laureates, and we continue to seek out the most exciting and innovative writers at work today.

Find out more about our authors and books
faber.co.uk

Read our blog for insight and opinion on books and the arts
thethoughtfox.co.uk

Follow news and conversation
twitter.com/faberbooks

Watch readings and interviews
youtube.com/faberandfaber

Connect with other readers
facebook.com/faberandfaber

Explore our archive
flickr.com/faberandfaber